The
TAO
of
ZEN

The

TAO

of ZEN

Ray Grigg

ALVA
PRESS

Acknowledgments

The following publishers and authors have generously given permission to use quotations from copyrighted works: "Events Are the Teacher" by Katy Butler, published in *Whole Earth Review*, Winter 1983, No. 40. reprinted by permission of Katy Butler, © 1983; *Civilisation*, by Kenneth Clark with permission of BBC Enterprises Limited, 1971; *Five Mountains: The Zen Monastic Institution of Medieval Japan*, by Martin Collcutt and published with permission of Harvard University Press, 1981; *Shifting Worlds, Changing Minds*, by Jeremy W. Hayward, 1987, and reprinted by arrangement with Shambhala Publications Inc., 300 Massachusetts Ave., Boston, MA 02115; *A Western Approach to Zen*, by Christmas Humphreys, published by Quest Books, and excerpts reprinted with permission of The Theosophical Publishing House, 1987; "Mysterium Coniunctionis" in Volume 14 of *Collected Works*, by C.G. Jung, published by Princeton University Press, 1963; *The Northern School and the Formation of Early Ch'an Buddhism*, by John R. McRae, published by University of Hawaii Press, 1986; *The Way of Chuang Tzu*, by Thomas Merton, © 1958 by The Abbey of Gethsemani and reprinted by permission of New-Directions Press; *Buddhism in Chinese History*, by Arthur F. Wright, published by Stanford University Press, 1971; *Zen Mind, Beginner's Mind*, by Shunryu Suzuki, published by John Weatherhill, Inc., first edition 1970; *The Great Religions*, by Richard Cavendish, published by Contact, 1980, and reprinted with permission of A.P. Watt Ltd., Literary Agents, London, England; *Zen Telegrams*, by Paul Reps, reprinted with permission of the Tokyo office of the Charles E. Tuttle Co., first edition 1959; *A Flower Does*

published by Bantam Books, 1990; *China: A History in Art*, by Bradley Smith and Wan-go Weng, published by Doubleday, 1972; *Zen and Zen Classics*, by Frederick Franck, published by Vintage Books, 1978; *Chuang Tzu: Inner Chapters*, by Gia-fu Feng and Jane English, published by Vintage Books, 1974; *Lao Tzu: Tao Te Ching*, by Gia-fu Feng and Jane English, published by Vintage Books, 1972; *Zen in the Art of Archery*, by Eugen Herrigel, published by Vintage Books, 1971; *Gödel, Escher, Bach: An Eternal Golden Braid*, by Douglas Hofstadter, published by Vintage Books, 1980; *The World of Zen*, by Nancy Ross, published by Vintage Books, 1960; *The Way of Zen*, by Alan Watts, published by Vintage Books, 1957; *Beat Zen, Square Zen and Zen*, by Alan Watts, published by City Lights Books, 1959; *Tao: The Watercourse Way*, by Alan Watts with the collaboration Al Chung-liang Huang, published by Pantheon, 1975.

Contents

PREFACE

Zen is Taoism disguised as Buddhism. When twelve hundred years of Buddhist accretions are removed from Zen, it is revealed to be a direct evolution of the spirit and philosophy of Taoism. Indeed, the literature known as the *Lao Tzu* and the *Chuang Tzu*[1] begins a continuous tradition that can be followed through the Ch'an of China to the Zen of present-day Japan. The formative writings of early Taoism are essentially the teachings of Zen.

The similarity of Taoism and Zen is first suggested when the term "Zen Buddhism" is separated into its component parts. This is implicitly done in some modern Zen teaching. But it is most apparent in the West's contemporary and nonsectarian sense of Zen, a fresh and innocent response with a clarity that is uncomplicated by the traditional interpretations and the historical assumptions which have seen Zen as an inseparable part of Buddhism.

This separation of Zen from Buddhism is clearly evident in the wide variety of popular literature that finds Zen to be a critical component in tennis, skiing, mountaineering, running, drawing, jazz, even "motorcycle maintenance." Indeed, Zen is understood in the common mind to be a ubiquitious, inseparable part of ordinary life. But always without Buddhism. Such a separation helps to reveal Zen's closeness to the essential character of Taoism. It is also a reminder of Zen's own admonition about the folly of becoming attached to any system of understanding—even Buddhism, and especially the religion of Mahayana Buddhism that has housed Zen in China and Japan for centuries.

Buddhism has its own doctrinal motives for connecting

Zen to the India of the Buddha rather than the China of the *Lao Tzu*, so its account of history is not objective when explaining the origin of Zen. But a critical examination of this history makes these motives fairly transparent and the inaccuracies fairly obvious. A less biased understanding of history relates Zen much more closely to Taoism, its kindred spirit in China.

The spirit of Zen is about naturalness, spontaneity, and inner freedom. But the centuries of company that Zen has kept with Buddhism in both China and Japan have created a formal practice that is stiff, austere, and monastic, qualities that are the antithesis of Zen's essentially organic identity. Once the trappings of Buddhism are removed, however, Zen returns to its original Taoist character.

Buddhism is the historical wedge that has separated Zen from its Taoist source. This separation has not been entirely unnatural. Buddhism does share with Taoism certain similarities that have accommodated their coexistence. These similarities can first be noticed in the reaction of Taoism to Buddhism's initial arrival in China during the first century, then in the creation of Ch'an in the seventh century, and later in the history of Buddhism in Japan.

But the similarities between original Taoism and pure Zen are far more striking: the simplicity, the directness, the intuitiveness, the paradoxes, the importance of being natural and the prevalence of natural images, the skepticism about words and explanations, about institutions and dogma. Zen is Taoism.

Indeed, throughout the history of Zen, its Way has been understood to be synonymous with the Way that is the Tao. Other basic words are related. The Chinese word *tao* is *do* in

Japanese, and the Japanese word *roshi*, which means both *master* generically and *Lao Tzu* specifically, is derived from the Chinese *Lao Chi*, an alternative name for the old Taoist sage.

The Way that is common to Taoism and Zen escapes definition. In both traditions it is undefineable and unexplainable, elusive, frustratingly near and far, always so close yet just outside intellect's reach. Indeed, the essential enigma of Taoism and Zen is the source of their wisdom and profundity—a freedom that is never enclosed by a system of understanding. As Frederick Franck writes of Zen in *Zen and Zen Classics*:

> *[We] have a belief which we need not believe in. No dogmas, no ritual, no mythology, no church, no priest, no holy book—what a relief!*[2]

He might have said the same of Taoism. Of course, Taoism has a book in the form of the five thousand characters of the *Lao Tzu*, and there are the so-called chapters of the *Chuang Tzu*. But these writings, like the literature of Zen, are really descriptive rather than prescriptive, instructive rather than sacred.

The *Lao Tzu* and the *Chuang Tzu* might be considered sacred if there was anything religious in them. They might even be the last words on Taoism if they did not reject the use of words altogether and thereby disqualify themselves from being a definitive statement on anything. At best they offer a somewhat sensible description of the world as it is and the process by which it seems to work. Regardless, both writings are too paradoxical, too confusing and too enigmatic to be the basis of any serious dogma. And they are certainly not holy. Like Zen, Taoism, too, is a relief.

This Preface must conclude by addressing some mechanical matters. In writing *The Tao of Zen*, deliberate and conscious distinctions have been made between a number of terms. If readers do not clearly understand these distinctions, the usual confusion that pervades any discussion of Taoism and Zen will simply continue.

Buddhism, unless qualified, is meant as religious Buddhism, not the philosophical Buddhism that was the essential teachings of Siddhartha Gautama. A clear distinction has to be made between these two traditions. The deification of the teacher and the resulting religious dogma have become the tenets of Mahayana Buddhism. This is the form of Buddhism that has accompanied Zen in China and Japan for more than a thousand years. There is some Zen in Gautama's original Buddhism; there is considerably less in the religion of Mahayana Buddhism.

Zen and Zen Buddhism are terms that are not used interchangeably. Zen refers to pure Zen, the practice in Chinese Ch'an and Japanese Zen that is likened to original Taoism but is wholly devoid of Mahayana Buddhism's religious allusions. Zen is also devoid of the inner analysis that is so characteristic of Indian Buddhist philosophy. Zen Buddhism, therefore, is the unlikely combination of Chinese and Indian sources; it began in Ch'an as a mixing of Taoism and Buddhism, and currently exists in Japan in the same combination. Because of the ubiquitious quality of Zen, it can be found in Zen Buddhism, but Zen and Zen Buddhism are not equivalent terms.

Taoism refers specifically to the philosophical or contemplative practice of this Chinese tradition, to the body of teaching and understanding relating directly to the literature known as the *Lao Tzu* and the *Chuang Tzu*. This original form of Taoism is different from the religion and the various sects of esoteric, yogic, and alchemic Taoism that have evolved from it. Except for historical distinctions, Taoism and Zen are terms that can be used interchangeably.

PART I

Taoism and Zen:
The Historical
Connections

As the consciousness of the early Chinese moved from superstitious defensiveness to volitional empowerment, what Arthur Waley refers to as the evolution from a "pre-moral" to a "moral" culture,[1] people began to realize that direct action was more effective than religious ritual in influencing events.

In early China this option of personal assertion as a response to unfolding circumstances first appeared in *The Book of Changes*, the *I Ching*. Its essential subject was the interplay between a constantly changing world and a self-conscious individual who was seeking options within these shifting circumstances. How was such a person to act within perpetual change and uncertainty, between what is and what will be? The obvious answer was to anticipate the changes by attempting to read the movement of circumstances, and then change them, avoid them, or be prepared for them.

For a culture closely connected to the soil and the rhythms of the seasons, the Chinese became aware that all changes were linked to the ordered change of natural processes. Changes were not random or meaningless; they were bound by the character of the world itself and could be read in the images and rhythms of Nature. Human nature was part of Nature. Together the two rose and fell in patterns and cycles of growth and decay, birth and death. The similarities between inner and outer movement were noticeable and clear.

The *I Ching* measured these movements so they could be harmonized with each other. But it also measured something else. The insight that defined individual volition became the first conscious separation between inner self and outer circumstances. The spiritual integrity of all being was consequently divided, and the magical wholeness of a solely religious existence was fractured by the effort to control events directly. Attention shifted from passive ritual toward active influence. Although *The Book of Changes* recorded and then described this newly emerging relationship between the inner and the outer, it did not offer a resolution to the resulting split that now divided the sense of spiritual oneness. A more sophisticated thinking was required to resolve this dichotomy. In the structure of the *I Ching* and within its underlying assumptions was the resolution.

The tradition that evolved from the *I Ching* held that two interactive elements influenced events. The first was the great force of circumstances, the universal principle that pervaded everything. This omnipresence was soft and nurturing but it was also hard and unfailing, both an energy of creative generosity and an inflexibility of order that was determined by the integrity of itself. Although immediate and obvious, this principle was also beyond thought and knowing. Because it was beyond words it was simply called the Way, the Tao.

The second element was the virtue-power of individual character, the Te. It could be reached through *tso-wang*, "sitting with blank mind,"[2] by finding "the mind within the mind," or *hsin tsung*, the still place in the center of consciousness that was somewhow connected to the Tao through the oneness of the inner and the outer—a relationship somewhat like the Atman to the Brahman in Hinduism. When this connection was entered, when the Te became one with the Tao, the result was a synchronistic accord between the inner person and the outer world. Thus people could live harmonious-

4

GREG J SPATUZZI
5300 POST RD
APT 321
E GREENWICH   RI 02818-3056   96

ly within the bounds of natural order by becoming one with it. They could be joint partners in the unfolding of circumstances, exerting their influence by taking part in the larger ordering process while remaining compliant to the larger ordering principle. Individual volition could become soft and cooperative, compliant rather than willful. By cultivating inner character, people could influence events but still be in accord with the great order of the Tao. Thus, the inner-outer dichotomy was resolved. This school of thought and practice became known as Taoism.

This original Taoism was known at first as Quietism and later as philosophical or contemplative Taoism to distinguish it from other forms. It was averse to supersitition. Based on personal experience rather than belief, it would have no part of organized religion, rituals, and priests. Knowledge and influence came from within, not from institutionalized systems. Although these early Taoists needed solitude, they were not reclusive. They engaged life in order to enter it; the inner and the outer had to remain connected. Individuals were empowered by the character of who they were, by the cultivated interaction of the Te with the Tao.

But what could be the nature of this interaction if the Tao was thought to be a universal principle that was unknowable? Could a separate self with personal power coexist with the omnipresent Tao? What could be the accord between individual volition and aquiescence to the great principle? What was the resolution between self-consciousness and Tao-consciousness? These crucial questions were at the heart of the dilemma posed by the inner-outer and self-not-self dichotomies. They were answered—in as much as such questions can be answered with words—in the early thinking of

Taoism that eventually coalesced into a book known variously as the *Tao Te Ching*, the *Te Tao Ching*, or simply the *Lao Tzu*.

Taoism is the resolution of the subject-object, active-passive paradox that was invented by self-conscious deliberation. It puts together the wholeness that personal willfulness took apart. In simplest terms this is done by entering the dichotomy and becoming the empty stillness in the center of the paradox. This Taoist strategy then moved through Chinese Ch'an and became the essential strategy of Japanese Zen.

The word for Zen comes from an abbreviation of the Japanese *zenna*, which comes from the Chinese *ch'an*, itself a contraction of *ch'anna*, which, in turn, is from the Sanskrit *dhyana*, meaning "meditation." In brief, this meditation is a stilling and focusing of consciousness, a process that is like the *tso-wang* and the *hsin tsung* of original Taoism.

The fact, however, that Zen's name can be traced to Sanskrit suggests that the Japanese practice has a connection to the spiritual traditions of India. The relationship of Te and Tao to Atman and Brahman has already been noted. Comparisons of "sitting with blank mind" and "the mind within the mind" can be made between Zen and Indian meditation techniques. If Zen is a direct extension of Chinese rather than Indian thinking, then what explains these similarities and the Sanskrit etymology of the word Zen? This raises an issue that must be addressed.

In Victor H. Mair's translation of the *Ma-wang-tui* texts of the *Lao Tzu*, he argues persuasively that parallels can be drawn between the old Taoist classic from China and the *Bhagavad Gita* of India. He writes:

6

*Certain distinctive aspects of Yoga that show up in Taoism can be
traced back to India beyond the first millennium B.C. . . .
However, in China they only begin to appear at the earliest
around the middle of the first millennium B.C.*[3]

Mair argues that a Yoga tradition in India traveled orally
to China about 1000 B.C. But the Chinese, in adopting it,
wholly recast its wisdom into their own form and purpose,
and then articulated it in the *Lao Tzu*, the so-called *Tao Te
Ching*:

The Tao Te Ching *was as much, if not far more, the product of
internal sociopolitical conditions as it was the reaction to radical-
ly new religious and philosophical stimuli from without. As a
result, it comes to very different conclusions from those of the*
Bhagavad Gita. *The Chinese classic emphasizes political skills
and social harmony in preference to the theistic orientation of the
Indian scripture.*[4]

If Mair is correct, the Chinese adapted this early Indian
yoga, this proto-Zen, into a teaching that was uniquely their
own. They totally reshaped it to fit the culture of China,
remaking it from the transcendental and theological into the
earthy and practical. This new system, now only remotely
similar to yoga, became Taoism.

But not all aspects of this oral teaching that came from
Indian philosophy could be reshaped into the Chinese mold.
Some ideas were too foreign and had to await a more oppor-
tune time for coherent expression:

*Certain distinctive aspects of Yoga [were presented] in a confused
and cursory fashion until after the advent of Buddhism around*

the first century A.D. when they are reinforced by a new and more
coherently conveyed wave of Indian influence.[5]

When this more recent "wave of Indian influence" arrived in China to bring some coherence to "certain distinctive aspects of Yoga," it also carried some of the original yoga that had been the genesis of Taoism. This ancient connection may account for Buddhism being recognized by the Chinese as a simplified form of Taoism. This recognition may also account, in part, for the acceptance of the foreign Buddhism into Chinese culture. If Buddhist philosophy carried some of the Indian proto-Zen that had given birth to original Taoism, this may also explain the later coexistence of Taoism and Buddhism as Ch'an. It would also give more credible depth to D.T. Suzuki's observation that: . . . "Zen is the product of the Chinese soil from the Indian seed . . . ."[6]

A comment made by Seung Sahn, a master of Korean Zen, is also relevant here. *In A Time of Complete Transformation* he writes:

> *When Bodhidharma came to China, he became the First Patriarch*
> *of Zen. As the result of a "marriage" between Vipassana-style*
> *Indian meditation and Chinese Taoism, Zen appeared.*[7]

This comment indicates some connection between Taoist and Indian practices, and gives further credibility to Mair's contention that Taoism has a distant Indian source. Seung Sahn's remarks clearly support a Taoist component to Zen. They also suggest that Bodhidharma may not have been as direct a link to the Buddha, as Japanese Zen Buddhism contends. Consequently, Mahayana Buddhism may not have been the principal historical element connecting Chinese Ch'an to Zen in Japan.

There is no doubt that Ch'an was a blending of Taoism and Buddhism, not such an unusual mix if the Chinese perceived Buddhism to carry traces of Taoist philosophy. Indeed, the Chinese recognized Buddhist philosophy as a simplified form of Taoism. Eventually, however, the philosophy of Buddhism that could be connected with Taoism was supplanted by the religion of Mahayana Buddhism. The connection between Taoism and this religious Buddhism was not sustainable, so that eventually Zen, the Japanese extension of Chinese Ch'an, found itself in the company of a belief system that was antithetical to its Taoist heritage.

Zen Buddhism in Japan should more correctly be called Zen Mahayana Buddhism. But anyone who knows a little about the secular character of Zen will realize that this term is an oxymoron. It identifies an interesting problem, namely, that Zen and Mahayana Buddhism are mutually exclusive. Their coexistence is a contradiction. Zen Mahayana Buddhism is the result of two related traditions that diverged into two distinctly different components yet remained in the same institution.

All this is to explain why unholy Zen, neither religious nor dogmatic, is in the company of a belief system like Mahayana Buddhism, which is both. It explains, too, why Frederick Franck can quite justifiably write: "I find no Zen in Buddha."[8]

But which Buddha? The Buddha of Buddhist philosophy or the Buddha of the Mahayana religion?

There is no discernible Zen in Mahayana Buddhism. The traces of the yoga/proto-Zen that may have been carried in the philosophy of Buddhism were largely displaced when Buddhism became religious. The deification of the Buddha so dramatically altered the context of his teachings that his Zen, whatever amount may have been present, disappeared. Any Zen that can be found in Mahayana Buddhism is in the philosophical Buddhism that accompanies its religious doctrines.

The majority of the Zen that appears in Japanese Zen Buddhism is, in fact, Taoism. This Zen, really an Indian yoga wholly reinvented by the Chinese, arrived in Japan through Chinese Ch'an. Slowly it was assigned a Buddhist origin by those who wanted to reinforce the Mahayana beliefs of the Zen Buddhist institution. Zen's history was revised to emphasize the religious half of the Zen Buddhist oxymoron. Such characters as Hui-neng and the early Ch'an masters were cast as Buddhists rather than Taoists. Bodhidharma was also redesigned to conform to Buddhist purposes. In fact, a good deal of Zen Buddhism's history was redesigned to justify the beliefs of its Mahayana component. The smile that Mahakasyapa offered in answer to the Buddha's flower was a real smile but it was a Taoist smile. The Zen of Zen Buddhism is in character far more Chinese than Indian.

A close comparison of Taoism with Zen reveals them to be virtually identical. The initial idea for Zen may have come from Indian yoga, but the Zen of Japan is an historical and philosophical extension of the distinctively Chinese version.

The information that is presented in Part I of *The Tao of Zen* does not purport to be a complete history of Taoism, Buddhism, Ch'an, and Zen. It merely attempts to show that there is a basis for concluding that Zen's roots are in China and Taoism rather than India and Buddhism.

Lao Tzu

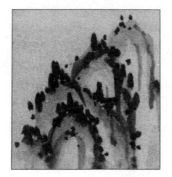

*t*radition has assigned the origin of Taoism to Lao Tzu, a mysterious sage who may have been born in 604 B.C. or 597 B.C. or perhaps in 571 B.C., at Ch'u Jen or Ch'en or K'uhsien. But he may have been born somewhere else at some other time, or perhaps not at all. The most basic information about Lao Tzu is either missing or is so mixed with contradiction or fancy that it argues against his existence.

One of the more credible stories has him Keeper of the Archives of the Chou court in 374 B.C., but this date does not coincide with the traditional time of his birth or with the conversations he reportedly had with Confucius, who by this time would have been dead for about a hundred years.

One fanciful story has Lao Tzu gestating in the womb for sixty-four years, another for eighty-one years. He is already silver-haired and speaking when born. At his birth he points to the plum tree where his mother was leaning and announces:

> "I take my surname from this tree." To Plum (Li) he prefixed
> Ear (Erh)—his being large—and so became Li Erh.
> However, since his hair was already snow-white, most people
> called him Lao Tzu, or Old Boy. After he died they called him
> Lao Tan, "Tan" meaning "long-lobed."[1]

Today, in a more scholarly understanding, *Lao* is still translated as "old" but *Tzu* is rendered as "master." So, in the same way that *Chuang Tzu* becomes "Master Chuang" and *Lieh Tzu* becomes "Master Lieh," *Lao Tzu* becomes "Old Master." Since definite and indefinite articles are not a part of written Chinese, however, there is no way of knowing whether his name is the specific *the* Old Master or the non-specific *an* old master. The name that seems to be coalescing out of the confusion is the Old Master, but the term is now being applied to the work as well as the author. As for the old sage himself, out of habit and convenience he is still called Lao Tzu even though all stories about him are historically questionable. Indeed, there is virtually no evidence that Lao Tzu ever existed.

Although the stories of Lao Tzu's birth are clearly fanciful, they do contain information that is useful in understanding the workings of the early Chinese mind and how it constructed and invented history. Sixty-four, one of the described gestation periods for Lao Tzu, is the number of hexagrams in the *I Ching*, an older Chinese literature than the *Lao Tzu*, and a significant element in Taoism's evolution. Eighty-one, the other gestation period, is the number of chapters assigned by custom to all modern versions of the book attributed to Lao Tzu. The sources of these translations, however, in their oldest forms, are essentially unchaptered. The eighty-one chapter divisions do not appear in any source material. Nor do they appear in the newly discovered texts from 168 B.C., the oldest extant sources by several hundred years. As Victor H. Mair notes in his translation of the *Ma-wang-tui* texts:

> *It is futile to attempt to provide any rational basis for the division into eighty-one chapters since the number is purely arbitrary and has no organic bearing on the systematic ordering of the text. This particular number . . . was probably picked up from the Buddhists who favored it because it is the square of nine, which was itself fraught with all manner of*

*symbolic significance for Indian mystics. One of the most hal-
lowed Buddhist scriptures, the* Prajnaparamitasutra *also had
eighty-one divisions.*[2]

With this kind of cultural mixing, the likelihood of finding
the authentic Lao Tzu becomes more remote.

Another curiosity in the traditional Lao Tzu story has to
do with Ear—*Erh*. Almost all depictions of the Buddha,
whether in India, Thailand, or China, show him with large or
long-lobed ears. That Lao Tzu should also be long-lobed is
more than a coincidence, a clear effort to connect Taoism and
Buddhism. Did Taoism affect the image of the Buddha or did
later Buddhists influence the story of Lao Tzu? The likely
answer is that the influence of Buddhism in China from the
first century onward retroactively altered the story of Lao
Tzu, making the details of his life even more elusive.

The various stories about Lao Tzu usually agree, however, that he become disillusioned with Chinese society, and
at age 90, 160 or 200 years he disappeared into the western
wilderness after presenting to the last gatekeeper of the
Middle Kingdom a written record of his wisdom. Later, when
Buddhism arrived in China, the Chinese recognized this
Indian teaching as a simplified version of Taoism, concluding
that it had been taught to the western barbarians by Lao Tzu
himself.

As modern scholarship and archeology examine early
Taoism, less and less of its traditional history remains credi-
ble. Even in 100 B.C., Ssu-ma Ch'ien, a reasonably reliable
Chinese historian, could not authenticate the existence of
Lao Tzu. Subsequent scholarship has not revealed a single
scrap of evidence to support the existence of the sage.
Present information suggests that he was probably a compos-

ite of a number of early writers or thinkers. The Old Master, therefore, can best be understood as a collective rather than an individual. Clearly, this has implications for the writing that is traditionally attributed to him.

Until recently the only texts of the *Lao Tzu* that existed were six Chinese versions, all of them at least copies or copies of copies, and all of them slightly different from each other; the number of characters alone ranging from 5,227 to 5,722.[3] The oldest versions are attributed to Yen Tsung (fl. 53-24 B.C.) or Wang Pi (A.D. 226-249).[4]

Then in 1973 at Changsha in Hunan province, archeologists excavated the tomb of the Horse King Mound (Ma-wang-tui) and found two nearly complete but slightly different versions of the *Lao Tzu*, a so-called *Text A* and a *Text B*. An enclosed inventory confirmed that both had been entombed in 168 B.C., making them at least several centuries older than previously existing copies. *Text B*, although not as old as *Text A*, shows indications of having been copied from an oral source.

Both Ma-wang-tui texts have a similar chapter order although, like other primary source material, they show only occasional breaks that do not correspond to the eighty-one chapters given to the traditional versions of the *Lao Tzu*. The two texts are more grammatically precise than the later copies but are still a formidable challenge to translate. In addition, the *Tao* and the *Te* halves of both manuscripts are reversed. The *Tao Te Ching*, which gets its name from the order of these two parts, should more rightly be called the *Te Tao Ching*. But a more accurate name would probably be the *Lao Tzu*; this is likely what it was called originally.

The Ma-wang-tui texts and their distinct but reversed

halves both clarify and confuse the puzzle of early Taoist history because they suggest a diverse rather than a particular beginning for Taoism, and argue against the creation of the *Lao Tzu* by a single author.

Such a diverse beginning does not bode well for the authenticity of Lao Tzu himself. Every question asked critically and answered objectively seems to point away from a specific historical character of that name. So Lao Tzu, the figure so large in Taoist history, moves closer to being the personification of a philosophical movement and a flesh-and-blood figment of the Chinese imagination.

Chuang Tzu

huang Tzu, the second most important figure in Taoism, is almost as enigmatic as Lao Tzu. The only historical reference to him is a brief description by Ssu-ma Ch'ien (145?-89? B.C.) in the *Shih chi*, or *Records of the Historian*.[1] The scant details of his life have been so mixed with legend that he is more a character of fiction than fact. And, as with the *Lao Tzu*, there is no way of knowing whether the work attributed to Chuang Tzu is the creation of one person or the compilation of a number of thinkers.

Chuang Tzu's life is traditionally set at 369-286 B.C. or perhaps 350-320 B.C., although he might have died as late as 275 B.C. He may have been a contemporary of the Confucian teacher Meng-tse, known as Mencius (372?-289? B.C.), but there is such a paucity of information about Chuang Tzu that scholars can only assume he existed. Since he is presently a part of Chinese consciousness it is easier to talk about him as if he existed than if he did not, which says something about the way historical figures can be created out of the thinnest of shadows. Scholarship, quite rightly, gives more attention to the writings than the writer.

No original version of the *Chuang Tzu* exists, however, and all the copies that do exist, like the traditional versions of the *Lao Tzu*, have been contaminated by either copying or editorializing. Kuo Hsiang, who died in A.D. 312, edited the versions of his day from a total of fifty-two sections down to thirty-three sections; he then divided these into seven "inner chapters," fifteen "outer chapters" and eleven "miscellaneous chapters."[2] Most of the inner chapters are presently considered to be authentic.

21

Present scholarship seems to agree that the aphoristic stories, the playful humor, and the brilliant logic of the *Chuang Tzu* have sharpened and elaborated the wisdom of the *Lao Tzu*. Furthermore, its style has lightened the sobriety of Taoism and has continued to shift it away from words, conventions, and systems.

But a critical reading of the *Chuang Tzu* provides no evidence that its author was or authors were even aware of a Lao Tzu or the writing attributed to him. In the body of literature that is assumed to be authentic, the *Chuang Tzu* neither refers to the Old Master nor quotes from him. Several similar phrases are used that could have come from the *Lao Tzu*, but they could also have come from the body of oral tradition that would have been widely available at the time.

Not only is there no definitive Lao Tzu or Chuang Tzu, there is no definitive link between the writings attributed to them. The possibility exists that the *Chuang Tzu* was a refinement and an amplification of the *Lao Tzu*, but it is more likely that the work is from an independent and parallel group of writers or thinkers whose ideas were later linked to the *Lao Tzu* by those who were trying retroactively to make sense of a style of thinking that was later known as Taoism. Indeed, if there was no actual character known as Lao Tzu, this may account for the failure of the *Chuang Tzu* to mention him. Even without Lao Tzu, however, why would the *Chuang Tzu* make no allusion to this earlier body of writing that was apparently of such seminal importance to Taoism? No one knows. One logical conclusion is that the *Lao Tzu*, at the time when the *Chuang Tzu* was taking shape, had not yet coalesced into a recognizable form of literature that could be cited. The work of Kuo Hsiang suggests that the *Chuang Tzu* also

22

evolved into existence from a diverse source. Its origin remains as enigmatic as that of the *Lao Tzu*.

Even with a text of the *Chuang Tzu*, the troubles do not end. The writings attributed to Chuang Tzu are subject to most of the problems that make so difficult any effort to translate the *Lao Tzu*. In addition to the corrupt texts and the inherent problems of translating from Chinese into English, the *Chuang Tzu's* thinking is unconventional and it uses words in unexpected ways. The subtleties and twists of logic would be difficult enough to understand if they had been written originally in English; in Chinese no one can be quite certain what they mean.

Still, what the *Chuang Tzu* seems to be saying is fascinating. Consider the following translation so superbly done by Gia-fu Feng and Jane English:

> *Now, I am going to tell you something. I don't know what heading it comes under, and whether or not it is relevant here, but it must be relevant at some point. It is not anything new, but I would like to say it.*
> *There is a beginning. There is no beginning of that beginning. There is no beginning of that no beginning of beginning. There is something. There is nothing. There is something before the beginning of something and nothing, and something before that. Suddenly there is something and nothing. But between something and nothing, I still don't really know which is something and which is nothing. Now, I've just said something, but I don't really know whether I've said anything or not.[3]*

This kind of convoluted thinking is incredibly difficult to understand, much less translate. However, there is a method in its madness. There is something unmistakably brilliant in the *Chuang Tzu*, a feeling that this intellectual play is maneuvering awareness toward a special kind of freedom.

This freedom is the result of a paradigm shift in understanding. In this respect the *Chuang Tzu* belongs in the company of the *Lao Tzu*. Together they are the basis of the Taoist experience. But the *Chuang Tzu* also belongs in the company of Zen, closer to the poetry of irrational logic than to the reason of rational philosophy. The comments in the *Chuang Tzu* about the "no beginning of . . . beginning" is like the riddles of Zen that precipitate the intellectual crisis preceding awakening.

In Burton Watson's book, *Chuang Tzu: Basic Writings*, his discussion of the Chinese master is very useful for drawing a comparison between Taoism and Zen:

> One device [Chuang Tzu] uses to great effect is the pointed or paradoxical anecdote, the non sequitur or apparently nonsensical remark that jolts the mind into awareness of a truth outside the pale of ordinary logic—a device familiar to Western readers of Chinese and Japanese Zen literature.[4]

Such "jolts" are characteristic of the *Chuang Tzu*, and they are also present, in a less anecdotal form, in the paradoxes of the *Lao Tzu*. These devices are later refined to become the *kung'an* of Ch'an and the *koan* of Zen.

Watson's further comments also reveal a good deal more about the closeness of Taoism and Zen:

> The other device most common in [Chuang Tzu's] writings is the pseudological discussion or debate that starts out sounding completely rational and sober, and ends by reducing language to a gibbering inanity. . . . Finally, [he] uses throughout his

writings that deadliest of weapons against all the pompous, staid and holy: humor.[5]

In intellectual tactic and in playful character this description of the *Chuang Tzu* could apply equally to Zen—not to the serious and austere Zen of Buddhism that would have come to China from India, but to the light and irreverent Zen of Taoism that was formed in China itself. From the perspective of history the figure called Chuang Tzu can be seen as the early Chinese equivalent of a Japanese Zen master. He thinks like one, he feels like one, he seems like one. All the similarities are present. What is missing is the solid biographical evidence that would give unquestionable certainty to the historical existence of Chuang Tzu.

This certainty is lost in early Taoist history. The evidence was compromised by the Chinese of the day who themselves either disregarded any sense of objective history—if there is such a thing—or had various motives, both honest and dishonest, for deliberately adjusting records to fit the circumstances of the occasion. Witness Kuo Hsiang's editorial efforts about A.D. 300 to find the authentic literature of the *Chuang Tzu*.

Any evidence of Chuang Tzu is compromised further by the overlay of later Buddhist history that rewrote or intermixed itself with Chinese history. Consider the following comments by Gia-Fu Feng and Jane English when introducing *Chuang Tzu: Inner Chapters*:

> *Chuang Tzu transcended the* whang cheng, *the illusory dust of the world—thus anticipating Zen Buddhism and laying the metaphysical foundation for a state of emptiness or ego transcendence.*[6]

Their comments suggest a close evolutionary relationship between Chuang Tzu and Zen Buddhism. If, however, no distinction is made between Zen and Buddhism, their comments also suggest a similarly close relationship between Chuang Tzu and Buddhism, an unlikely connection when "the dust of the world," the *whang cheng*, is much more an Indian than a Chinese notion. Historical timing precludes the possibility that the *Chuang Tzu* could have carried original Buddhist philosophy because Buddhism had not yet arrived in China. The likely explanation for the *whang cheng* in the *Chuang Tzu* is that it was added later by Buddhism's subsequent influence on Taoism. A less likely explanation is that the notion came to China orally with the Indian yoga that arrived about 1000 B.C. and somehow survived in opposition to centuries of Chinese attitude about the beneficence and generosity of life. Furthermore, original Taoism does not understand "emptiness or ego transcendence" in the same way that Buddhism does. For Taoists such release from ego is a means of reconnecting to wisdom and body of Earth, to the Great Mother; for Buddhists it is a way of disconnecting from the burden of *samsara*, the "Wheel of Life."

What does this mean with respect to the *Chuang Tzu*? It means that an exact version is impossible to find, and that following only the literal meaning of its words will mislead and confuse. Here is the paradox of garbled history. So the *Chuang Tzu* requires as well a subjective response that comes from the perspective of its general feeling, rather than the narrowness of its literal details. These details can be useful and they can be compared to Zen, but it is the overall feeling of the *Chuang Tzu* that finally reveals so convincingly its similarity to Zen.

As for Chuang Tzu the person, he is an unsolved mystery, a wish and a habit more than a fact. Like Lao Tzu, he remains in historical limbo. But the writings, whoever wrote them, are crucial to the character and spirit of Taoism. Without the *Chuang Tzu* there would probably be none of the playful irreverence that eventually became the wit and smile of Zen.

Taoism—
A Brief History

f the early history of Taoism is vague because of a lack of solid information, its later history is confusing because a profusion of shifting and intermixing relationships. Original Taoist philosophy eventually combined with superstition, folk practices, mythology, Buddhism, and Confucianism in a myriad of arrangements. The last two thousand years of Taoist history does not organize into a simple evolutionary pattern because it has been a constantly shifting mosaic of appearing and disappearing movements, of converging and diverging combinations.

Throughout this turmoil, however, the essential core of Taoist literature has survived because of conscientious efforts to preserve it, despite conscientious efforts to change it, and by sheer good luck. This literature has provided a relatively stable center around which the history of Taoism has churned and swirled in typically Chinese style. This history has been selected and simplified to trace more easily the connections between Taoism and Zen.

By the fourth century B.C. Taoism had become a pervasive part of the Chinese psyche and thereafter appeared in a widening spectrum of expression. At one extreme was the peaceful purity of the Quietists who lived simple and reclusive lives of contemplation and study, the philosophical descendents of Lao Tzu and Chuang Tzu. Others interpreted the metaphors of the original Taoist writings in a literal manner and followed an esoteric path. They became known as *hsien*, or "immortals." By yogic, alchemic, and hygienic means they attempted to cultivate supernatural powers, even to overcome death. One such branch sought the elusive Isles of the Blessed, *P'eng Lai*, for the fountain of eternal life or, as other stories contend, the sacred mushroom. At the other end of the spectrum were the folk practices that reduced Taoism to a religion of gods and goddesses, of supplicant prayer which was supposed to bring wealth, good fortune, and influence, even of a promised afterlife in paradise. In this folk form, Taoism existed with all the trappings of common religion, complete with sin, priests, demon control, and even orgiastic rituals. The only remnant of the *Lao Tzu* and the *Chuang Tzu* that remained was the aversion of each parish to any larger authority.

Whereas religious Taoism was practiced by the masses of Chinese, the more philosophical and contemplative forms remained the choice of the literary Chinese. They gave Taoism an intellectual and scholarly stability that weathered radical adulteration and provided a solid base against the ebbs and flows of popular fashion. This Taoism has remained relatively true to its original source and is the constancy connecting its early and later history. It is also the link to Zen.

The Chinese themselves divide Taoist history into *chia* and *chiao*, schools and sects.[1] The schools are philosophical or contemplative, and regard the wisdom of the *Lao Tzu* and the *Chuang Tzu* as the focus of their attention. Consequently, they have been largely responsible for maintaining the integrity of original Taoism. The sects, which have flourished since at least A.D. 25, have taken *hsien*, "immortality," as their objective. They use a variety of esoteric practices to reach this end, and interpret the original Taoist writings accordingly. This portion of Taoism, by far the most popular because of its promise of material benefits, deserves only mention here. The Taoist religion is placed in the *chiao* category. Zen evolved from the *chia* category.

But not all Taoist history fits into the categories of *chia* and *chiao*. Taoism mixed freely with both native and foreign traditions. After the first century A.D. some Taoist practices were influenced by the arrival in China of Indian Buddhism. Variations of this Buddhism later influenced Taoism by combining with it to create Ch'an, the Chinese form of Japanese Zen Buddhism. Taoist history even involved neo-Confucianism, which was the creation of its interaction with Confucianism. Even neo-Confucianism, in an indirect way, managed to reinforce the Taoist character of Ch'an.

Ch'an, in Taoist terms, branched Taoism away from its solely Chinese character by combining *chia* with Buddhist philosophy. Ch'an is really Taoism with an overlay of Buddhism and, as such, has divided loyalties between China and India. Later, when Ch'an migrated to Japan to become Zen Buddhism, its Buddhist component, for religious reasons, chose to recognize its Indian connection to Buddhism rather than its Chinese evolution from Taoism.

But Taoism has been the founding force in Ch'an. Indeed, the pervasive and persistent influence of the *Lao Tzu* and the *Chuang Tzu* have existed as an unbroken thread throughout the whole formative history of China, influencing practically everything that became a part of Chinese thought. Ch'an was no exception. Taoism influenced Ch'an directly and indirectly. It was Ch'an's foundation, and through Ch'an, Taoism became the foundation of Japanese Zen. But Taoism also influenced Ch'an indirectly. Some of these indirect influences must be explained.

Neo-Taoism originated in the third century A.D. and was a kind of reconstituted Quietism. Some of the new interest in Quietism may have been generated by the growing popularity in China of Buddhism and the apparent similarities between it and Taoism. As the various sects became more occupied with organizing Taoist churches and interpreting the *Lao Tzu* and the *Chuang Tzu* in fanciful ways, this caused others to return with fresh interest to consider carefully and contemplate seriously the original Taoist literature. These neo-Taoists engaged in what was called *ch'ing t'an*, or pure conversation, an activity that implied "philosophy for its own sake."[2] So the *Lao Tzu* and the *Chuang Tzu* were considered for their own sake. This not only gave a more public profile to the contemplative form of Taoism, but it also resulted in the preservation of its literature; the traditional sources of both the *Lao Tzu* and the *Chuang Tzu* came from this neo-Taoist period. Wang Pi (A.D. 225-249) was a cofounder of *ch'ing t'an*, and to him is owed one of the most reliable of the traditional *Lao Tzu* texts. He and others also revived the connection between the *Lao Tzu* and the *I Ching*.

To these neo-Taoists is also owed the notion that Taoism should not be the pursuit of the recluse, that it should be an integral part of common life. This view was echoed later in the *Ox Herding Pictures* of Ch'an and Zen in which the enlightened sage returns to the community to become a part of its daily life. The followers of *ch'ing t'an* did not support the esoteric, immortal, alchemic, and hygienic traditions of the *hsien* Taoists and lived like ordinary people. One group known popularly as the *Seven Sages of the Bamboo Grove*:

> *used to walk in the heat of the afternoon, making up poetry,*
> *drinking a little wine, and playing the lute. Here, too, they*
> *indulged themselves in "pure conversation" which would end,*
> *as Fung Yu-lan puts it, when they reached the Unnameable*

34

*and then "stopped talking and silently understood each other
with a smile."[3]*

Not only are the silence and the smile pure Zen, but the conversation and the music are reflected later in Japanese Zen's
pastime of writing *tanka* and making spontaneous music.
These attributes of the Zen tradition entered Japan through
neo-Taoism's influence on Ch'an.

There were two indirect and unexpected ways in which
Taoism helped to shape the character of Ch'an and then Zen.
Curiously enough, these were through the Taoist religion and
neo-Confucianism.

The first evidence of Taoist religion can be dated to
about A.D. 150 with Chang Tao-ling of the *Celestial Master
Sect*.[4] Although this sect should not be confused with philosophical Taoism, some of the wisdom of the *Lao Tzu* and the
Chuang Tzu was carried within its religious practices. By the
sixth century its Taoist churches began to copy the successful
Buddhist monasteries by establishing convents for women
and issuing certificates of proficiency for practitioners.[5] By
the tenth century there were some eighty-six different Taoist
sects in China, roughly classed into a northern and a southern
group.[6] By more than coincidence these two groups corre-
sponded to the division in the Ch'an schools of the same
time, the same schools that later in Japan became Soto and
Rinzai Zen.

The northern Taoist religion, said to have been founded by Wang Che (A.D. 1112-1170), was known as *Ch'uan Chen*,
or Perfect Realization.[7] It reveals the synthesis that had taken
place in what were now the three principle traditions of
China: native Taoism and Confucianism, and adopted
Buddhism. Although a fanatical ascetic:

> *Wang was by no means exclusively a Taoist. He acknowledged*
> *"the Three Doctrines," i.e., the Confucian Doctrine of the*
> *Mean; the Ch'an Buddhism of Bodhidharma; and the Taoism*
> *of Lao Tzu. His successor, Ch'ang Ch'un considered Lao*
> *Tzu's doctrine the original one. . . .⁸*

This synthesis in *Ch'uan Chen* of Confucian virtue with the spiritual elements of the Taoist and Buddhist religions is wonderfully illustrated in a quote by Ch'ang Ch'un, Wang Che's successor:

> *Sweep, sweep, sweep!*
> *Sweep clear the heart until there is nothing*
> *left.*
> *He with a heart that is clean swept*
> *is called a "good man."*
> *A "good man" is all that is meant*
> *by "holy hsien" or "Buddha."* ⁹

It is clear that Ch'ang Ch'un understood the Chinese notion of immortals in terms of the Mahayana belief in the Buddha, and that he had integrated the emptiness in Taoist practice with a similar practice in Buddhism. In *Ch'uan Chen*, Buddhism and Taoism became indistinguishable.

The southern Taoist religion, founded by Liu Hai-ch'an and his successor, Chang Po-tuan (A.D. 983-1082),¹⁰ was substantially the same as the northern one. Whereas in the north they "cultivated life," *ming*, in the south they "cultivated nature," *hsing*,¹¹ to the same purpose. The two terms, *ming* and *hsing*, correspond to the differences between the two schools of Ch'an that existed at the same time. Holmes Welch writes in *Taoism: The Parting of the Way*:

*As for the classification into North and South, I suspect that it
. . . arose from analogy with Ch'an Buddhism. The Southern
School of Ch'an advocated sudden rather than gradual
enlightenment. It is significant that Chang Po-tuan claimed to
have acquired "the highest degree" from Hui Neng, the Sixth
Patriarch of the Southern School of Ch'an.*[12]

Chang Po-tuan must have received "the highest degree" by some magical means because Hui-neng would have been dead for some three hundred years. The claim is clearly fanciful but it is important in connecting Taoism with Zen because it identifies Hui-neng as a Taoist rather than a Buddhist. Hui-neng, the traditional founder of Zen Buddhism and its sixth Patriarch, was regarded as a prime authority in the Taoist religion. Furthermore, the parallel structure between the two Taoist religions and the two Ch'an schools suggests a deeper than coincidental connection between Taoism and Ch'an.

What was gradually occurring in China was a convergence of the Taoist and Buddhist religions such that:

*the Taoist monastic system became so similar to the Buddhist
that in recent times Taoist monks were welcome to stay in
Buddhist monasteries and vice-versa.*[13]

Taoism's other unexpected influence on Ch'an came through Confucianism, the other founding tradition of Chinese culture. In its original form, Confucianism lacked a spiritual dimension. By the third century, at the same time that the Taoist religion was becoming less distinguishable from Chinese Buddhism, Confucianism was filling its own deficiency by adopting the essential spiritual qualities of

37

philosophical Taoism. Neo-Confucianism, as it came to be called:

> adopted the Taoist goals of minimizing desires, returning to the purity of one's original nature, identification of the individual with the universe, and even the self-expression of feng lui.[14]

Feng lui, literally "wandering from convention,"[15] means following the impulse, becoming free from the rigid controls that guide traditional Confucianism. The feng lui of neo-Confucianism and the tzu-jan of philosophical Taoism, a personal and inner allowing of "spontaneous arising" or "what happens of itself," are virtually identical. This is the same spontaneity that is cultivated in Ch'an and Zen.

The neo-Confucians borrowed heavily from Taoism but they also borrowed so heavily from Ch'an that they became nearly indistinguishable from it, too. Consequently they intermixed with the Ch'an schools so that attributes of philosophical Taoism were fused into Ch'an by this unlikely and indirect Confucian means.

As for Taoism itself, it continued to be a distinctly Chinese tradition expressing the philosophy of the Lao Tzu and the Chuang Tzu. But it also branched into Ch'an. Because of the Indian influence in China, Ch'an became an extension of Taoism with an overlay of Buddhist religion, rituals, and organization.

Not that Buddhism in its purely philosophical form was wholly incompatible with Taoism—remember that the Chinese first recognized Buddhism as a simplified form of Taoism. Enlightenment, so explicit in Buddhism, has always been implicit in Taoism as an equivalently profound experience. For Buddhism, however, enlightenment creates a metaphysical disconnectedness; for Taoism it creates an earthy reconnectedness. At a superficial level the two forms of awakening seem similar. Both cultivate an attitude of separation, of detachment, but at a deeper level they are quite different. For Buddhism the separation is an objective; for Taoism it is a means. Buddhism separates from the world to transcend it; Taoism dissolves back into the world to become one with it. Later, in Japanese Zen Buddhism, this difference is clearly expressed in the distinction between Buddhist and Zen attitudes.

The superficial similarity of Taoism and Buddhism has accounted for the ability of these different traditions to coexist in China as Ch'an and then in Japan as Zen Buddhism. At the same time, however, the deeper differences between their Chinese and Indian components have created within them an inherent contradiction.

Ch'an, then, when understood without the overlay of Buddhism—when its Indian element is removed—is almost indistinguishable from Taoism. In personality, philosophy, and intellectual character, Ch'an without Buddhism is almost identical to Taoism.

Taoism has been such a pervasive part of the Chinese culture that it has been an unavoidable influence on nearly everything that has happened in China. It directly formed the essential character of Ch'an, and indirectly it was a formidable influence through the Taoist religion and neo-Confucianism. When Ch'an arrived in Japan to become Zen Buddhism, Taoism came along as a fundamental ingredient. When the Buddhist attitudes and practices in Zen Buddhism are removed, they reveal its Taoist character. As Holmes Welch puts in bluntly: "[Zen's] roots in Lao Tzu are clear."[16]

Exposing these roots and tracing their importance reveals that the trunk of Zen, hidden beneath the branches and foliage of Buddhism, is also Taoism.

Buddhism
in China

y its own account, Zen Buddhism was officially brought from India to China by Bodhidharma in A.D. 520. Of course, Buddhism had been in China long before Bodhidharma's arrival and by his time it was already well established in Chinese courts and monasteries. As early as the end of the first century, monks had founded a Buddhist community in Loyang, the capital of the Han emperor.

Over the next five centuries the Buddhist presence in China grew, and texts—mostly Mahayana—were translated. When the Han Dynasty collapsed in the third century, the resulting disorder increased the appeal for softer and gentler philosophies such as Buddhism and Taoism.

These two traditions had enough basic similarities to coexist comfortably. Some political disagreements occurred between Buddhists and organized Taoists but, for the most part, their relationship was cordial. Taoism's initial resistance to Buddhism was little more than cultural protection and pride. As Richard Cavendish notes in *The Great Religions*:

> *Scornful Chinese intellectuals regarded the foreign religion as an inferior variety of Taoism. Lao Tzu was said to have gone to the west and taught Taoism to the barbarians—in a simplified form appropriate to their limited intelligence—and from them it had now returned. Taoists claimed that Lao Tzu and the Buddha were the same person.*[1]

Indeed, associating the Buddha with Lao Tzu could be interpreted as a tacit expression of China's respect for Buddhism, and acknowledgment of the recognized similarities between the traditions.

As religious Buddhism changed shape to fit its new environment in China, religious Taoism was also evolving to fit the needs of the Chinese. Sometimes the two were nearly indistinguishable:

> *This early Buddhism was generally regarded as a sect of religious Taoism . . . [and] Taoist communities may have served to spread certain Buddhist symbols and cults.*[2]

In many instances the two traditions melded so that mountains once sacred to the religious Taoists also became sacred to the Buddhists.[3]

Meanwhile, those who followed the original form of philosophical Taoism, Quietism, recognized that their objectives were similar to those in Buddhist philosophy:

> *The Buddhist contemplative practice struck a responsive chord in Chinese society in part, at least, because of its resonance with the older Taoist philosophical mystical tradition and the Taoist ideal of attaining an intuitive awareness of the underlying Way of the natural universe.*[4]

The Quietists were attempting to accomplish essentially the same thing as these Buddhists. By penetrating deeper and deeper into consciousness, they hoped to reach the *hsin tsung*, "the mind within the mind," and thereby stop the intellectual mindfulness that obstructed profound insight. The Buddhist philosophers believed that reaching this level of awareness would constitute enlightenment. The Quietists had the more worldly objective of balancing and harmonizing social and natural relationships by attuning the inner virtue-

44

power, the Te, with the way of the universe, the Tao. The Buddhists would have understood this process to be somewhat like the Hindu notion of reaching Brahman through the inner realization of Atman. In Buddhism the terminology was different but the process was similar. Buddhist and Taoists would have recognized that all three processes could be equated to each other.

So similar were these elements of Taoist and Buddhist philosophy that by the third century Buddhism even became useful for Taoist interests. When philosophical Taoism was losing some of its vitality from decades of thorough exploration, and its essential teachings were being adulterated by popular interpretation, the discussion and practice of Buddhism added a new vitality to Taoism.[5] In the fourth century, writes Burton Watson, in *Chuang Tzu: Basic Writings*:

> *The gradual spread of Buddhism . . . helped to foster [a]*
> *revival of interest in Taoism, often referred to as Neo-Taoism,*
> *because so many of the doctrines of the Indian religion*
> *appeared, on the surface at least, to be strikingly similar to*
> *those of Lao Tzu and Chuang Tzu.*[6]

As Buddhism was being adopted by China, its teachings were being adjusted to fit the Chinese temperament. Eventually, three somewhat distinct forms of Chinese Buddhism evolved: *Ching-t'u*, *T'ien-t'ai*, and *Hua-yen*.

Ching-t'u, later to be known as *Jodo* in Japan and *Pure Land* in the West, reduced the sophistication of Buddhist psychology and philosophy into a simple belief system in which a reincarnation of the Buddha, such as the popular female figure of *Kuan-yin*, could offer direct and immediate salvation.

T'ien-t'ai became a Chinese version of Mahayana Buddhism. As for *Hua-yen*, it tried:

> to explain the nature of things by pointing out the inseparability of phenomena and principle: all phenomena are identified with each other and are representative of the same supreme mind of the Blessed One; thus the One contains the many and the many contain the One.[7]

With only minor adjustments in terminology this summary of *Hua-yen* could quite comfortably describe the Chinese understanding of the Tao. What is apparent is the degree to which Chinese thinking had entered Buddhism because of the related similarities of Taoist and Buddhist philosophy.

The first effect of these similarities was to gain for Buddhism access into China. Then, as this Indian philosophy began to adopt a Chinese character, its popularity increased. Slowly, philosophical Buddhism found itself more and more comfortable in the company of philosophical Taoism. At the same time, original Taoism was feeling less and less comfortable with the folk and esoteric practices of the *hsien*, the "immortals," and with all the sects that seemed to be drifting farther from the writings of the *Lao Tzu* and the *Chuang Tzu*.

Taoism even drew closer to such unlikely company as *T'ien-t'ai*. This Chinese form of Mahayana Buddhism would have remained incompatible with Taoism had it not emphasized instant enlightenment arising out of a relationship with the particulars of the everyday world.[8] Seng-chao (A.D. 384-414), a monk who was a Taoist and a Confucian copiest, found these connections during his study with Kumarajiva, an

Indian scholar and monk who was translating Mahayana sutras into Chinese between A.D. 384 and 413.[9]

The main importance of this sutra for China and for Zen was the point that perfect awakening was consistent with the affairs of everyday life. . . .[10]

Seng-chao's fusion of Mahayana Buddhism and Taoism in *The Book of Chao* was supported by Tao-sheng (A.D. 360-434)[11] and was later reinforced by the famous Ch'an patriarch Hui-neng (A.D. 637-713), who initiated in China about two hundred years of flourishing Ch'an activity.

What evolved between philosophical Taoism and Buddhism during this time was an increasing compatibility such that their essential teachings and character became inseparable. Together they formed the Ch'an monasteries. In Ch'an, the Tao was thought to be "Buddha-nature immanent in nature."[12] This was one of the major ways in which Taoism would eventually become a part of Japanese Zen Buddhism.

At first, when Buddhism began to become popular in sixth-and-seventh century China, Confucians and court representatives of Taoism objected to this intrusion of a foreign teaching into their culture. So in A.D. 624 a forum was initiated by the T'ang court in the hope of showing that: "Though the three teachings are different, their benefits are the same."[13]

The forum continued until A.D. 870, and during these 251 years:

the struggle was resolved in typical Chinese fashion—synthesis rather than exclusiveness, compatibility rather than conflict.[14]

47

For Confucianism this synthesis eventually created neo-Confucianism, a blending of all three traditions. For Buddhism it meant that Taoism could be comfortably integrated into its thinking. For Taoism it ratified and legitimized its incorporation into both Confucianism and Buddhism.

To understand the process by which Taoism and Buddhism were able to coexist to become Ch'an, it is necessary to understand in greater detail the essential philosophical similarities of the two traditions. Without these similarities Ch'an could not have been created as an institution, and Zen Buddhism would not have existed.

Taoism and Buddhism share some essential insights that form important common ground: desire is a source of problems; self is an impediment to spiritual insight; guiding others or helping society at large is a stated or implicit obligation. Some of their principles are comparable: the Middle Way of Buddhism can be related to the Taoist notion of balanced harmony; Buddhist compassion is similar to the Taoist teachings of humility and softness; emptying, the same process that permits the Taoist to become one with the Tao, permits the Buddhist to achieve enlightenment. Differences do exist between Taoism and Buddhism. Buddhism is shaded with Hindu mysticism whereas Taoism has its roots in Chinese practicality, but these differences are small enough that their teachings can be applied to a common purpose.

These teachings in Buddhism are embodied in *Meditations on the Four Acts*, attributed to Bodhidharma.[15] Each of these Acts is directly convertible into the language and thought of Taoism: "the Requital of Hatred" can be understood as an unqualified acceptance of the world and the things in it; "Following Circumstances" engenders trust by acknowledging an inherent wisdom in the unfolding of events; "Asking for Nothing" not only reflects an absence of desire but also affirms the poignancy and importance of each moment; "Accordance with Reality" can be interpreted in Taoism to mean that a thoughtless suchness is the nature of each thing and the nature of the Tao itself.

The philosophical similarities shared by Taoism and Buddhism even extend to their basic intellectual tactics. Both are fundamentally processes of negation by which the Way of Taoism and the Buddha-nature of Buddhism are found through emptying—no self, no permanence, no bliss. "*Neti! Neti!*" is the Indian expression, "Not this! Not this!"[16]

Or compare the first and second of Buddhism's Four Noble Truths—very roughly interpreted to mean that suffering is a condition of existence and that desire perpetuates this suffering—to the pronouncement in the *Lao Tzu*:

Accept disgrace willingly.
Accept misfortune as the human condition.

What do you mean by "Accept disgrace willingly?"
Accept being unimportant. . . .

What do you mean by "Accept misfortune as the human condition?"
Misfortune comes from having a body. Without a body, how could there be misfortune?[17]

Taoists would have recognized the validity of the Buddhist concepts of detachment and selflessness, although they would have interpreted these notions in more practical than metaphysical terms—the absence of possessing, interfer-

49

ing or controlling for Taoists was a strategy for entering the world, not escaping it. The whole cultural climate of China disposed Taoists toward a useful and grounded existence. But they would have concurred with the operative principles in Buddhism and, in general, they would have been sympathetic with Buddhist philosophy.

The philosophical qualities of Buddhism had an intellectual character that would have appealed to those who followed the principles of original Taoism. Both Taoism and Buddhism experience from within systems of understanding that must finally negate and abandon themselves; both practices can only happen when they are free of the constraints of themselves. Much of Taoist literature is an admonishment against becoming caught in any system, whether moral, political, philosophical, linguistic, or religious. With such freedom, belief is replaced by experience. A traditional Buddhist dialogue reflects the same principle:

> *The Buddha was asked, "Are you God?"*
> *"No," he said.*
> *"Well, then, what are you?"*
> *"Awake," said the Buddha.*

In a more abrupt and much less comfortable form the same idea is expressed in Zen Buddhism, "If you meet the Buddha, kill him!"

To become a pure Buddhist, a Buddhist must ultimately renounce Buddhism just as the Buddha renounced self and all attachment. this principle pervades Taoism as well. Taoists cannot live Taoism if they hold to the system called Taoism. Individuals who practice either Taoism or Buddhism are inevitable inclined toward inconspicuousness and, finally, invisibility as the system that contains them dissolves itself. In this regard Chuang Tzu's sense of freedom[18] can be likened to the Buddha's sense of emancipation.

As Buddhism became a part of Chinese culture, Taoists would have identified with its philosophical qualities, partly because of similarities but partly because of their disaffection with the practices of the Taoist sects and religions of the time. Of course, philosophical differences did exist between the Taoists and Buddhists. But the relevant history here is that the Chinese recognized similarities and this common ground became the basis for Ch'an.

As for Mahayana Buddhism, it would have appealed to those in the Taoist religions; the philosophical Taoists would have had some fundamental differences with its religious qualities. However, during the formation of Ch'an from Taoism, both the philosophy and the religion of Buddhism were involved. As China became more Mahayana, so too did Ch'an. Eventually, the Taoists in Ch'an found themselves in the company of Mahayana Buddhism, which is how Zen came to find itself in the same company.

As Buddhism in China was adjusted to fit Chinese sensibilities, the distinction between it and the Taoist sects and religions began to blur. In the common mind a synthesis of Buddhism and Taoism began to take place:

Chinese versions of the Buddhist scriptures were adapted to Chinese ideas, and Buddhism and Taoism were often mingled together in popular belief.[19]

This mingling did not take place among the more literary and scholarly Taoists. For them the integration of Buddhism into China helped to define and invigorate the

Taoism of the *Lao Tzu* and the *Chuang Tzu*. Their Taoism involved, ostensibly, no belief; it was and continues to be an aesthetic philosophy rather than a religion. Mahayana Buddhism is a religion that evolved from a philosophical base. Taoism and Buddhism can be reconciled philosophically but not religiously. Those following the original form of Taoism have been unable to relate to the Mahayana aspects of Buddhism.

Even in the popular mind some of these differences were not so easily resolved:

> *Buddhism was in many ways distinctly un-Chinese. The Indian belief that human beings live over and over again on earth was entirely unknown in China. The Chinese reverence for the family clashed with the Buddha's teaching that family ties were a hindrance to enlightenment, and the celibacy required of Buddhist monks. Where Buddhism saw life as suffering, Chinese tradition regarded the order of nature as fundamentally good and the right life as one lived in harmony with nature. Far from wanting to escape from the body and individual personality, most Taoists wanted to prolong their individual existence indefinitely.*[20]

In other words, a basic difference separates the character of Indian Buddhism and the native Chinese traditions of Confucianism and Taoism.

Taoism is earthy. It is basically optimistic. It accepts in general terms that life is worth living and that nature, personified in the metaphor of the Great Mother, is essentially a balanced beneficence. Buddhism's character is more sober, less optimistic. As Richard Cavendish notes:

> *Although it has often been observed that Buddhism is a cheer-*

52

ful and good-humored religion, the Buddhist attitude to life is intensely pessimistic. Life on earth is evil, painful and transitory. It is full of suffering and nothing lasts, nothing stays the same.[21]

One of the characteristics of Zen that argues for a Taoist rather that a Buddhist origin is its lightness, its playfulness, its appreciative acceptance of life. Buddhism is serious, leaden, weighted down by Gautama's traumatic realization that suffering lies beneath the veneer of life's comforts, and pleasures. The story of his own evolution from innocent prince to enlightened being is a revealing process. The emphasis is on the endurance and perseverance that the quest for enlightenment demands. He struggles through seven years of wilderness meditation and asceticism before reaching realization. The same long struggle is reenacted later in China by Bodhidharma who sits persistently for nine years facing a wall. The literal truth of these stories is less important that the underlying attitudes they reveal.

The heavy, plodding feeling that pervades Buddhism has none of Zen's sprightly freedom and intellectual adroitness. This spirit of Zen comes through Taoism. The *Lao Tzu* and the *Chuang Tzu* represent the dancing and darting intellect, the wit and humor that accept and celebrate the human condition.

The Chinese embrace life as worth living, and they seek ways of living it wisely and well. This is evident in the popular Kuan-yin, a maternal incarnation of the Buddha, who bestows fertility, safety, and comfort to her supplicants. This same positive attitude is seen in the round and jovial folk-Buddhas of modern China who sit big-bellied and contented, or stand wide-legged and laughing. These images of the

Buddha, unlike the austere and emaciated ones from India, invite a full and happy life.

Even in religion the Chinese enjoy life too much to waste it on esceticism and metaphysical exercises. They would gladly sacrifice a few years for immortality as a good investment of time. They would willingly do *t'so-ch'an* (Japanese: *zazen*, literally "sitting meditation") to effect social harmony or attain worldly gain and influence. But they would not expend much energy for something as abstract and metaphysical as enlightenment. "Once you had enlightenment," they would ask, "what would you do with it?" This question is expressed with an appropriate mixture of playfulness and practicality in a Zen story:

> A Zen roshi *and a Hindu guru were walking together along a riverbank and decided to visit an adjacent island.*
> *"Let's walk to the island," said the guru.*
> *"Why not take the ferry?" suggested the* roshi.
> *"Because," said the guru, "I've spent twenty years learning to walk on water."*
> *"Why take twenty years learning to walk on water," asked the* roshi, *"when you can take a ferry for a penny?"*

The same grounded practicality characterizes the Lao Tzu. As Victor H. Mair points out:

> *The Chinese classic emphasizes political skills and social harmony in preference to the theistic orientation of the Indian scripture.*[22]

The Mahayana religious component in Ch'an and Zen Buddhism emphasizes the *zazen* in emulation of the sitting Buddha of India. Very practical reasons exist for doing *zazen* but they have been overlayed with exhortations to persevere, to be like the Buddha, to sit until all sentient beings are saved. In contrast, the Taoist element in Ch'an and Zen Buddhism is not interested in such theological objectives. The purpose of protracted sitting is not to perpetuate itself but to release the practitioner into the spontaneity and freedom of merely being. The end of all the searching and discipline is a full and balanced life lived gracefully and harmoniously in wonderful simplicity. The sitter returns to the village to become fully engaged in the profoundly ordinary business of day-to-day existence.

The *Lao Tzu* dedicates about half its wisdom to the affirmation of such worldly affairs. Although its treatment lacks the playfulness of the *Chuang Tzu*, it is nonetheless a clear confirmation of this life in this earthy place, fully committed to the worth that is inherent in the whole social and natural world. Any discipline in Taoism is used to reenter fully what is already present. This is also the case in Zen. Buddhism's discipline does not complete the cycle of leaving, returning, and reaffirming. It spins outward to become removed, unearthly, and austere, reluctantly present in the world as if living were a kind of selfless sacrifice.

Bodhidharma

odhidharma (circa A.D. 470-543) is a critically important figure in Zen Buddhism. Without him there is no direct connection between its present practice in Japan and the original teachings of the Buddha in India. Zen Buddhism's own history attempts to support this connection with Bodhidharma. He is both the Zen and the Buddhism of Zen Buddhism.

According to Zen Buddhism's account, the actual enlightening process employed by Siddhartha Gautama himself was passed from teacher to teacher through a thousand years of Indian history to Bodhidharma. Then he brought this teaching to China where it became Ch'an, and later, Zen Buddhism in Japan. Zen Buddhism, according to its own account, possesses the original instructional technique of the Buddha. The alleged authenticity of Bodhidharma serves philosophcially and theologically to connect Japan with India and to establish that Zen and Buddhism are the same thing.

But which Buddhism? A considerable difference exists between the religion of Mahayana Buddhism that presently houses Zen and the psychological gymnastics that led to the awakening experience of the Buddha. If Zen Buddhism purports to be the very process that the Buddha employed in his own awakening, then the Mahayana flavor of Zen Buddhism has to be dismissed as superfluous trappings, as theological baggage. The Buddha was no more a Mahayana Buddhist than Jesus was a Christian.

The next pertinent question is whether Zen Buddhism employs the Buddha's technique for awakening. Since Bodhidharma is supposed to be the connecting link between the Buddha of India, the tradition of Ch'an in China, and its successor as the present practice of Zen Buddhism in Japan, then the pertinent answer lies in the authenticity of Bodhidharma as Zen Buddhism describes him.

Bodhidharma is his Indian name; it comes from *bodhi*, meaning "truth," and *dharma* meaning, approximately, "teachings." In Japan he is known as *Daruma* and in China he was named *Pu-ti-ta-mo*.[1]

Bodhidharma's arrival in Canton in A.D. 520—legend describes that he crossed the sea riding on a reed—is Zen Buddhism's account of the formal introduction into China of the essence of Buddhism. But it is important to note that Buddhism—mostly Mahayana—had already been in China for more than four hundred years, and by Bodhidharma's appearance was a well-established part of Chinese culture. This new teacher, only one of a number who had been arriving from India at that time, purported to be offering the authentic form of teaching that was transmitted directly from the Buddha.

Emperor Wu of Liang was already an avid Mahayana Buddhist, and he was not impressed with either the new teacher or the new teaching. Its abrupt and enigmatic style confused him, and Bodhidharma's efforts failed to convert him. In *Zen Buddhism*, D.T. Suzuki[2] describes this meeting. The following is an adapted and abbreviated version of that account:

> *Emperor Wu of Liang asked Bodhidharma, "Ever since the beginning of my reign I have built many temples, copied many sacred books, and supported many monks and nuns. What do you think my merit might be?"*
>
> *"No merit whatsoever, sire!" Bodhidharma bluntly replied.*

"Why?" demanded the astonished Emperor.
"They are inferior deeds," said Bodhidharma.
"What then is the first principle of the holy doctrine?" asked
the Emperor.
"Vast emptiness. And there is nothing in it to be called holy,
sire!" answered Bodhidharma.
"Who is it then that is now confronting me?"
"I know not, sire!"

There was not a meeting of minds. Emperor Wu, it seems, was already too steeped in Mahayana thinking to grasp the simplicity and the subtlety of Bodhidharma's point or even to pursue it further. So Bodhidharma retreated to a monastery, reportedly the Shao-lin Temple on Mount Wu-tai in Honan,³ where, facing a wall, he sat in continual meditation for nine years.

What exactly Bodhidharma was attempting to teach the Emperor was simple, but incredibly difficult to convey precisely because of its simplicity. It remains enigmatic because this simplicity cannot be explained. Zen Buddhism's account of Bodhidharma's insight reaches back to the Buddha himself. A traditional story is recounted—with varying degrees of elaboration—of a group of disciples who had gathered around the Buddha to be tested on their understanding of his teachings. When he held up a single flower they unsuccessfully tried elaborate explanations in terms of it. Only one disciple, Mahakasyapa, seemed to know. He simply smiled silently. And in his smile the Buddha recognized Mahakasyapa's understanding. In this silent and inexplicable smile, according to Zen Buddhism, was the essence of Buddhism, the essence of Bodhidharma's teaching, and the essence of Zen.

Zen Buddhist tradition acknowledges Mahakasyapa

through to Bodhidharma as the direct successors of the essential process by which the Buddha attained enlightenment. In *The Way of Zen* Alan Watts writes:

> *Bodhidharma is represented as the twenty-eighth of a somewhat fanciful list of Indian Patriarchs standing in a direct line of "apostolic succession" from Gautama.*[4]

As a result of Bodhidharma's arrival and teaching in China, he is considered by Zen Buddhism to be its first Patriarch. But why not its twenty-eighth? He is that, too. Then why two categories? If Zen is the uninterrupted extension of the Buddha's teachings, why are there separate Chinese and Indian counts of its patriarchs? Because two different forces define Zen Buddhism. One is Indian and the other is Chinese. Zen Buddhism wants to be Indian because its belief and theology demand Buddhism; it has to be Chinese because its history and philosophy demand Taoism. Its own conflicting identity is evident in the two systems of counting its patriarchs. Bodhidharma is crucial to understanding this divided condition.

At Shao-lin, according to Zen Buddhism's account, Bodhidharma's long meditation lasted until a suitable disciple came to receive his teaching. This was Shen-kuang, later renamed by Bodhidharma as Hui-k'o [5] (A.D. 487-593) (Japanese: *Yeka* or *Eka*).

To attract the attention of Bodhidharma and to show the seriousness of his intention, Hui-k'o stood outside throughout a night of heavy snowfall. When the snow had risen to his knees, according to the traditional story, with his own sword he cut off his left arm and proffered it to Bodhidharma as a token of his resolve to become his student.[6] Hui-k'o was accepted and eventually became the second Patriarch of Zen.

As for Bodhidharma, the first Patriarch, his nine years of meditation at the wall and his nine years of teaching in China before he decided to return to India are suspicious coincidences, given the value of the number nine, "which was . . . fraught with all manner of symbolic significance for Indian mystics."[7]

Other elements in the Bodhidharma story are also questionable. The proffering of Hui-k'o's severed arm has the exaggerated markings of a fiction invented to impress irresolute and naive converts about the importance of diligence and absolute resolve. The nine years of meditation is a handy encouragement used later, particularly in the Soto sect of Zen, for those who were to find protracted meditation very difficult. It is also a clear echo of the Buddha's seven years of meditation in the wilderness before he attained enlightenment. Of course, care was given that Bodhidharma did not reach awakening more quickly than the Buddha.

In another curious coincidence, legend describes Bodhidharma as a prince from southern India who came to China as a 150-year-old monk,[8] a rather transparent effort to relate Bodhidharma to the princely origin of Gautama himself. Furthermore, Bodhidharma's testing of his disciples is suspiciously close to the testing done by the Buddha. Each of Bodhidharma's disciples attempts with only partial success to summarize his understanding of the teachings until Hui-k'o answers with a reverent bow of silence. The silence is the same as Mahakasyapa's, but the bow has now replaced the smile.

A critical examination of the Bodhidharma story casts

most of it in doubt. The first historical reference to Bodhidharma, according to D.T. Suzuki,[9] was not until A.D. 645, more than a hundred years after his death. At this time Bodhidharma was described in Tao-hsuan's *Biographies of the High Priests* as:

> *merely one of those "masters of meditation" whose conception of dhyana did not differ from the old traditional one as was practiced by Hinayana followers.*[10]

So Bodhidharma was hardly an exception to the many Buddhists who for centuries had been coming from India to teach in China. In addition, he is described as Hinayana, not Mahayana, a detail that even places him in the wrong branch of Buddhism if he is to be the first Patriarch of Zen.

The next mention of Bodhidharma was not until A.D. 1004 when his teachings and activities were noted in *Records of the Transmission of the Lamp* by the Ch'an monk Tao-yuan.[11] By then Ch'an was well established in China as a Mahayana institution. Because it needed spiritual authority, there was now justification for elevating Bodhidharma to special status and inventing a mythology that connected him, and therefore Ch'an, to the Buddha.

Before Bodhidharma arrived in China, other influential Indians had already come and significantly affected Chinese thinking:

> *Kumarajiva [had arrived] before 400, Bodhiruci just after 500 and Paramartha was at the court of Liang about the same time as Bodhidharma.*[12]

It is now fairly clear that Bodhidharma's influence in China was exaggerated by later efforts of the Ch'an Buddhists to justify their authority by inflating his reputation. As Alan Watts notes in *The Way of Zen*:

> *The creation of Zen [Buddhism] would seem to be sufficiently explained by the exposure of Taoists and Confucians to the main principles of Mahayana Buddhism. Therefore the appearance of trends very close to Zen can be seen almost as soon as the great Mahayana sutras became available in China—that is to say, with the work of the great Indian scholar-monk Kumarajiva.*[13]

Seng-chao (A.D. 384-414) was a Taoist and a Confucian. Together with a fellow student, Tao-sheng (A.D. 360-434), the two of them studied with Kumarajiva. Both were strongly influenced by him, both were converted to Buddhism, and both wrote about the experience. Of Seng-chao:

> *Here is one of the main links between Taoism and Zen, for the style and terminology of the* Book of Chao *is Taoist throughout though the subject matter is Buddhist.*[14]

And of Tao-sheng, he was:

> *The first clear and unequivocal exponent of the doctrine of instantaneous awakening. . . . It must be realized in a single flash of insight, which is* tun wu *or, in Japanese,* satori, *the familiar Zen term for sudden awakening. . . . Tao-sheng's even suggests that instantaneous awakening is more appropriate to the Chinese mentality than to the Indian. . . .*[15]

Buddhism may have affected the Chinese but they also affected Buddhism by reshaping it into their own character. Because of Seng-chao and Tao-sheng, Chinese Buddhism already had a strong Taoist flavor by A.D. 520. As Alan Watts observes:

> *One of the reasons for suspecting the Bodhidharma story is that Zen is so Chinese in style that an Indian origin seems improbable.*[16]

Furthermore, adds Watts, the doctrine described by Tao-sheng:

> *even suggests that instantaneous awakening is more appropriate to the Chinese mentality than to the Indian, and lends weight to [D.T.] Suzuki's description of Zen as the Chinese "revolution" against Indian Buddhism.*[17]

Thus it would seem that Bodhidharma could not be the Chinese connection to Zen Buddhism. Instead it is the fifth-century writing of Seng-chao and Tao-sheng. Zen itself, therefore, is distinctly Chinese rather than Indian, a Japanese name with a Taoist source. Watts's conclusion is that Bodhidharma's purported arrival in Canton in A.D. 520 and his succession from the lineage of the Buddha are:

> *a pious invention of later times, when the Zen School needed historical authority for its claim to be a direct transmission of experience from the Buddha himself. . . .*[18]

Even the solid literature that is said to have been written by Bodhidharma is of questionable authorship:

> *Only one work, it is generally agreed, can legitimately be attributed to Bodhidharma:* The Treatise on the Two Entrances and Four Practices . . . *but it is uncertain whether [this work] was actually written by him.*[19]

All the evidence suggests that the character and ideas of Bodhidharma are largely fabrications of a later time, and that Indian thought was totally reformed in China to be more compatible with the Chinese mind. Bodhidharma was nearly irrelevant in this process. And he was not the Zen connection between India and Japan.

The credibility of the Bodhidharma story and thus the Buddhist source of Zen is widely questioned by many scholars. Even the great Japanese scholar D.T. Suzuki, a staunch supporter of the Buddhist roots of Zen, obliquely acknowledges that Zen was a Chinese movement. Another eminent authority on Chinese, Arthur Waley, also argues for a Chinese origin to Zen, and argues further that there is no historical evidence for the existence of the Bodhidharma that is described by Zen Buddhist history:

> It is now recognized that the [Zen] sect was an internal movement in Chinese Buddhism and owed nothing to India. The whole story of Bodhidharma is late legend, designed to give status and authority to the movement.[20]

Finally, when examining Zen Buddhism's history of Bodhidharma as the foundation of Zen, it should be possible to find in India a tradition of meditation that corresponds to the practices instituted in China by him. There is none. According to Watts:

> The absence of any record of a Dhyana School in Indian Buddhist literature, or of Bodhidharma in connection with it, is perhaps due to the fact that there was never any Dhyana or Zen School even in China until some two hundred years after Bodhidharma's time.[21]

67

No evidence supports a Bodhidharma as he is traditionally represented by Zen Buddhism. He is largely a fictitious character invented by Ch'an and later reinforced by Zen Buddhism for historical and theological convenience.

As Ch'an gradually institutionalized in China and became more and more an expression of the Mahayana religion, it needed to associate itself with the Buddha. The story of Bodhidharma was invented to serve this purpose. Now, with an invested Buddhist origin, Ch'an had to justify its Chinese Taoist character in Indian terms. Bodhidharma served this purpose by making the Buddha the originator of Ch'an's Zen character. Thus Mahayana Buddhists in China used Bodhidharma to construct their own version of history and then sanctified it with the final authority of the Buddha.

When Ch'an spread to Japan to become Zen Buddhism, the Japanese quite naturally adopted and entrenched the Bodhidharma fiction because they were Mahayana Buddhists rather than Taoists. Declaring Bodhidharma to be the first Patriarch of Zen Buddhism is really the historical remnant of the actual Chinese origin of Zen. There is in Buddhism some trace of the original Zen impulse that arose in ancient Indian yoga, but the actual character of what is now called Zen was a Chinese invention called Taoism.

The Zen in Zen Buddhism did not come from Bodhidharma, from India, from Buddhism, or from the Buddha. It came from China and Taoism. It is Chinese. If the history of Zen Buddhism is to be accounted accurately, perhaps the two Taoist-Confucian monks Seng-chao and

Tao-sheng should replace Bodhidharma as the first
Patriarch.

Ch'an

*C*h'an is Zen Buddhism's predecessor in China. The two traditions are so closely related that as late as the eighteenth century Zen Buddhists in Japan were commonly instructed in Chinese,[1] Ch'an masters were often invited to instruct in Zen Buddhist monasteries,[2] and all Ch'an masters, both current and past, were given Japanese names and regarded, without distinction, as part of the Zen Buddhist tradition.

But the history of Ch'an is inaccurate for the same reason that the history of Zen Buddhism is inaccurate. Just as Zen Buddhism adjusted the role of Bodhidharma to connect itself with the Buddha, so it adjusted the story of Ch'an to connect itself with Bodhidharma. Hui-neng is a key figure in this story. There was such a person. But, as with Bodhidharma, his relevance has been skewed by the Mahayana need to be associated with India and Buddhism rather than China and Taoism. A more objective perspective of history makes these inaccuracies quite clear.

The early history of Ch'an is not so clear. An Indian tradition of sitting meditation may have come to China with Buddhist sutras as early as the second century A.D.[3] but this practice was probably not widely adopted because of its similarity to the Taoist schools and sects that would have offered comparable experience in a Chinese manner. Any such practice was not likely called Ch'an. And its relationship to comparable and existing Taoist practices is also uncertain.

Such a shortage of reliable information about Ch'an's early history is not surprising. One reason is simply the absence of existing records. The other has been the consistent inclination of Mahayana Buddhism to chart its history through Hui-neng to Bodhidharma rather than from Hui-neng to Lao Tzu. Since Ch'an evolved into an expression of institutionalized religious Buddhism, its concern has been to construe itself in terms of Buddhism rather than Taoism. Any information on its Taoist heritage was either deleted or overlooked. Furthermore, any solid history of Ch'an's association with Taoism through this early period is unlikely to be made because of Taoism's own inclination to be organic and reclusive; order and formality are contrary to its nature, so it would leave few written records and other historical footprints. All that can be accurately assumed is that some forerunner of Ch'an was practiced in China prior to Bodhidharma's arrival.

In his definition of Ch'an in *Zen Dictionary*, Ernest Wood describes an early practice devoid of Buddhism and sounding remarkably similar to the contemplative form of Taoism that was first known as Quietism, very much in character with the tradition of the *Lao Tzu* and the *Chuang Tzu*:

> *At first Ch'anists were isolated men whose idea was to lead a life in harmony with everything in Nature, and to meditate for the attainment of peace or tranquillity and the opening up of intuition. They had no temples, but some of them had groups of followers or disciples. . . . [M]ost of the early Ch'anists did not give much attention to Buddhist literature, which began to provide much material description of meditation and its results for them only after the arrival from India of Kumarajiva, Bodhidharma and others.*[4]

Clearly a Ch'an-like practice did exist in China before the arrival of Kumarajiva, and certainly before the official introduction of Buddhism by Bodhidharma. But what was it

74

like? It was not called Ch'an. It probably did not have a strong Buddhist component since the early Buddhism in China was Mahayana, emphasizing good works and salvation rather than personal awakening. This early Ch'an practice may have been Quietism itself, or a modified version of it since Taoists recognized Buddhist philosophy as a simplified version of their own, and the two may have integrated in this instance. It is possible, too, that the meditation in this early Ch'an was not the formal sitting of later Ch'an, but simply a meditative attitude practiced under a variety of informal conditions. Given the Taoists' antipathy for imposed structure and their near reverence for being natural and spontaneous, formal sitting for them would have been a contradiction in terms. There was potentially an irreconcilable difference between the *t'so-ch'an* of a formal sitting meditation and the *tzu-jan* of Taoism, an organic what-comes-of-itself spontaneity. Early Ch'an meditation was very likely more organic than the disciplined sitting of later Ch'an when Mahayana Buddhism had stiffened and ritualized its practice.

The details of Ch'an's formative period from Bodhidharma to Hui-neng are only slightly clearer. But they, too, exist only according to Mahayana Buddhism's interpretation. As John R. McRae writes in *Zen: Tradition and Transition*:

> *There is virtually nothing that is known about Ch'an during the seventh century that does not come down to us filtered through the perspective of the eighth century or later periods.*[5]

An objectively considered history does not suggest that Bodhidharma significantly increased the receptivity of the Chinese to Ch'an, and the second and third Patriarchs, Hui-k'o and Seng-tsan (A.D. ?-606), are not usually mentioned as influential teachers. Not until the seventh and eighth centuries did Ch'an begin to congeal into a solid movement that clearly displayed both the attributes of Chinese Mahayana Buddhism and the spontaneous, intuitive qualities of Taoism. The circumstantial evidence suggests that Ch'an began as an extension of Taoism and gradually incorporated Buddhism into its practice.

In a manner suggestive of the Taoist tradition, the first recognized practice of Ch'an occurred in "relatively isolated alpine monastic communities"[6] chosen for their natural beauty. The first was at Huang-mei where the fourth Patriarch, Tao-hsin (A.D. 580-651), was invited to the retreat of Hung-jen. Students were attracted there "from diverse backgrounds"[7] to a practice that already had in language and philosophy a strong Buddhist component. Meditation was also being stressed.[8]

Hung-jen (A.D. 605-675) succeeded Tao-hsin as the fifth Patriarch in A.D. 651 but Ch'an was still not a solid, identifiable movement. Indeed, at this time and into the next century it did not even have a specific name:

> *The most common term for Ch'an during the early eighth century was the "East Mountain Teaching," derived from the location of Hung-jen's monastery at Huang-mei.*[9]

Even more than Tao-hsin, Hung-jen seems to have been influential in drawing students and spreading the reputation of Ch'an, although the details of his teaching are not clearly known. Like Taoists, he stressed the importance of seeking the wisdom that is within, exemplified in the ancient Chinese proverb:

76

The treasures of the house do not come in through the gate.

As a person Hung-jen seems to have been more interested in this innate wisdom than in Buddhist doctrine:

> *[He] was described by contemporary followers as a quiet, unassuming man, not disposed toward doctrinal exposition of scriptual study but always on the mark in his personal instructions to students.*[10]

Although this early Ch'an was evolving toward a more formal, institutionalized practice, at this stage in its history it seems to have possessed more of the organic freedom of Taoism than the doctrinal truths of Mahayana Buddhism. Also, at this time, it still very likely carried Taoism's aversion to the stultifying effects of Confucian organization:

> *Taoism has for some time been in quiet revolt against Confucianism; the early Taoist teachers had stressed that a practitioner could go directly to the Tao, the Way, without having to master the Confucian sayings or classics and without having to be governed by the* li, *the Confucian rites and ceremony. This implicit directness was welcomed by Ch'an leaders.*[11]

Indeed, Indian Buddhism carried with it some of the same sense of order as the Confucians. This order, too, would have been anathema to the Taoists. Several modern scholars, therefore, have defined Ch'an as a reaction against Indian Buddhism. Christmas Humphreys, for example, writes that:

> *The Ch'an school of China was founded . . . to deflate the extravagance of Indian Buddhist thought and to drive the mind with earthy violence back to the origin of "Buddhism". . . .*[12]

77

This "origin" could be the ancient yoga that would have been shared by the philosophies of both Buddhism and Taoism.

It is possible, too, that Confucianism itself may have contributed to the eventual institutionalization of Ch'an simply because it was an influential part of Chinese consciousness. Regardless, Ch'an was a growing movement that eventually required some kind of organization and management. In the order and structure of later Ch'an, in its discipline and hierarchy, was a quality that could have been Confucian. What is historically important is not that these organizational influences were literally or necessarily Confucian but rather that they happened and the Chinese felt comfortable with them.

If the heads of these early Ch'an masters were considering Confucianism or Buddhism, their hearts were still following Taoism:

> *The old Chinese Zen masters were steeped in Taoism. They saw nature in its total interrelatedness, and saw that every creature and every experience is in accord with the Tao of nature just as it is. This enabled them to accept themselves as they were, moment by moment, without the least need to justify anything. . . .*
> *"In the landscape of Spring there is neither better nor worse.*
> *The flowering branches grow naturally, some long, some short."*[13]

Whether the meditation practiced in these eighth-century Ch'an schools was formal or informal is not clear. Evidence suggests, according to Alan Watts, that the teachers of the time placed little or:

no stress on meditative exercises but often dismissed them as irrelevant. Their entire emphasis was upon immediate intuitive insight. . . .[14]

These early, formative years of Ch'an reflect most of the essential attributes of philosophical Taoism: a thoughtless spontaneity in both action and inaction; a merging of self with a larger natural oneness; an honoring of nature through experience and imagery; an aversion to the dogma imposed by words and institutions. In many ways early Ch'an seems to have been a Taoist practice mixed with escalating amounts of Indian Mahayana doctrine.

The popularity of Ch'an did not begin to increase dramatically until the sixth Patriarch. Because of Hui-neng something happened to Ch'an. Perhaps it reached critical mass. But a more likely explanation is that Hui-neng adjusted the character of Ch'an and made it more acceptable to the Chinese. He, more than anyone, helped to reconcile the differences between the native sensibilities of China and the Buddhism from India that was beginning to dominate Ch'an. Hui-neng was, in the words of D.T. Suzuki; "the real Chinese founder of Zen. . . . The rise of Zen after [Hui-neng] was phenomenal."[15]

By the tenth century Ch'an was the largest Buddhist sect in China and by the twelfth century most Buddhism practiced in China was Ch'an.

As Ch'an rose in popularity, the other practices of Buddhism fell proportionally:

With the rise of the Sung dynasty (960-1279) Zen reached the height of its development and influence while the other sects of Buddhism showed signs of rapid decline.[16]

By the fourteenth century almost all sects of Buddhism that were not Ch'an had disappeared from China. There was, it seems, a fundamental incompatibility between Indian Buddhism and the Chinese character, and this incompatibility was only resolved in Hui-neng's version of Ch'an. As D.T. Suzuki speculates:

> *Perhaps they were to die out anyway on account of their not having been completely assimilated by Chinese thought and feeling; there was too much of an Indian element which prevented them from being fully acclimatized.*[17]

Of course, the very success of Ch'an worked against its essentially Taoist spirit. As Ch'an institutionalized, the philosophy of Taoism found a home but became entrapped by the walls. Scholarly arguments suggest, for example, that the *zazen* tradition in Ch'an did not grow out of any legitimate spiritual motive but out of the practical necessity of managing large numbers of undisciplined practitioners. Even the early Ch'an practices of the *East Mountain Teaching* were barely small enough to remain places that were personal and casual. As the popularity of Ch'an grew, the populations of monasteries increased beyond manageable limits. The practice of sitting meditation and the disciplines of a rigid monastic life were thereby introduced as organizational imperatives. Even by Hung-jen's time he was said to have been the head of five hundred to a thousand monks.[18] And, after Dogen visited China in A.D. 1223, he reported:

> *I personally saw in great Sung China Zen monasteries in many areas, each built to include a meditation hall, wherein from five or six hundred to one or two thousand monks were*

housed and encouraged to devote themselves to zazen *day and night.*[19]

The problems inherent in dealing with such numbers of people required organization and regimens. The option was pandemonium. The onerous responsibility of teaching all these monks, keeping them occupied, and measuring the level of their insight meant that instruction had to standardize and that discipline was required.

The cost and logistics of operating these large Ch'an monasteries required new organization. It was Pai-chang (A.D. 720-814), also known as Nich-p'an and Hwei-hai (Japanese: Hyakujo), who was one of the first to organize the Ch'an movement into formal monasteries that operated by strict rules:

He insisted on work and was the originator of the expression, "No work, no food."[20]

By implication, the earlier Ch'an communities must have been more organic, informal places.

In the large monasteries, without the close and congenial atmosphere in which each student was intimately known, the task of finding successors became more complicated. So the *kung-an* (Japanese: *koan*] was devised. It fit comfortably with the Taoist notion of spontaneity, it could quickly measure levels of insight, and it served to transmit with reasonable fidelity the essential Ch'an experience. As expected, the *kung-an*, with its immediate and intuitive grasp of insight, grew out of the Southern School of Ch'an, the one that was closer to the Taoist tradition of China—the Northern School followed the slower, more intellectual course associated with the original Buddhism of India.

Zen Buddhism's inclination has been to explain the origin of the *kung-an* in terms of Indian philosophy. But a closer and more obvious course is to trace it through Taoism to the *Chuang Tzu* and the *Lao Tzu*, and even to the *I Ching*. The polarity between the apparent opposites of *yin* and *yang* are the same energies that must be surmounted in the *kung-an* exercise. The *kung-an* uses this polarity to create a paradox of opposites which can be suspended only by a holistic balancing that negates and then encompasses the polarity. Essentially, these opposites are the same irresolvable elements that Taoism has to wrestle into a condition of emptiness and, therein, a special kind of receptive opening. This process is clearly a part of the *Lao Tzu* and is a conspicuous strategy in the playful wisdom of the *Chuang Tzu*. It is also a crucial part of Ch'an, which Arthur Waley describes as:

> a *"wordless doctrine." Like Taoism it discarded outward ceremonies, and like Taoism is startled the novice, loosened his sense of "is" and "isn't" by conundrums and paradoxes. Thus Zen which has played so great a part in the spiritual life of China and Japan . . . is psychologically if not doctrinally the heir of 4th and 3rd century [B.C.] Chinese Quietism.*[21]

So the philosophical strategies of Taoism pervaded the character of early Ch'an. The eventual success of the *East Mountain Teaching* in the eighth century and the mass popularity of later Ch'an can best be explained when they are considered as expressions of Chinese culture, as "thought and feeling" that are essentially Chinese rather than Indian. So Ch'an and its Mahayana Buddhism became a structural and institutional framework in which the spirit of Taoism expressed itself.

Even Taoism's vocabulary pervaded early Ch'an, and Taoist expressions were often used interchangeably with Ch'an ones. "The Way of the Tao," for example, was meant to mean the "Way of Ch'an." The following is a Ch'an dialogue involving the young Chao-chou who lived, incidentally, to be nearly one hundred and twenty years old (A.D. 778-897):

> *Chao-chou asked, "What is the Tao?"*
> *The master replied, "Your ordinary (natural) mind is the Tao."*
> *"How can one return into accord with it?"*
> *"By intending to accord, you immediately deviate."*
> *"But without intention, how can one know the Tao?"*
> *"The Tao," said the master, "belongs neither to knowing nor not-knowing. Knowing is false understanding; not knowing is blind ignorance. If you really understand the Tao beyond doubt, it's like the empty sky. Why drag in right and wrong?"* [22]

Taoist and Buddhist terminology also intermixed in Ch'an. This illustrates the syncretic character of Chinese thinking. It also illustrates the prevalence of Taoism in Ch'an. Buddhist philosophy that occupied Ch'an thinking was often translated into Taoist concepts, suggesting that Taoism was the base reference in which Buddhism was interpreted:

> *Important Taoist terms were used by Ch'an and other Buddhists teachers to a wide extent.* Tao *became the established Chinese rendition of the Buddhist word* dharma, *meaning teaching or even the wider concept of reality. Sometimes* Tao *was used to translate the word* bodhi, *or enlightenment.* [23]

But such historical connections between Taoism and Ch'an have been constantly overlooked or undermined by the effort of later Mahayana Buddhism to establish a doctrinal link between itself and the Buddha in India. The quasi-fictional rendering of Bodhidharma and Hui-neng are two more prominent examples. The more obvious connection of Zen to Taoism has been so effectively avoided by Buddhist history that the bias now perpetuates itself like unquestioned dogma. Consider, for example, the reference under "Zen" in *Zen Dictionary*:

> *In China, Zen is called* hsin-tsung, *which means "the teaching of the Mind," referring of course to the Buddha-mind, with its enlightenment.*[24]

But *hsin-tsung* could as easily refer to a practice in early Taoism that had comparable objectives and similar techniques as philosophical Buddhism. Indeed, *hsin-tsung* was originally a term of Quietism having to do with the "mind-within-the-mind." The Tao, like Buddha-mind, could only be found when thoughts were quiet and empty enough to enter a special condition of receptivity. To call "the teaching of the Mind" Buddhist is simply the bias of the Buddhist view that keeps imposing itself on the history of native Chinese thought.

Sometimes this historical bias of Buddhism offers revealing contradictions. Again from *Zen Dictionary*:

> *Zen is described . . . as the "apotheosis of Buddhism," and a "direct assault upon the citadel of Truth, without reliance upon concepts (of God or soul or salvation) or the use of scripture, ritual or vow."* [25]

84

Here, in summary, is the contradiction inherent in the expression "Zen Buddhism." Zen, as it must be lived, and Mahayana Buddhism, as it must be practiced, are antithetical. The "apotheosis of Buddhism" and all its concomitant religious and ritual baggage is exactly the opposite of Zen. Zen cannot exist until there is no Buddhism, no Buddha. Indeed, Zen itself cannot exist until there is no Zen.

The consequences of attempting to mix Zen and Buddhism soon became apparent. In A.D. 732, soon after the death of Hui-neng, Ch'an divided into two schools—the same division, incidentally, that took place in the Taoist religion. Shen-hui (A.D. 668-760), a student of Hui-neng, argued that the insight of enlightenment could not be attained in partial measures because it was indivisible; it either happens totally or not at all. This "flash of revelation"[26] came to define the Southern School of Ch'an, Lin-chi, whereas the Northern School, Tsao-tung, held to "the principle of gradual enlightenment."[27] These two schools later spread unchanged into Japan as the Rinzai and Soto traditions of Zen Buddhism.

The differences that divided Ch'an into these schools were clearly the result of doctrinal disputes, and they measured the degree to which the essential spirit of Ch'an had become lost as the details of an organizing process hardened into an institution. The softness of pure Taoism would have found these opposite positions nothing more than the two inevitable sides of the same wholeness, a problem of dogma that was entirely irrelevant outside the context of institutionalized Ch'an. How could it matter whether the Way was found quickly or slowly? Indeed, this was the kind of squabbling that would have left Chuang Tzu dragging his tail in the mud rather than joining the Imperial Court of the Emperor.

But Ch'an took the dispute seriously. Of the two schools that evolved, the Southern one retained more of the character of Taoism and the Northern one adopted more Buddhist qualities. The differences were minor, matters of detail that gave one a more Chinese personality, the other a more Indian disposition.

But the details seemed different enough that each school chose a different sixth Patriarch, officially ending this tradition of succession for both schools. Beneath the current of differences, however, was the bedrock of Taoism. Arthur Wright in *Buddhism In Chinese History* describes the situation like this:

> *The [sudden] branch of Ch'an had closer affinities with the native tradition of Taoism but both branches can best be understood as complex amalgams of Buddhist and Taoist ideas. The distrust of words, the rich store of concrete metaphor and analogy, the love of paradox, the bibliophobia, the belief in the direct, person-to-person and often wordless communication of insight, the feeling that life led in close com-munion with nature is conducive to enlightenment—all these are colored with Taoism. Indeed, Ch'an may be regarded as the reaction of a powerful tradition of Chinese thought against the verbosity, the scholasticism, the tedious logical demonstra-tions, of the Indian texts. And, in its [sudden] branch, which became dominant, it asserts an ideal of salvation that echoes the persisting Chinese belief—alien to caste-bound India—that a man may, in his lifetime, rise to the heights through his own efforts.*[28]

The two schools of Ch'an were united by their common Chinese values and by their shared Taoist instincts.

Eventually, sitting meditation became a major part of both practices. The Southern School, to confound the intellect, emphasized the *kung-an*; the Northern School, to prepare the intellect, stressed the study of *sutras*. This difference, essentially representing the inclination of Ch'an toward its Chinese or its Indian component, is a distinction that even today is the basis of quiet dispute between the two major sects of Zen Buddhism.

When Zen Buddhism was transposed to the West in the latter part of the twentieth century, two things happened: it either continued to be practiced in its institutional form as traditional Rinzai and Soto, or it relaxed its Buddhist component and reverted to its intrinsically Taoist character. Zen became widely discussed, recognized, and practiced in the fresh informality of its new environment without any mention of the Buddha.

Perhaps the Taoist character of Zen is best exemplified in the West by Alan Watts, a free-spirited iconoclast who did much to popularize Zen and separate it from Buddhism. Zen's Buddhist character is represented by all those who teach traditional forms of either Rinzai or Soto, and particularly by the eminent Japanese scholar D.T. Suzuki. Under earlier circumstances he might have become Zen Buddhism's seventh Patriarch.

Watts argued that meditation was only used informally in early Ch'an and that its practice is inherently unnatural to Zen.[29] At issue is whether Zen is to be regarded in terms that are organic or formal, primarily Taoist or Buddhist. Watts identified the problem this way:

> *The history of Chinese Zen raises one problem of great fascination. Both Rinzai and Soto Zen as we find them in Japanese*

87

> *monasteries today put enormous emphasis on* za-zen *[sic] or sitting meditation. . . .*[30]

Why, he asked, is there deliberate sitting meditation when such a practice is so contradictory to spontaneous awakening? How can nonattachment be attained when *zazen* must be devotedly practiced? What could be the possible relationship between sitting and self-realization?

> *[T]here are several references [in the Zen tradition] that prolonged sitting is not much better than being dead. There is, of course, a proper place for sitting—along with standing, walking and lying—but to imagine that sitting contains some special virtue is "attachment to form."* [31]

Being natural, being profoundly ordinary and spontaneous, is the way of Zen for Watts. It is also the heart of Zen from the Taoist perspective. Even Hui-neng is reported to have said of Shen-hsiu's instructions for concentrating on quietness and doing *zazen*:

> *To concentrate the mind on quietness is a disease of the mind, and not Zen at all.*[32]

Those with a Buddhist understanding of modern Zen tend to endorse *zazen* because of its Indian qualities and its association with the stories of Bodhidharma and the Buddha. This endorsement and supporting position for a Buddhist origin for Zen is exemplified by D.T. Suzuki. Despite recognition of Taoism as the shaping force of Ch'an and, therefore, Zen, the old Japanese scholar remains Buddhist by both culture and belief. He becomes another of many who sees Zen through Buddhist glasses. After discussing the importance of Hui-neng in the evolution of Ch'an, after saying that this man "was the real Chinese founder of Zen," he leaps to add the entirely unsupported opinion, without accounting for more than a thousand years of very vague history, that:

> *The spirit of Zen was of course the same as the one that came to China transmitted without interruption from the Buddha....*[33]

D.T. Suzuki represents the side of Japanese Zen that is connected by belief to India and the Buddha. Alan Watts, if he will forgive being cast into any category, represents Zen's secular quality, the natural and spontaneous expression of personal freedom that comes through the Chinese tradition of Taoism. These two positions have existed in an unresolved condition since the earliest history of Ch'an. They summarize the divided character of Zen Buddhism that came into being when the irresolvable energies of India's religious Buddhism met with ancient China's philosophical Taoism during Ch'an's formative years.

Hui-Neng

ui-neng (A.D. 638-713) (Japanese: *Eno* or *Yeno*) is more fascinating for what is said about him than for what is known about him. In either case, he is a crucial figure in the history of Zen Buddhism and its present practice in Japan.

The Zen Buddhist tradition considers Hui-neng to be its sixth Patriarch, the last one in an official series that can be traced to its first Patriarch, Bodhidharma, and finally to the Buddha himself. Without this official position for Hui-neng, Zen Buddhism has no valid connection to Bodhidharma and thus to Buddhist history of both China and India. And yet, ironically, Zen Buddhism's own account of Hui-neng serves to sever its Buddhist connection in China by creating a "philosophy of living"[1] that is essentially Chinese rather than Indian.

Together with the Buddha and Bodhidharma, Hui-neng is considered by Zen Buddhism to be one of the three most formidable influences on its character. And yet "virtually nothing"[2] is known about him:

> *Like Bodhidharma and Hui-k'o before him, and Ma-tsu and Lin-chi after him, Hui-neng is in part a creation of the collective Chinese religious imagination.*[3]

Historical accuracy seems to be of secondary concern when these characters and their stories are adopted into the Chinese and Japanese psyche. So the traditional story of Hui-neng is worth examining in some detail because it is laden with significant information that is relevant to understanding the workings of Zen Buddhist history and the connective relationship between Taoism and Zen.

Hui-neng is described as a poor, illiterate farm boy who was drawn to Hung-jen's monastery by a reading of Buddhism's *Diamond Sutra*, which he inadvertently overheard while delivering firewood. One story recounts that this reading created his "first awakening"[4]—without, incidentally, the guidance of any master.

At the Huang-mei monastery Hui-neng is brought before Hung-jen:

> *"Where do you come from and what do you want here?"*
> *"I am a farmer from Hsin-chou and wish to become a Buddha."*
> *"So you are a Southerner," said the Patriarch. "But Southerners have no Buddha-nature. How can you expect to attain Buddhahood?"*
> *"There may be Southerners and Northerners, but as far as Buddha-nature is concerned, how can you make such a distinction?"* [5]

Of course, Hung-jen's observation about Southerners is appropriately ironic. Not only does Hui-neng become the next patriarch of Zen Buddhism, but he is eventually responsible for creating the Southern School of Ch'an, the one that stresses sudden rather than gradual enlightenment. In other words, the story has been contrived by the Southern School to elevate the status of Hui-neng and to endorse its own authority. Hui-neng's allusion to the equality of the Northern and Southern Schools is a diplomatic gesture of Zen Buddhist politics.

Hung-jen is appropriately pleased with Hui-neng's

reply and assigns to him menial tasks at the monastery. For the next eight months Hui-neng serves at Huang-mei[6] as a rice pounder and a wood gatherer. Then the fifth Patriarch lets it be known that his successor, the sixth Patriarch, will soon be chosen. Shen-hsiu, the likely candidate because he is so studied and learned, is secretly dubious about his own credentials however, so he anonymously writes and attaches to the outside wall of the meditation hall a poem that illustrates his level of mastery of Ch'an:

> *This body is the Bodhi-tree,*
> *The mind is like a bright mirror standing;*
> *Take heed to always keep it clean,*
> *And allow no dust to ever cling.*

Everyone is amazed by the wisdom in the poem, and incense is lit before it as a reminder to all monks of the importance of diligent meditation. The next morning a response by Hui-neng is found posted beside it:

> *There never was a Bodhi-tree,*
> *There never was a mirror shining bright;*
> *Since there was nothing from the first,*
> *Where, then, is the dust to cling?*

The translations of the poems vary, as do the detailed accounts of the story. One version has Hung-jen as the only one aware of the authorship of the poems. Another has the whole monastery buzzing with discussion of Hui-neng's poetic challenge to Shen-hsiu. The stories agree that Hui-neng is secretly awarded the title and is advised to flee the monastery until the furor subsides and his authority as the sixth Patriarch can be established.

The consequences of Hui-neng's appointment are significant. Politically, the patriarchate disappears in confusion and contention as Hui-neng's authority remains unresolved and Shen-hsiu claims the title.[7] Then Hui-neng's successor, Shen-hui, is acknowledged as the seventh Patriarch by the Imperial Court but not by the Ch'an movement itself.[8] Hui-neng has become the wedge that splits Ch'an into its Southern and Northern Schools, a split that later carries into Japan as Rinzai and Soto Zen.

The symbolic consequences of Hui-neng being named sixth Patriarch are equally significant. The very robe and begging bowl of Bodhidharma, the same ones that had been passed from patriarch to patriarch and were even awarded to Hui-neng, disappear. Their loss represents a symbolic severing of Ch'an's direct connection with the tradition of Bodhidharma and the philosophy of India. It also affirms that early Zen Buddhism has a style of understanding that is fundamentally Chinese. Buddhism continues to be a component of Ch'an but the defining terms are no longer Indian. The Hui-neng story marks the end of China's efforts to reconcile itself to Indian thought.

The most important symbolic, philosophical, and political effect of Hui-neng's appointment was that he could now be acknowledged in the Chinese imagination as an archetypal Taoist. This was necessary if Ch'an was to be popularly accepted in China. Because of Hui-neng, Ch'an could officially recognize the Taoist character at the heart of itself. As D.T. Suzuki writes of Ch'an of later centuries:

> *Zen dispensed with the images and concepts and modes of thinking that were imported from India along with Buddhist thought; and out of its own consciousness Zen created an origi-*

*nal literature best adapted to the exposition of the truth of
Enlightenment. This literature was unique in many senses, but
it was in perfect accordance with the Chinese modus operan-
di and naturally powerfully moved them to the core.*[9]

These comments confirm the Chinese character of Zen.
But they are revealing in other regards and deserve some
examination because they disclose Zen Buddhism's ambivalence to Hui-neng and they expose the contradiction within
the term "Zen Buddhism." Although "Zen dispensed . . .
with Buddhist thought," according to D.T. Suzuki, he continues to mix Zen and Buddhism. An expression such as "the
truth of Enlightenment" is Buddhist; Taoists are averse to
talking about absolutes such as truth, and they do not mention Enlightenment—a tradition, incidentally, that is still
largely respected in the practice of modern Japanese Zen.
D.T. Suzuki's expression illustrates the difficulty that Zen
Buddhists have relinquishing their tradition to a solely
Chinese source. So they don't; and at the same time they do.
They acknowledge the importance of Hui-neng but they also
deny his Taoism by connecting him to Bodhidharma and
Indian Buddhism. Thus the Zen portion of Zen Buddhism
becomes undeclared Taoism in a fictionalized Hui-neng, and
the Buddhist portion is declared in a fictionalized
Bodhidharma.

Zen Buddhism misrepresents its two key historical
characters to avoid confronting the incompatibility of its two
principal components. Hui-neng is disguised so he does not
appear to be a representative of Taoism, and Bodhidharma is
disguised so he does appear to be a representative of the
Buddha. This is the consequence of Zen Buddhism's efforts

to maintain its contradictory character. Consider D.T. Suzuki again:

> *Hui-neng . . . was the real Chinese founder of Zen for it was through him and his direct followers that Zen could cast off the garment borrowed from India and [begin] to put on one cut and sewn by the native hands. The spirit of Zen was of course the same as the one that came to China transmitted without interruption from the Buddha, but the form of expression was thoroughly Chinese, for it was their own creation.*[10]

The contradiction is obvious. And the "of course" shifts the argument from scholarship to belief. Certainly there is Zen in Buddhism; Zen is everywhere. Except for Mahakasyapa's smile, however, there is little Zen to be found in Buddhism, and there is even less to be found in the articulated philosophy of the Buddha. As for Bodhidharma, it is impossible to attribute Zen to him. Such an attribution by Zen Buddhists illustrates the blinders that they wear when it comes to Zen's history. D.T. Suzuki's position, the orthodox one offered by the Buddhist context in which Japanese Zen exists, is not supported by the history of Bodhidharma, and it is neither credible nor logical that an Indian Buddhist should come to China and reform the Chinese to think like Chinese.

So the effect of Hui-neng on the history of Ch'an was to separate its indigenous Taoism from its imported Buddhism, and to reclaim its native character by establishing a recognizable Taoist as its figurehead. This permitted the Chinese, who were philosophically Taoist but now religiously Buddhist, to feel wholly comfortable in Ch'an because it filled both their practical and religious needs. For people who had been living for centuries as Taoist-Confucians, the

Taoist-Buddhist contradiction did not concern them. They could live quite contentedly with Zen as one thing and Buddhism as another. Bodhidharma defined their Buddhism as Indian; Hui-neng defined their Zen as Chinese.

Even D.T. Suzuki tacitly acknowledges this when he attempts to explain how little Zen is actually present in Buddhism:

> *When we read Zen literature without being told of its relation to Buddhism, we may almost fail to recognize in it such things as are generally regarded as specifically Buddhist. . . . Zen looks as if it had nothing to do with Buddhism, and some critics are almost justified in designating Zen as a Chinese anomaly of Buddhism. . . .*[11]

Put succinctly, Zen is Chinese but Buddhism is not; Zen Buddhism is the anomoly of putting together two incompatibles. Ch'an became a form of Taoism housed within the institution of Mahayana Buddhism. The interplay of these contradictory styles of Chinese and Indian thought has still not been officially resolved because the present form of Ch'an in Japan is still called Zen Buddhism.

In further support of a Taoist source for Zen, again consider Hui-neng. He was a poor farmer, and at the monastery a pounder of rice and splitter of wood. He was unschooled and unsophisticated. Indeed, some accounts stress this point by describing that he was unable to read or write, an attribute which does question his poetic duel with Shen-hsiu. D.T. Suzuki confirms this description of Hui-neng:

> *. . . in the narratives of his life we can trace some systematic effort to make him more unlettered than he actually was . . . [to emphasize] the real character of Zen as independent of*

learning and intellectuality. If Zen is . . . a "special transmission outside the scriptural teaching", the understanding of it must be possible even for the unlettered and unphilosophizing. The greatness of Hui-neng as Zen master is all the more enhanced. This was in all likelihood the reason why the sixth patriarch [sic] was unreasonably and sometimes even dramatically made unlettered.[12]

In other words, Hui-neng was uncontaminated by society. His wisdom was natural and intuitive. He was the model Taoist and thereby became the catalyst for the soaring popularity of Ch'an when the Chinese recognized in him the perfect symbol of themselves.

Until Hui-neng, Ch'an had been evolving as a somewhat ambivalent mix of Chinese and Indian thought. The pull between its Taoist and Buddhist qualities left the Chinese uncommitted. But Hui-neng—or the story of him and the subsequent teaching attributed to him—changed that. He naturalized Ch'an, made it fully Chinese, and thereby offered something for everyone. He also transformed the emphasis of Ch'an. Because of Hui-neng's influence, notes R.H. Blyth in *Games Zen Masters Play*, there was a definite shift in:

the way in which the quietism and negativism of early Zen, which was still Indian flavored, changed to activism and positivism [with] the Sixth Patriarch. . . .[13]

Hui-neng offered to the Ch'an practitioner the possibility of becoming a model Chinese sage. He grounded Ch'an and made it seem easy and normal. And he departed from the traditional Buddhist notion of what constituted meditation. In effect, he dispensed with the necessity of formal sitting and reconnected those who practiced Ch'an with the more natural and organic meditative tradition of Taoism:

> *The Sixth Patriarch Hui-neng offered some novel formulations of* zazen. *In his* Platform Sutra *(*Liu-tsu t'an ching*), he says that if one were to stay free from attachment to any mental or physical realms and to refrain from discriminating, neither thoughts nor mind would arise. This is the true "sitting" of Ch'an. Here the term "sitting" is not limited to physical sitting but refers to a practice where the mind is not influenced or disturbed by anything that arises, internally or in the environment.*[14]

In other words, sitting meditation defeats its own purpose by deliberately attempting to eliminate the very thing that can only be done by not deliberately doing it. The situation is exemplified in the classic paradox, "Now, I want you to forget what I just told you." Chuang Tzu expresses Hui-neng's sense of meditation when he says:

> *The sound of the water*
> *says what I think.*[15]

In an account that stresses the same point, Huai-jang (A.D. 677-744), a disciple of Hui-neng, chastizes the monk Ma-tzu for doing *zazen* all the time. Ma-tzu, who eventually became a great master, is advised that:

> *Self-nature is to be found in . . . the "mind-ground" not in the realm of form. Later Ma-tzu reiterated this point in his concept of "ordinary mind"* (p'ing-ch'ang). *One sense of this expression is a mind that is involved in the ordinary world, moving as usual but not clinging to anything. Another sense comes from the root meanings of* p'ing *and* ch'ang, *which*

suggest a mind that is "level" and "constant" or in a state of constant equanimity. In either sense, there is no attachment.[16]

Level, constant, and equanimity are Taoist expressions. "Ordinary mind" is what Confucius was describing when, sounding like a Taoist, he said:

To serve one's own mind, unmoved by sadness or joy, accepting whatever happens, is the true virtue.

The special virtue of Hui-neng was his apparent ability to see the Taoist essence of Ch'an through accumulating Buddhist complications and to return it to its Chinese roots. These roots, although not specifically called Taoism by Ch'an, can be identified as none other.

When Hui-neng was being honored posthumously, it was supposedly Liu Tsung-yuan who wrote on the tombstone an inscription that read:

According to his doctrine, non-doing is reality, emptiness is the truth, and the ultimate meaning of things is vast and immoveable. He taught that human nature in its beginning as well as in the end is thoroughly good . . . for it has its root in that which is serene.[17]

Here in Liu Tsung-yuan's inscription is a fairly succinct description of Taoism, complete with some Taoist terminology, phraseology, and the philosophical assumptions that distinguish it from Buddhism.

Even D.T. Suzuki's description of the four essentials of Hui-neng's teachings are a summation of Taoist philosophy. They are as follows in abstracted form:

1. Zen is seeing into one's nature, and not of practicing

dhyana *(meditation) or obtaining liberation.*
2. The truth, which transcends dualism in all forms, comes
abruptly. When the abrupt doctrine is understood there is no
need of disciplining oneself in things external.
3. When the seeing into self-nature is emphasized and intuitive
understanding is upheld against learning and philosophizing,
we know that as one of its logical conclusions the old view of
meditation begins to be looked down on as merely a discipline
in mental tranquillization.
4. Hui-neng's method of demonstrating the truth of Zen was
purely Chinese and not Indian. He did not resort to abstract
terminology or to romantic mysticism. The method was direct,
plain, concrete, and highly practical.[18]

Of course, the Buddhist disposition of D.T. Suzuki leaves
traces of Indian thought and expression; liberation and *dhyana*
are obvious examples. And truth, in as much as it even
deserves mention, is sufficiently abstract that Taoism offers
the reminder: "Knowing is the way of fools."

So one of the effects of Hui-neng's Chinese identity
was to rescue Ch'an from the abstraction of Indian Buddhism
by returning truth, and all such notions, to a level of fundamental and elemental experience that never once mentions
itself:

Hui-neng's simple-mindedness, not spoiled by learning and
philosophizing, could grasp the truth first hand.[19]

This complimentary description of Hui-neng's "simple-
mindedness" cannot be applied to Buddhism. Despite
Mahakasyapa's smile, the Buddha said a great deal about
truth, and the subtle intricacies of Buddhist philosophy are
hardly simple. Although each person has Buddha-nature, the

Indian tradition has not advertised this attribute to be manifestly obvious and immediately accessible. The personality of Buddhism is essentially pessimistic and laborious rather than light and playful. The inherent wisdom of a natural simple-mindedness is a Taoist notion founded on the trusting attitude that life is worth living and that Nature is inherently wise and generous. Life creates death for a Taoist; the incomparable experience of being alive requires an end that enhances the value of living. Bliss and suffering are the inevitable opposites of the same whole process. To declare life to be suffering is a perspective too narrow and bleak for the Chinese.

The solely Chinese character of Hui-neng made Ch'an immensely popular. His teachings caught the spiritual imagination of China because his thinking and understanding were indigenous. He was a Taoist speaking to a culture that was spiritually Taoist. Hui-neng, in the popular Chinese imagination, became the archetypal image of itself.

The story of this man resonated deeply in the Chinese psyche. But it is also explained by other considerations:

> *The attraction of Hui-neng was that he was the antithesis of everything that upper-class society cherished: he was from the far South; he had no education or social standing; and he was not even a monk. The figure of Hui-neng represents a prototypic religious antihero, a legendary image that could develop only because Hui-neng's actual biography was almost entirely unknown.*[20]

Almost entirely unknown! The only authoritative record of him is in a list of Hung-jen's disciples as a minor figure in the Northern School of Ch'an.[21] Where, then, is the source of all his stories and teachings? It is Shen-hui:

Hui-neng's name would almost certainly be forgotten today were it not for the efforts of his student Shen-hui (A.D. 684-758).[22]

Indeed, it seems to have been Shen-hui who lectured, taught, and argued Hui-neng's notion of sudden insight into popularity. However:

Shen-hui's greatest impact was not directly related to his doctrinal claims regarding suddenness and gradualism or his version of the transmission from Hung-jen to Hui-neng. Rather, he was most influential in the area of Ch'an rhetoric. Shen-hui was a master storyteller; he inspired his congregations with exciting new anecdotes about Bodhidharma, Hui-k'o, and other early patriarchs. The popularity of his stories helped Ch'an to focus attention on the words and deeds of individual masters and to adopt a more colloquial style of expression.[23]

Undoubtedly these "exciting new anecdotes" took considerable liberties with facts, and so Shen-hui was largely responsible for creating the character of Hui-neng that is presently understood by history. He also coined the term "Northern School," a perjorative expression even though he himself had studied with both Hui-neng and Shen-hsiu.

Remember Shen-hsiu? He was the disciple of Hung-jen who was defeated by Hui-neng in the poetry contest, the result of which split Ch'an into two schools. Shen-hsiu was recognized by the Northern School as the sixth Patriarch, whereas the Southern School gave this title to Hui-neng. The politics of Ch'an were becoming complicated.

But politics, being what it is, became even more complicated when a third school, the Ox-head, discredited the bickering of the other two by offering its own account of the controversy in the popular *Platform Sutras*. This document raised the profile of Hui-neng to his present status in Ch'an history, reduced Shen-hsiu to an incidental figure, and practically obliterated Shen-hui from history by barely even mentioning him:

> *Undoubtedly, one purpose of the* Platform Sutra *account was to provide a rationale for Hui-neng's identity as sixth Patriarch without reference to Shen-hui.*[24]

As politics appeared in Ch'an, its history became complex and convoluted. The illusion of a simple history collapsed with the linear succession of patriarchs. Curious anomalies arose:

> *Traditionalists may be disappointed to learn that the* Platform Sutra *account is completely inaccurate as history and that the conventional interpretation errs at almost every point.*[25]

Shen-hsiu and Hui-neng, it seems, could not have been together with Hung-jen because reliable biographies do not locate them at the same place at the same time. The famous poetry encounter could not have happened. Indeed, the two poems show signs that they both came from the Northern School.[26] Thus the sudden and gradual distinctions between the Southern and Northern Schools are at least exaggerated if not incorrect. And the *Platform Sutra*, written around A.D. 780, about a hundred years after Hung-jen's death, was created by a later motive to write history retroactively. John R. McRae, writing in *Zen: Tradition and Transition*, summarizes the matter nicely. His comments reflect not only on Hui-neng and the characters surrounding him, but also on Bodhidharma and his immediate successors:

> *One of the lessons we can learn from this inquiry is that in Ch'an lore things are not as they appear; indeed, the reality is often contrary to appearances. Though Shen-hsiu was pivotal in the history of Ch'an, his biography was simply too well-known for him to be transformed into a legendary hero.*[27]

So, in one of history's curious reversals, the facts of Ch'an became the fiction so the fiction could become the facts.

As a footnote to Hui-neng, two more related characters must be mentioned because they help to illuminate the relationship between Taoism and Zen. They are Huang-po and Lin-chi.

Huang-po (A.D. ?-850) (Japanese: Obaku) was Lin-chi's teacher and was the third after Hui-neng by the reckoning of the Southern School. He was also known as Hsi-yun or sometimes T'uan Chi—a point, incidentally, that illustrates the problem of identifying historical characters in China when they are known variously by a formal name, an informal name, a monastic name, and a place name.

In Huang-po's *Treatise on the Essentials of the Doctrine of Mind (Ch'uan Hsin Fa Yao)*,[28] he uses Taoist ideas and language, even quotes Taoist sages in this Ch'an document. The version cited by Alan Watts in *The Way of Zen* is worth quoting because it is so resonant with Taoist thinking:

> *Fearing that none of you would understand, they [the*

Buddhas] gave it the name Tao, but you must not base any concept upon that name. So it is said that "when the fish is caught the trap is forgotten." (From Chuang-tzu.) When body and mind achieve spontaneity, the Tao is reached and universal mind can be understood. . . . In former times, men's minds were sharp. Upon hearing a single sentence, they abandoned study and so came to be called "the sages who, abandoning learning, rest in spontaneity." In these days, people only seek to stuff themselves with knowledge and deductions, placing great reliance on written explanations and calling all this the practice.[29]

These "Buddhas" are clearly more Taoist than Buddhist; they could be Lao Tzu and Chuang Tzu. And Huang-po's *Treatise* is Taoist in both content and style.

The successor to Hui-neng, by the accounting of the Southern School and thus Rinzai Zen, was not Shen-hui but Lin-chi (A.D. ?-867) (Japanese: Rinzai), also known as I-hsuan. His teachings, recorded as the *Lin-chi Lu* (Japanese: *Rinzai Roku*), illustrate the continued presence of Taoist thinking in Ch'an. He dispensed teachings that were Taoist in subject, mood, philosophy, and even terminology:

Why do I talk here? Only because you followers of the Tao go galloping around in search of the mind, and are unable to stop it. On the other hand, the ancients acted in a leisurely way, appropriate to circumstances (as they arose).[30]

The "ancients" is a traditional expression for old Chinese sages and the "leisurely" response "to circumstances" is pure Taoism. Lin-chi continues:

There is no place in Buddhism for using effort. Just be ordi-

nary and nothing special. Relieve your bowels, pass water, put on your clothes, eat your food. When you are tired, go and lie down.[31]

This avoidance of effort that opposes natural momentum is the *wu-wei* of Taoist philosophy. Lin-chi's advice could have been from any of the old Taoist ancients.

Lin-chi was the official founder of the sect that was later to bear the Japanese version of his name. The return of the ordinary to special status was expressed in his teaching strategy:

Lin-chi had a fourfold system for snatching away his students' attachments to subjects and objects. The first part of the process was removing the subject and keeping the object, next removing the object and keeping the subject, then removing both subject and object, and, fourthly, keeping both subject and object.[32]

The end, in effect, is a return to the beginning, a beginning that has been transformed by the very process of losing it and then reclaiming it. The idea, repeated later in the more recent versions of the *Ox Herding Pictures*, reconnects the student to the grounded and real world of concrete experience that is so characteristic of both Chinese thinking and Taoist philosophy.

This Taoist philosophy is the central teaching of Zen. But this fact has been obscured by the insistence of the Ch'an schools of China and the Zen Buddhist sects of Japan that their teachings be defined in terms of Mahayana Buddhism. Since the operating principles of Taoism could not integrate with either religious beliefs or Buddhist philosophy, they were overwritten by Buddhist ideology and methodology.

The result has been a tangle of misrepresentations that have attempted to disguise the contradictory character of both Ch'an and Zen Buddhism. Bodhidharma is one such example. Hui-neng is another.

There was a Hui-neng. He was thoroughly Chinese. But he was unlikely a Buddhist, although later efforts attempted to make him one. All the evidence suggests that he was the archetypal Taoist, or at least he was invented as such by the Chinese need to express its own character through him.

So Hui-neng, perhaps more an invention than a person, became a pivotal event in the history of Ch'an. Native Chinese sensibilities were revitalized and expressed through him. Taoism's spontaneity and naturalness were renewed as the heart of Ch'an; Confucianism declared itself in the order and structure, in the discipline and hierarchy, in the institutions and monasteries of Ch'an. The historical importance of Hui-neng is that he was thoroughly Chinese and through him China cast Ch'an in the form, spirit, and consciousness of itself.

But the long story of Zen Buddhism in China and then Japan has been complicated by the insistence of the Mahayana religion that all this history be related to India and the Buddha. Because of this insistence, Zen Buddhism could not be honest about its Chinese heritage or Hui-neng. So Hui-neng was divided to comply with the historical fact and to satisfy the religious need. He became the same contradiction as Zen Buddhism.

Clearly, Zen Buddhism could not have existed as an institution without leaving unresolved the contradiction of its Taoist and Buddhist components. This unresolved condition is the dynamic of Zen itself, and is Zen Buddhism's best excuse for its depiction of Hui-neng. So the sixth Patriarch became a Buddhist with none of the attributes of one, and a Taoist who could not be called a Taoist. Hui-neng became a contradiction and thereby a symbol for Zen Buddhism itself.

Zen
in Japan

C h'an was probably known to the Japanese as early as the eighth or ninth century[1] but it was not officially introduced until 1191 by Eisai (A.D. 1141-1215). He was a Buddhist monk who returned from China with the Rinzai teachings, those of the Southern School of Ch'an known in China as *Lin-chi*. Another Japanese monk, Dogen (A.D. 1200-1253), returned to Japan in 1227 with Tsao-tung, the other major branch of Ch'an teachings; they became known as Soto. Zen Buddhism, commonly shortened to Zen, became the generic Japanese term for Ch'an.

The directness and simplicity of this new style of Buddhism first appealed to the newly established military class of the Kamakura Era.[2] Its widespread acceptance in Japan occurred slowly, however, considering that the culture had for centuries been Buddhist and that Japan had a common written language with China. Several centuries passed before Zen fully integrated into the Japanese culture. In 1654 the Ch'an master Yin-yuan[3] brought a third Ch'an to Japan. These were the teachings of Huang-po who was historically related to Rinzai—he was Lin-chi's teacher. Obaku is presently the least influential of the three major sects of Japanese Zen.

The differences between the two major sects, Rinzai and Soto, still reflect the differences between the two schools of Ch'an. Both traditions place value on sitting meditation (Japanese: *zazen*, Chinese: *t'so-ch'an*) but Rinzai holds that *kensho* (Chinese: *tzu-hsing*), literally "seeing into one's own nature,"[4] comes from using the *koan* (Chinese: *kung-an*) to force the mind to an abrupt awakening. Soto Zen holds that each individual can be slowly brought to awakening by ritual sitting (Japanese: *shikantaza*) and by studying Buddhist literature.

> *"Rinzai's teaching is like the frost of the late autumn, making one shiver, while the teaching of Soto is like the spring breeze that caresses the flower, helping it to bloom." There is another saying: "Rinzai's teaching is like a brave general who moves a regiment without delay, while the Soto teaching is like a farmer taking care of a rice field, one stalk after another, patiently."* [5]

Perhaps the gentler and less dramatic practice of Soto is more compatible with the Japanese Buddhist character, for it presently maintains a three-to-one popularity over Rinzai.

The differences that divided Ch'an in China during the eighth and ninth centuries continued and multiplied in Japan. Of the three sects that were initially introduced from China, there are now:

> *twenty-two independent organizations [that] consider themselves heirs to the Zen lineage. These groups relate to one another like cousins who accept each other's claim to membership in the extended clan, but who prefer to think of themselves as representing the most direct line of descent.*[6]

This "line of descent" through Bodhidharma to the Buddha is a belief that has been reinforced in Zen Buddhism throughout the centuries of company that it has kept with the Mahayana religion in both China and Japan. Such a religious connection has been in effect since Ch'an was first identified by name in late eighth-century China, and since it came to Japan as Zen Buddhism. Both Ch'an and Zen Buddhism became inseparable from the Mahayana religion. Most Zen

Buddhist temples, therefore, celebrate occasions such as the birth, enlightenment, and death of the Buddha. They also generally reflect the cultural and religious disposition of Japan, including the ritual honoring of the ancestral dead, an event that is also practiced in China.

So the Chinese thread that connects Taoism to Ch'an and Zen becomes thinner and thinner in Japan as the particular language and rituals of religious Buddhism continue to overshadow the elusive qualities of Zen. To repeat D.T. Suzuki: "Zen looks as if it [has] nothing to do with Buddhism. . . ."[7]

Tracing a single source along a single course is also made difficult by the syncretic character of the East. Religious, philosophical, and aesthetic movements mix, converge, and diverge with apparent abandon. With respect to Ch'an and Zen alone:

> *Literary minded Ch'an masters . . . who were active in Japan in the early fourteenth century, found it perfectly natural, while instructing their patrons in Zen, to make use of the [Confucian]* Analects, Lao-tzu *or* Chuang-tzu, *and to encourage the study of Chinese poetry, painting and calligraphy.*[8]

Although the spoken language was a barrier between the exchange of culture from China to Japan, the written language was not. The Japanese had adopted and continue to use the Chinese ideograms called *kanji*, so the written language became a conduit for the flow of innumerable Chinese influences. Ideas moved easily from an older China to a younger Japan, and the maturity of Chinese culture had a significant and formative effect on the thought and character of

Japan. One of these influences was Taoism. But tracing Taoism through Japan is not as easy as tracing it through China because Japanese ingredients come into play.

It would be unrealistic to think that Ch'an and the naturalistic Taoist philosophy at its heart did not in some way influence the Japanese. But the influence is also influenced. Just as the Buddhism of India was altered by the Chinese, so the Taoist element in Ch'an took a somewhat different shape as it expressed itself in Japanese Zen. A comment by Frederick Franck in *Zen and Zen Classics* is useful here:

> *What the Japanese added to Zen was the most difficult thing in the world, simplicity; this was their own innate, potential Zen.*[9]

Simplicity has been one of the foremost philosophical impulses that has moved through the long history of Taoism. In China it cultivated the traditional image of the Chinese sage, formed the basis for both the pursuit and character of wisdom, and expressed itself throughout Chinese art. The best of life, beauty, and worth was grounded in simplicity. So the Japanese inclination toward simplicity came to be expressed with even greater refinement as the Taoist influence moved through Zen to complement the existing aesthetics. Two things happened to Zen:

> *[O]n the one hand it became aristocratic, in the artistic sense; Zen served poets and painters and sculptors in confirming their tastes, and deepest judgements of value. On the other hand, Zen spread among the common people, those who could not read or write, who were completely ignorant of the Mahayana philosophy, who did not and could not know,*

intellectually speaking, what Zen was, and had not heard even the word.[10]

Zen entered the common people organically, in exact concurrance with the character of Taoism. In the artistic consciousness of Japan, the Zen influence reinforced and refined the meaning and significance of nature. As in China, the images of nature were incorporated into the language of poetry and brushpainting, but with a special blending of spontaneity, simplicity, and dignity. Nature, already a large part of the Japanese consciousness, became even more sharply focused in thought and feeling, more acute, an integral and refined part of their very being.

Water, the predominant image of Taoism, flowed through Ch'an into Zen and spoke in both new and old ways. Here is Dogen, the thirteenth-century Zen master who introduced Soto into Japan, sounding like both Lao Tzu and Chuang Tzu. Of course, he has a Buddhist accent:

> *The color of the mountains is Buddha's body; the sound of running water is his great speech.*[11]

Dogen's metaphors are clearly Chinese. But the Japanese sensitivity to nature is not all traceable to Ch'an and Taoism. A huge undercurrent of nature consciousness was native to Japan. This was Shinto.

Like Confucianism, Shinto venerated ancestors, but like Taoism, it also honored the spirit and power of nature. The *kami* were the spirit forces of natural things and, as such, gave each thing its identity or life force, *musubi*. Because venerated people could have both *kami* and *musubi*, no separation was made between human and nature:

> *Shinto was, and remains, essentially directed to making the best of life, the religion of people who live in rapport with nature, who respect the natural order and the traditional social order which is regarded as part of it, and whose over-riding priorities are prosperity and social harmony. . . . It has little to say about life after death. . . .*[12]

Shinto, in fact, might be described as Japan's own original, blended version of Confucianism and Taoism. Because of its similarity to the basic elements of Chinese culture, it is easy to understand how a Taoist influence could have entered Japan through Ch'an and been adopted without difficulty into the Japanese psyche. This process was made even easier by the earlier meeting of Shinto and Buddhism.

Buddhism had come to Japan about seven hundred years before the arrival of Ch'an. It first came through China and Korea in the sixth century and was practiced mainly in the courts of the aristocracy. Over the centuries it integrated with the wider population and established a comfortable relationship with Shinto. Each influenced and accommodated the other such that their deities coexisted in Shinto shrines and Buddhist temples. In modern Japan this tradition still exists with temples and shrines often adjacent to each other, and in Japanese houses icons of the two religions are commonly seen adorning opposite walls of the same room.

This blending of Shinto and Buddhism expressed itself in Tendai and Shingon, two Japanese religious traditions with connections in China. Tendai is a form of Chinese *T'ien-t'ai*, an early Mahayana Buddhism, and Shingon is a more esoteric form of Buddhism with tantric connections to India. In Japan these two forms of Buddhism:

each made room for the Shinto kami in its system. . . . In
Shingon, *a distinctly Japanese sect of Buddhism, the Shinto*
kami are regarded as Japanese manifestations of the great
Mahayana Buddhas and Bodhisattvas.[13]

By the time Ch'an arrived in Japan in the late twelfth
and the early thirteenth centuries, Japanese Buddhism
already had a strong Shinto component that would have recognized as familiar the Taoist element in Chinese Ch'an—
the same process, incidentally, that had occurred more than a
thousand years earlier when the Chinese recognized in Indian
Buddhism a form of Taoism. Because of this established
Shinto component in Japanese Buddhism, there were clearly
defined distinctions between it and the Chinese Buddhism of
Ch'an such that Shinto:

cast its spell over [Ch'an] in at least two ways, helping to
make the Zen of Japan different from the Ch'an of China.[14]

Curiously, this "spell" of Shinto that created a distinctly
Japanese Buddhism also gave to Zen some of the qualities of
early Chinese Ch'an that had been diluted by the influence
of Indian Buddhism.

The first of these Shinto influences was the way in
which the spirit of natural objects, the *kami*, and their life
force, the *musubi*, moved Chinese Ch'an toward a deeper spiritual regard for nature, in effect shifting Ch'an closer to its
Taoist origin. The essential result was that Japanese Zen
Buddhism would have appeared to be more like earlier Ch'an
than the later one that migrated to Japan. So Shinto moved
Ch'an toward the same respect it had for nature before it
became saturated with religious Buddhism. Noteworthy, too,

was the fact that the *kami* and *musubi* were "caught but not caught,"[15] an expression which meant that the Shinto frame of mind was already prepared to approach the paradoxical Taoist thinking that was at the core of Ch'an.

The second influence of Shinto on Ch'an was the way in which:

> *the* musubi *of all objects had to be felt, smelled, touched, seen, heard.*[16]

Shinto, therefore, in modifying Ch'an from a Chinese to a Japanese form, reconnected it to the grounded, direct experience of original Taoism. Simplicity, directness, earthiness, and groundedness became attributes of Zen Buddhism. From Shinto came a focused experience of things, a sense of profound empathy and oneness with nature such that the *kami* could be thought of as the Zen's suchness of a thing (Japanese: *sonomama*).

Indeed, much of the art of Zen, whether in writing or calligraphy, painting or potting, is an expression of this same spirit of essential identity with nature that is the heart of both Shinto and Taoism. Furthermore, the paradox of something being "caught but not caught" induces the creative tension that is so wonderfully a part of the living energy in both Zen and Taoism.

Because the Taoist and Shinto attitudes to nature are so similar, it is, perhaps, impossible to separate Zen's response to nature into a Chinese or a Japanese component. It is sufficient to note that Taoism and Shinto, when they met, would have felt comfortable in each other's company. Indeed, they were so similar in so many ways that the Taoism in Ch'an probably helped Ch'an's adoption into Japan.

Although Taoism and Shinto both arose out of a spirituality that was grounded and earthy, they also possessed a wisdom that was intuitive and organic, qualities that caused neither of them to be organized or formalized enough to leave clear, historical trails. The origin of early Taoism is still the subject of speculation. And Shinto, before Buddhism's arrival in Japan in A.D. 552, did not even have a name for itself.[17] Furthermore, the spiritual directness of Taoism and Shinto makes neither of them an orthodox religion:

> *Japanese simplicity is seen most clearly in Shinto, which is a religion without a religious idea in it.*[18]

When Zen is considered separately from the religious and organizational force of Buddhism that keeps it company in Japan, it has the same sense of spiritual freedom that is common to Shinto and Taoism. Zen has deliberately burned its own books and statues, denounced its own teachings, even refused to utter its own name. Like the Tao, any concept of Zen is somehow extraneous to Zen itself. It is as if:

> *The history of Zen is the history of moments. It cannot be like the history of ideas. . . . Zen seems to become deeper sometimes, shallower, broader, narrower sometimes, but there is no progress of the ordinary kind.*[19]

Zen is like Taoism in this regard; any concept of it is a contradiction of terms. Nothing can be done with it. It arrived. It became. It is. And that is that.

123

Zen Without Buddhism

*t*he Buddhism in Zen Buddhism provides the institutional context in which Zen is found. But the Buddhism is not Zen. Indeed, a Zen aphorism offers the rather stunning reminder, "If you meet the Buddha, kill him!" This advice is to be understood metaphorically, and makes perfect sense when interpreted in the spirit of the Buddha's original teachings. But it does not make sense in Mahayana Buddhism, the religious tradition with which Zen became associated in China and Japan. Killing the Buddha comes from the Zen in Buddhism, not from the Buddhism in Zen Buddhism. The aphorism illustrates the polarity of difference between Zen and Mahayana Buddhism.

For the last thousand years Zen has found itself in the company of Mahayana Buddhism. The relationship began innocently enough:

The Schools [of Mahayana Buddhism] in China which emphasized meditation . . . blended their purposes and ideas with those of the Tao with the result that Ch'an, and later Zen, came to mean that kind of meditation which is specifically aimed at the Tao and the Buddha-mind or Buddha-nature. [1]

In Ch'an, Tao and Buddha-mind or Buddha-nature became synonymous. Since both meditation and teaching took place in the early monasteries, those with an interest in Buddhism would have experienced the meditation in terms of Buddha-nature, and those with an interest in Taoism would have experienced the teaching in terms of the Tao. Of course, this process of melding the two systems was neither conscious nor contrived; it just happened inadventently as a result of a combination of circumstances.

The arrangement was advantageous for both Buddhism and Taoism. For the newly forming Buddhist monasteries, the Taoism at the roots of Ch'an would have guaranteed their popularity; and for Taoism, the institutionalized order of Buddhism would have guaranteed its security. Thus their amalgamation in Ch'an appeared to meet the needs of both traditions. For those who wanted the unequivocal certainty of religion, there was Mahayana Buddhism; for those who wanted the paradoxical subtleties of Chinese thinking, there was Taoism. The unintentional arrangement evolved naturally and was simply practical, although not always comfortable.

The Taoist voice in Ch'an has always expressed ambivalence about this shared arrangement, as if it could never quite relax in the formal and proper company of Mahayana Buddhism. Taoism is not religious like Buddhism; it is more inclusive and less restrained. It never felt comfortable being confined in an institutional structure. There has always been in Ch'an a slight and irresolvable tension between the abstract qualities of the Indian philosophy and the earthy practicality of its indigenous Chinese character. Taoism has often indicated, throughout its history with Buddhism, uneasiness with these differences. Zen has continued to do so. Here is the Chinese master Mu-mon (A.D. 1183-1260) (Japanese: Ekai) in the *Wu-men-kuan* (Japanese: *Mumonkan*):

> *That broken-toothed old Hindu, Bodhidharma, came thousands of miles over the sea from India to China as if he had something wonderful. He is like raising waves without wind. After he remained years in China he had only one disciple and*

that one lost his arm and was deformed. Alas, ever since he has had brainless disciples.[2]

So the first Patriarch and his disciples have been a constant source of bother. But Hindu? Not Buddhist? This *Zen Flesh, Zen Bones* translation by Paul Reps is interesting for that one word alone.

Or consider the words of the Zen scholar, R.H. Blyth, from *Games Zen Masters Play*:

The Buddhas and the Patriarchs of Zen are doctors who cause the disease they pretend to cure.[3]

Consider also the poem by Ikkyu (A.D. 1394-1481), a Zen abbot from Kyoto whose wit and irreverence express the same sentiment more playfully:

Since that mischievous creature
called Sakya [the Buddha]
Was born into the world,
How many, many people
Have been befooled![4]

More dramatic still are the words attributed to Zen Master Fang in *Zen and the Comic Spirit*:

The Buddha is a bull-headed jail-keeper, and the Patriarchs are horse-faced old maids.[5]

And Frederick Franck expresses Zen's uneasiness with Buddhism this way:

Zen, supposed to be the essence of Buddhism, is closest, not to the moralizing of Confucius or the philosophizing of [the]

Buddha but to the silent bowing of the head before what is neither good nor bad, neither true nor untrue.[6]

Zen Buddhism in Japan is the result of the long coexistence of Taoism and Buddhism as Ch'an in China. It is, consequently, an institutional system with a dual personality. This condition is quite different from the paradoxes within Zen itself, although Zen's accommodation of paradox probably permitted the opposing elements of this personality to coexist. But accommodation hides the differences between Zen and Buddhism. There are similarities between them, but the differences are great enough that the two must be regarded as separate systems.

Buddhism, in effect, rejects the world, viewing it as a place of suffering, transience, and imperfection; Zen accepts the world exactly as it is, unconditionally receiving whatever experience is offered. Desire, according to Buddhism, is the nemesis of the human condition, the burden of being that can only be overcome by insightful consciousness; according to Zen, desire becomes a problem only when it is owned or personalized, and thereby becomes an interference in an individual's equanimity and balance.

The Buddha's essential realization under the Bodhi tree was that suffering is inseparable from living, that life is death. But his insight was treated in an Indian style, not a Chinese one:

Nirvana is release from life, from life and death, calling and answering. This was the Indian, the Buddhist idea.[7]

But the Chinese, when they received the insight of the Buddha, understood it differently:

130

The Zen, the Chinese experience, was that this was only half
Nirvana. The other half was not to be released from life and
death, from calling and answering. So we must call as not
calling, not call as calling, answer as not answering, not
answer as answering—a tall order, indeed. . . .[8]

This Chinese insight is the essential paradox of Zen. In a style that is characteristically Taoist, it leaves experience similtaneously connected and disconnected. This is the source of Zen's groundedness, a distinctive reconnection with a world that can only be experienced and honored from an intimate distance. This special distance creates the closeness, and the closeness creates the distance as the two contrary energies move unresolved in a delicately balanced counterpoint. The Chinese harmonized this duality in their particularly Taoist way to create a sense of balanced wholeness:

Zen perceived that just as our joy and suffering are indivisi-
ble, so are Nirvana and the world, the absolute and the rela-
tive. Buddhism is thus always a duality, and Zen tends to fall
into unity.[9]

This unity of duality was the contribution of Chinese Taoism. And herein lies the contradiction in Zen Buddhism, as its Buddhism tries to remain connected to India through the invention of Bodhidharma while its Zen is directly connected to Taoism through Chinese Ch'an. Zen includes Buddhism but Buddhism does not include Zen. This inclusiveness is what makes Zen so contradictory and so elusive. It also permitted Taoism and Buddhism to coexist as Ch'an. But it was not the only reason.

When Indian Buddhism came to China during the first century it was reshaped to fit the Chinese mind. The Chinese were not sympathetic with the asceticism and metaphysics of India so the Indian form of Buddhism evolved into Chinese Mahayana,[10] which was more practical, more earthy, and more immediate. The Buddhism with which Ch'an, and later Zen, came to coexist was no longer the original Indian system.

The argument that claims Zen to be the direct heir of the teachings of the Buddha is compromised in three ways. The first is doctrinal. The Buddhism associated with Ch'an in China and Zen in Japan is Mahayana, not the austere silence of Gautama sitting alone on the bank of the Gaya's Neranjara River. Obviously, the Buddha himself was not Mahayana; he was not even Buddhist. His search for insight was existential, not religious. His conclusion was to believe and trust nothing but experience. The second is stylistic. The Buddha taught with a system of principles and clearly enunciated processes, but not, as all evidence suggests, in the abrupt and seemingly illogical style of Zen. There are moments of Zen in Indian Buddhism, but these are largely incidental to Buddhism's claim that it is the source of Zen. The third is historical. There is no traceable or supportable link from the Buddha to Bodhidharma and onward to Hui-neng and Japanese Zen. The amount of Zen that can be traced to Indian Buddhism is not much more than Mahakasyapa's small smile. And this smile, if indeed it was ever smiled, may have been the modicum of ancient yoga that filtered through Indian thought into Buddhism.

Beyond the issues of doctrine, style, and history that argue against a Buddhist source for Zen, Zen Buddhism's own case is confused by the ambiguity of its terminology, an ambiguity that has served to hide the insufficiency of

Buddhism's claims to Zen. Confusion is created because Zen is not the same as Zen Buddhism, and the Buddhism that is practiced in Japan's Zen Buddhism is the religious Buddhism of Mahayana but not the philosophical Buddhism of the original Indian Buddha. What then accounts for the coexistence of Zen and Buddhism if there is so little to support their connection?

Remember that the Buddhism that first came to China was recognized, so the Taoists contended, as a simplified form of Taoism. Beneath its veneer were qualities that the Chinese Taoists recognized as familiar; they felt comfortable with Buddhism. The similarities were numerous: the awakened Buddha in the flesh was comparable in character to the Taoist sage; the path of Buddhism's middle way was similar to the Taoist's method of resolving the mutually arising opposites of *hsiang sheng*; anyone could become enlightened just as anyone could become a sage—indeed, everyone was enlightened, just as everyone, conscious or not, willing or not, followed the Tao; the Mahayana pledge for collective enlightenment could easily be equated to the sage's guidance of society toward individual and collective harmony; Buddhism and Taoism both shared a profound empathy with people and all other things; both trusted the consequences of self-awareness; both held that selflessness provided access to deep insight.

When the two eventually came together in the Ch'an monasteries, the Chinese, with their usual syncretic skill, were able to integrate the philosophical similarities of Taoism and Buddhism with the religious elements of Mahayana without sacrificing the identity of any of the three constituents. This balanced integration was accomplished with typical

Chinese pragmatism such that all sides were able to benefit from the arrangement. Because of this syncretism, however, the single word Ch'an came to denote the coexistence of the three quite distinct traditions.

But Taoism, the Zen portion of the partnership, always chafed at the confinement imposed on it by the other two:

> *[The] Buddha, according to Zen, warned his followers of the confusing maze of dogma which often confronts anyone attempting to practice a religion.*[11]

The focus of Zen has always been toward engendering sensitivity and an insight into the world itself, not the teachings of the Buddha per se, and certainly not the religious dogma of Mahayana. The goal of Zen is to follow the Way, a process that ultimately—even initially—has nothing to do with any systemized or institutionalized process of understanding. Indeed, the Way in Zen and Taoism has nothing to do with anything but itself, not even goals. But for those who need a system, Chuang Tzu offers the reminder that the fish trap is only needed to catch the fish; once the fish is caught the fish trap is no longer needed—so much the better if the fish can be caught without the trap. The only purpose of any consideration of Zen is eventually to be freed of that consideration. Therein lies the only relevance of the *zazen* and the *koan* in the practice of Zen Buddhism.

The function of the *zazen* and *koan* is to undo the system that contains them. They are meditational and intellectual devices to show the Way; they are not ends in themselves. Paradoxically, however, they must be declared as such in order to fulfill their purpose; they will not work if they are purposeful. The *koan* and the *zazen* must be taken seriously so that attention to them becomes more important than the objective of using them. They are, in effect, deliberate tricks of self-deception, intentional contrivances, that can be effective only when they are disregarded as such.

The purpose of the formal sitting of *zazen* is to become calm and empty, to shed everything—even the shedding—so that there is no sitting, no sitter, not even Buddhism or the Buddha. Hui-neng, according to Zen Buddhism's history of him, understood this and argued against formal *zazen* as unnecessary. What could be the purpose of a process whose purpose was to show that there was no process? Hui-neng knew that *zazen* had become entrenched as the principal activity in institutionalized Ch'an and he would not endorse its formal practice. He said that an empty mind with no thoughts arising from it constituted "sitting" (Chinese: *t'so*; Japanese: *za*) and that any inward reflection on one's own nature was meditation (Chinese: *ch'an*; Japanese: *zen*). Zen Buddhism, in its story of Hui-neng, symbolically abandons its institutional self. But this gesture is only symbolic. The *zazen* continues, and the actual effects are the loss of patriarchal succession and the fracturing of Ch'an into separate schools.

If Hui-neng, who is considered by Zen Buddhism to be its last great patriarch, did not advocate formal *zazen*, why is it practiced with such diligence and insisted upon with such vigor by roshis of the past and present? Because it reinforces Zen Buddhism's self-proclaimed historical association with Bodhidharma and the Buddha. *Zazen* is about Buddhism, not about Zen. With formal sitting Zen Buddhism attempts to assert its link to India and the Buddha and thereby avoid its actual connection to China. It is ironic that the teachings of one of Zen Buddhism's most venerated sages, Hui-neng, are effectively disregarded in the interest of maintaining an ordered Buddhist institution.

Alan Watts, with the spirit of a modern Hui-neng, argues vigorously that there is no substantial evidence in Ch'an literature or practice to support the emphasis given to *zazen* by Zen Buddhism. The evidence, he says:

> corroborates the view that the T'ang masters of Ch'an
> deplored the use of meditation exercises as a means to the
> attainment of true insight (wu, or Japanese satori). I had fur-
> ther confirmation of this view in private discussions with D.T.
> Suzuki and R.H. Blyth, both of whom regarded compulsive
> "aching legs" za-zen [sic] as a superstitious fetish of modern
> Zen practice.[12]

Elsewhere, when the clear voice of Zen is heard above the rigid pronouncements of institutionalized Buddhism, R.H. Blyth writes of the Buddha that, "his sitting was no different from his walking. . . ."[13]

In other words, *zazen* is not distinguishable from any other activity as a means to enlightenment. In *A Western Approach to Zen*, Christmas Humphreys is less generous:

> Meditation is at best a means and not in itself an end. To
> some extent all meditation is unnatural, and no "sitting" for
> however long will itself produce enlightenment.[14]

Even the great Dogen, who brought to Japan the Soto Zen that emphasizes formal sitting, is purported to have seen *zazen* as only a part of Zen. Our everyday life should have the same single-mindedness as sitting:

> To cook or fix some food, is not preparation; it is practice. . . .
> Whatever we do, it should be an expression of the same deep

activity. We should appreciate what we are doing. There is no
preparation for something else.[15]

The only purpose of *zazen*, then, is to prevent the "something else" that distracts from a sense of total presence. Any activity will suffice. This is precisely how Zen is popularly practiced in the West.

The *koan* has the same strategic purpose: to draw the mind out of its own miasma of abstract speculation, to bring to an end the self-invented thoughtfulness that becomes lost in its own cogitations and thereby misses the total sense of grounded presence that is the Zen experience. The *koan* stills and empties the mind by forcing it to confound itself with its own devices. The process is commonly described as "mind beating out mind." When mind is totally overcome by itself, when it is stopped in absolute confusion, when it is still and empty, what then is the correct answer to a *koan*?

There are many right answers and there are also none. . . .
For the koan itself is the answer, and by the time there is a
right answer to it Zen is dead.[16]

The aliveness of Zen has entirely to do with eliminating the conceptualizations that organize, categorize and institutionalize experience. Any answer becomes the "something else" that kills the vitality of Zen.

Unlike *zazen*, the *koan* is more an instrument of Chinese than Indian thought. The *Lao Tzu* is full of logical conundrums that leave deliberate consciousness with nothing to do but let go of its rational, linear, systematic style of understanding. The *Chuang Tzu*, too, is full of the *koan*-play that was later perfected in Ch'an. The *koan* is principally a Taoist device perfected by the Chinese for institutional use.

The *koan* was not a traditional part of the original teachings of Buddhism, but in retrospect, it can be found there. The flower held up by the Buddha to test the insight of his disciples can be interpreted as a *koan*; Mahakasyapa's ringing smile was the only possible answer. And there is a *koan* in the words attributed to the Buddha in the so-called *Diamond Sutra*:

> *... I obtained not the least thing from unexcelled, complete awakening, and for this very reason it is called "unexcelled, complete awakening."*[17]

Perhaps these were the words heard by Hui-neng, causing him to seek out Hung-jen's monastery and altering forever the course of Ch'an and Zen Buddhism. But the words are also a sharp reminder that all the teachings of Buddhism and all the disciplines of Zen Buddhism are not Zen. Everything thought and said about Zen turns against itself. Like Chuang Tzu who sees the Tao's wisdom in the thoughtless freedom of a wild turtle, Zen survives alive and whole only when it is left to drag its tail in the mud.

The natural spontaneity that allows the turtle its Zen is what causes Frederick Franck in *Zen and Zen Classics* to be so uncomplimentary about organized and institutionalized Zen:

> *To an occidental, the forms and ceremonies of a Zen temple, and the feudalistic, not to say militaristic ranking of the priests may seem un-Zen-like, and worse still, disagreeable. The rules and regulations, the chantings and genuflections. . .* [18]

Change the metaphor from turtle to snake and Franck's criticism of Zen Buddhism continues. He describes as odious:

> *the photographs of Zen monks in their fanaticism, bigotry,*

superstition, and standardisation; the pettifogging and infan-
tile personal stories supposed to exemplify moments of enlight-
enment; the commentaries . . . with their esotericism and supe-
riority-complex; [and the] foreigners (no exceptions) who pre-
tend to understand Zen, and bamboozle themselves and (some
of) their readers by adding their own legs to the snake.[19]

Even writing about Zen is an effrontery, as self-contradictory as adding legs to the snake! Yet silence is not enough.
The dilemma is that Zen, once it seems to be lost, can only
be found by becoming more lost. The snake that cannot walk
because it thinks it has legs must ponder until it discovers
that it has no legs. This is the long search of finding what to
forget so that everything that is not Zen can be forgotten.
The process of searching for Zen seems at first to be a further
violation of Zen.

Something undeniably simple and profoundly ordinary
demands to be remembered, whether it be the legless snake
or Chuang Tzu's turtle. The equivalent human image is the
Taoist sage, living peacefully and unnoticed among others.
This is a person who belongs everywhere and nowhere,
someone who seems deeply ordinary and yet subtly different,
an inner outcast who follows some unknowable wisdom of
great grace. Induced silence and enforced stillness are not
Taoism or Zen. Monasteries are not the places to find those
who follow the ordered freedom of nature. What other freedom is there? What other Zen is there?

Perhaps in Japan this Zen spirit is best expressed in the
poet-monks who left their monasteries to become mendi-
cants. Seeming to belong nowhere, those such as Ikkyu,
Basho, and Santoka wandered the countryside, writing *haiku*
and visiting with simple folk. Ryokan, with his "certified"

enlightenment, called himself the "Great Fool" and chose to roam the mountains and valleys, chatting and drinking with earthy farmers. These monks were the embodiment of Zen, as close as possible to resolving the paradox of being detached and thereby connected to the rhythmical softness of the hard Earth's breathing.

This resolution tugs apart institutionalized Zen, pulls at the unnatural legs of the snake, and turns the turtle toward the mud of the riverbank. In condensed form, here is one of many such stories that turns Zen free to be itself:

> *The winter night was so cold that Tanka took the wooden Buddha of the monastery, chopped it into pieces and lit a bonfire to keep himself warm.*

Or here, from *The Gateless Gate*, is the same message:

> *On [the day of his enlightenment], in front of the lecture hall, Tokusan burned to ashes his commentaries on the* sutras. *He said: "However abstruse the teachings are, in comparison with this enlightenment they are like a single hair to the great sky. However profound the complicated knowledge of the world, compared to this enlightenment it is like one drop of water to the great ocean." Then he left that monastery.*[20]

An old Zen adage not only recalls the same theme more poetically but also echoes with Taoist images and metaphors:

> *Though the bamboo forest is dense,*
> *Water flows through it freely.*[21]

When Zen expresses itself without the company of Buddhism, it takes the shape and language of Taoism.

Ch'an was brought to Japan to become Zen, so the last

word should go to Dogen, the founder of Soto, the sect that eventually became the most popular in the country. He declared:

> *"Anyone who would regard Zen as a school or sect of Buddhism, and call it* Zen-shu, *Zen School, is a devil."*[22]

Nonin and Bankei

Zen in Japan has been expressed officially in the context of Mahayana Buddhism, although by instinct Zen is not Mahayana, not Buddhist, not anything but itself.

This nonsectarian and nonreligious nature of Zen has been revealed in small glimpses throughout its history. In persistent anecdotes, aphorisms, and stories, Zen has asserted its independence from all categorization and confinement. But few roshis have formalized an even partial separation of Zen from Buddhism. Nonin and Bankei are exceptions.

Nonin (A.D. ?-1196?) is an enigmatic figure who is almost unknown in the official history of Zen Buddhism. Biographical sketches were not written about him until five hundred years after his death, and they are undoubtedly inaccurate. But Nonin is worth some attention because he was probably the first roshi to acknowledge an official difference between Zen and Buddhism. Unfortunately, the end that came to him and his sect does not speak well for a Zen Buddhism that is traditionally known for compassion, perspective, and religious tolerance. Intolerance, in fact, may account for the near absence of Nonin from the history of Zen Buddhism.

Nonin initially studied Tendai Buddhism but he apparently became dissatisfied with it, even abandoning the traditional teacher-disciple relationship by declaring himself to be a self-enlightened Zen roshi.[1] His early popularity rose dramatically. When his lack of certification was challenged by the Zen Buddhist authorities of the day—probably Eisai—he dispatched two disciples to China to petition for recognition

from an appropriate Ch'an master. Nonin's letter and generous gifts promptly procured the necessary recognition, which
suggests something about the politics of twelfth-century
Ch'an. His popularity continued to rise.

Although Nonin's sect came to be known as Nihon
Daruma (Japanese Bodhidharma), little of its teaching seems
to have involved the traditional Zen Buddhist treatment of
Bodhidharma and the Buddha. It did not require adherence
to Buddhist religious practices and observances. Special
respect was given to Bodhidharma as a teacher, but:

> *"a separate transmission outside the scriptures" was champi-
> oned as the essence of Zen. Nonin denied the need to engage in
> customary Buddhist practices or observe the precepts. He fur-
> ther claimed that rewards and blessings are obtainable in the
> present life.*[2]

Nihon Daruma received very pointed censure from the
other newly established Zen Buddhist communities. When
Eisai, the Japanese founder of Rinzai Zen, was reportedly
asked about Nonin's Zen, he complained that those in the
Daruma sect had the audacity to say:

> *"There are no precepts to follow, no practices to engage in.
> From the outset there are no passions; from the beginning we
> are enlightened. Therefore we do not practice, do not follow
> precepts. We eat when we are hungry, rest when we are tired.
> Why recite the Buddha's name, why make offerings, why give
> vegetarian feasts, why curtail eating?" How can this be?*[3]

The response of the orthodox Zen Buddhists to Nonin's
teachings is noteworthy for it reveals the narrowness and
zealotry that are the usual marks of religious bigotry. Eisai

became so "outraged"[4] that a portion of the famous work for which he is known, *The Propagation of Zen in Defense of the Country*, was an attack on the teachings of Nonin.[5]

And Dogen, who later founded Soto Zen, also became critical of Nonin's teachings. Although he was initially tolerant of such independent instruction, he eventually openly condemned it and anything else that did not conform to Soto precepts.

This kind of sectarian bickering became common; in the case of objections to Nonin, they also became vicious. Nonin was killed, apparently by his own nephew—the circumstances were suspicious, to say the least. By the 1230s militant Buddhist monks had destroyed most of the temples established by Nihon Daruma, and Nonin's sect eventually dissolved into Soto and disappeared as a distinct expression of Zen.

Bankei (A.D. 1622-1693) came to a more fortunate end than Nonin, and his influence was significantly greater. But he had the same streak of stubborn, independent determination that promised a somewhat distinct course for his life. His story is worth exploring because the style and substance of his teaching became Taoist-like once he relaxed the overt formality and stiffness of Zen Buddhism. He did this in two ways.

First, Bankei took the position that all questions, answers, discussion, and instruction in Zen Buddhism should be conducted in Japanese, that this should be the language of use rather than the classical Chinese still used as a residue of Ch'an's introduction to Japan four centuries earlier. This suggested change of practice, incidentally, gives some sense of the pervasive influence that Chinese thinking must have had

147

on Zen Buddhism. Second, he made a point never to talk about the Buddha or his teachings. This is best expressed and explained in his own words:

> *I never cite the Buddha's words or the words of Zen patriarchs when I teach. All I do is comment directly on people themselves. That takes care of everything. I don't have to quote either the "Buddha Dharma" or the "Zen Dharma." I don't have to, when I can clear everything up for you by commenting directly on you and your personal concerns right here and now. I've no reason to preach about "Buddhism" or "Zen."*[6]

As a boy of eleven years old, Bankei ran away from home to search for the meaning of a quotation from the *Great Learning*, a neo-Confucian book that was still widely used by the Japanese. The event was triggered by an innocent encounter at the village school where:

> *Bankei was subjected to the same curriculum given all Tokugawa schoolboys, the recitation of Confucian texts repeated over and over until they came automatically to the lips.*[7]

Bankei memorized the text but became obsessed with understanding the meaning of "the way of great learning lies in clarifying bright virtue."[8] No one in his community could explain it to him.

Aside from revealing something of Bankei's character, the incident offers another insight into the degree to which Chinese thinking was influencing Japanese consciousness even as late as the seventeenth century. Remember, too, that neo-Confucianism, to compensate for the spiritual limitations of Confucianism, contained a large proportion of Taoism.

Bankei's search led him from Confucian scholars to

Buddhist priests. He wrestled with "the intrinsic good of each person" and each person's "fundamental nature." Eventually he reached Zen Buddhism, the seventy-year-old Rinzai abbot Umpo, and *zazen*. The year was 1638.

In the following years, Bankei maintained contact with Umpo and Zen Buddhist monasteries, but much of his search took place on his own as an independent ascetic. Finally, at twenty-five years of age and nearly dead from austerity, he realized that:

All things are perfectly resolved in the Unborn.[9]

What was Bankei's realization? Fortunately, an explanation is available. Even though he strictly forbid that his teachings be written down, his disciples apparently recorded them surreptitiously. So, in Bankei's own words:

The unborn Dharma disappeared in both Japan and China,
and it has long since been forgotten. But now it has appeared
in the world again. . . .
Once you come to know without any doubt that the marvelous
illuminative wisdom of the Unborn is the Buddha-mind and
that the Buddha-mind puts all things in perfect order by
means of the Unborn, then you can no longer be deluded or led
astray by others.[10]

Bankei was a Buddhist in a Buddhist culture so he cast his insight of the Unborn into the form and language of Buddhism. But the unborn Dharma is Zen without Buddhism. It is preconceptual consciousness, a wordless and formless knowing that takes the shapeless shape of unordered order. This teaching that "has long since been forgotten" and puts "all things in perfect order" has the essential markings of

Taoism. Of course, Bankei was not a Taoist but he was an independent thinking Zen Buddhist who would have known about Taoism, and as such he inadvertently returned to the Taoist attitudes that were at the heart of Zen. Here he is again trying to explain his insight. This time the Taoist qualities are even more striking:

> *The unborn Buddha-mind deals freely and spontaneously*
> *with anything that presents itself to it. But if something should*
> *happen to make you change the Buddha-mind into thought,*
> *then you run into trouble and lose that freedom.*[11]

Simply change "the unborn Buddha-mind" to "following the Tao" and Bankei is describing the paradoxical dynamics of Taoism.

How did the people respond to Bankei's teachings? At first they rejected them, thinking that perhaps he was crazy:

> *When I was young and first began to declare the unborn*
> *Dharma, people had trouble understanding it. They thought I*
> *was preaching heresy, or they took me for a Christian. They*
> *were afraid of me. No one would come near. . . . Now, instead*
> *of their staying away as before, I'm besieged by too many*
> *callers, imploring and pressing me to meet with them. I don't*
> *have a moment to myself.*[12]

The common Japanese people grew to love Bankei because he was so unpretentious, so ordinary. He met them at their level, and he taught and answered with a simplicity they could understand:

> *The Master Bankei's talks were attended not only by Zen students but by persons of all ranks and sects. He never quoted*
> sutras *nor indulged in scholastic dissertations. Instead, his*

words were spoken directly from his heart to the hearts of his listeners.[13]

But the Zen Buddhist institution and traditional Mahayana Buddhists had reservations about Bankei and his teachings. The exception was his old abbot Umpo, who, as his dying wish, officially recognized the teachings of the Unborn by declaring Bankei to be his successor.

Others continued to express their concerns, but Bankei paid no attention. And they even continue to express them today. D.T. Suzuki complains that Bankei is not "Buddhist" enough.

Bankei's freer form of Zen was a fresh breeze in the stuffy air of institutionalized Zen Buddhism. In Alan Watts's words:

Bankei found a way of presenting Zen with such ease and simplicity that it seemed almost too good to be true. He spoke to large audiences of farmers and country folk, but no one "important" seems to have dared to follow him.[14]

No one "important" followed him because his Zen was too different from the Zen Buddhism of the day. Bankei taught in Japanese. He never mentioned the Buddha or the Dharma. As for *zazen*, it was practiced at his monastery because that was what the monks themselves decided they wanted to do:

Here, I always urge people simply to live in the unborn Buddha-mind. I don't try to make anyone do anything else. We haven't any special rules. But since everyone got together and decided they wanted to spend six hours (for a period of twelve sticks of incense) doing zazen, *I let them do as they wish.*[15]

As for the *koan*, the heart of Rinzai Zen, Bankei condemned its use and its effect. The *koan*, along with its purpose of generating a "great ball of doubt" that is overcome
with sudden insight, he referred to as "old tools"[16] and
declared that those who use such things were eyeless monks
who:

> . . . *if they don't have their implements to help them, they*
> *aren't up to handling people.*
> *What's worse, they tell practicers that unless they can raise a*
> *"great ball of doubt" and then break through it, there can't be*
> *any progress in Zen. Instead of teaching them to live by the*
> *unborn Buddha-mind, they start by forcing them to raise this*
> *ball of doubt any way they can. People who don't have a*
> *doubt are now saddled with one. They've turned their*
> *Buddha-minds into "balls of doubt." It's absolutely wrong.*[17]

And to a monk who had wrestled unsuccessfully with a
koan called *Hyakujo's Fox*, Bankei said:

> *I don't make people here waste their time on worthless old doc-*
> *uments like that.*[18]

Part of Bankei was unorthodox, spontaneous, even outwardly disrespectful of the formalities and rigidities of the
Zen Buddhist tradition. He was a free-spirited Zen being who
was Japan's version of the archetypal Taoist sage. But this
image is not the complete picture. Bankei was also a Buddhist
and the abbot of a Rinzai monastery. He was steeped in the
thinking and responsibilities of both. In the records of his life
and teachings there are adequate details to confirm that he
was culturally Japanese and wholly Buddhist. However, he
had a trace of something rare that distinguished him from

other roshis and made him exceptional; it was a special sense of perspective and inclusiveness that made his Zen larger than Zen Buddhism.

Bankei's special sense gave him the ability to play with Zen Buddhism itself. He could dismiss as "worthless" the *koan* of Hyakujo. Or he could recommend against mandatory *zazen* knowing full well that the monks of his monastery were not yet wise enough to follow his advice—they still needed Zen Buddhism because they were too studied to find Zen. Others, particularly the common people to whom he spoke in a simple and honest way, needed Zen because they were too ordinary to find Zen Buddhism. So Bankei filled the needs of everyone.

He was not cunning or hypocritical; he was just wise. He played Zen Buddhism like a game. And because he was just as easy inside as outside its rules, he escaped the confinement of its institutional walls. This was Bankei's Zen. It was free. Like the Tao, it could not be contained by anything. Not even itself.

Everyday Zen

ll the scholarly literature and all the searching discussion about Zen are merely intellectual exercises that have little to do with Zen itself. Did Bodhidharma really exist? Is there Zen in Buddhism? What are the inherent similarities between Zen and Taoism? What really matters is everyday Zen.

The real purpose of any exploration of Zen, aside from realizing the ultimate futility of the exercise, is to point to what cannot be said, to return all the speculation and thought into Zen itself. Zen just is. It takes control of itself. It has nothing to do with Lao Tzu or Bodhidharma, with the patriarchs or even Bankei. All these things are distractions, fingers that point away from themselves. Understanding them is not Zen.

Zen, like Taoism, is natural and intuitive, so ordinary that it is easily missed. This is why Zen without Buddhism seems so close to Taoism. When stripped of formality and returned to its natural shape, Zen is earthy and ordinary, nothing special.

But everyday Zen is not as simple as nothing special; it is everything special so that nothing can be deemed special. Separating Zen from the ordinary is the very process that destroys it; the reflexive awareness that distinguishes it also spoils it. Zen is not the dismissal of awareness; it is awareness uninhibited by reflection upon itself. This awareness is the clear and uncluttered distinction between what is authentically real and what is an intellectual contrivance. The late Suzuki Roshi describes the situation succinctly in *Zen Mind, Beginner's Mind*:

When you say, "Whatever I do is Buddha nature, so it doesn't matter what I do, and there is no need to practice zazen *[sic]," that is already a dualistic understanding of everyday life. If it really does not matter, there is no need for you even to say so. . . . Of course whatever you do is* zazen, *but if so, there is no need to say it.*[1]

Everyday Zen, then, is not quite the same as being ordinary. It means that the ordinary is given the same attentive mindfulness as *zazen*, that everyday moments become the stillness of sitting meditation. There is no duality, no division between now and some other time, between what is being done and what might or ought or should be done. There are no hypotheticals. Instead, a total, undivided presence transcends the duality of here or somewhere else. When packing water, there is only packing water. When chopping wood, there is only chopping wood. When sitting, there is no wobbling.

Immersion in the everyday is the essential practice of the Taoist sage. Without a separation between inner and outer, between self and not-self, the world is entered. In Taoist terms, the *te* of virtue-power is lived and manifested. Without separation, there is no division; without division, there is no opposition. The way of the world's wholeness is entered when nothing resists because nothing is disturbed.

Everyday Zen stresses the ordinary as the expression and realization of Zen. This is a "a method of no method,"[2] a process that shifts the emphasis from *zazen* to chopping wood or washing dishes. Ordinary activity becomes meditation so that, in effect, the practitioner is always doing the equivalent of *zazen*. As a result, the detached and institutionalized monasticism of Zen Buddhism breaks free of the walls and becomes everyday Zen. Its purported goal of connecting the inner world of consciousness with the outer world of form is dealt with directly rather than indirectly such that the practice becomes the attainment itself. This, incidentally, is a very Zen-like approach to Zen.

No visible practice of Zen is apparent in this process. There are no institutions to organize and formalize. Nothing is invented to intervene between means and end, to attract attention away from direct awareness and focused doing. No one is enlightened; no one is not enlightened. To use Zen's own metaphor, there is no finger pointing to a distant moon. Institutionalized Zen Buddhism has its purpose just as a finger has its purpose, but the finger and the moon are not each other.

Of course, at the deepest level, the pointing finger and the distant moon are each other, equal and one within the great Oneness. The two are the same in a consciousness that does not make distinctions. So thinking about Zen or attending to duties in a Zen monastery is not different from seeing the moon, digging in the garden, or eating peas. Being a conscientious husband or wife, father or mother, gravedigger or surgeon, requires the same discipline as being a diligent monk. With no inside Zen and no outside Zen there is not a thing that is not Zen and Zen practice. Zen Buddhism, by objecting to Nonin and Bankei, has mistaken the finger for the moon.

The deliberate, conscious practice of Zen is a self-defeating process, an exercise in futility. Bankei said it is like, "Wiping off blood with blood."[3]

This self-defeating process is ended when the practice of Zen becomes the same as ordinary activity. When nothing noteworthy distinguishes Zen from anything else, Zen becomes unpretentious and inconspicuous. Thus those who practice everyday Zen, like the archetypal Taoist sage who follows the Way, simply disappear into the ordinary. Lin-chi said of being ordinary:

> When it's time to get dressed, put on your clothes. When you must walk, then walk. When you must sit, then sit. Don't have a single thought in your mind about seeking Buddhahood. . . . What Dharma do you say must be realized, and what Tao cultivated? What do you lack in the way you are functioning right now? What will you add to where you are?[4]

The simplicity is the difficulty. R.H. Blyth explains in *Games Zen Masters Play*:

> Zen means doing ordinary things willingly and cheerfully.[5]

But ordinariness recognizes distinctions, and Oneness must include separateness. Thus, at a more profound level, differences must be embraced in the practice of everyday Zen. This is difficult to understand, particularly at the beginning of a process whose intention is to turn the end into the beginning and to transform the extraordinary into the ordinary. That is why any practice of Zen must be inclusive enough, paradoxical as it may seem, to allow everything that is ordinary—even deliberation about itself, and the sadness and grief of tragedy. Zen must "willingly and cheerfully" accept this, too. It must accept everything. And it must somehow integrate the serious with the playful, the deliberate with the impulsive, so that there is, as in Taoism, a balanced and inclusive wholeness of being that welcomes differences as if they were not different from each other. From a traditional

Zen story comes the following account:

> *A young monk who was respected and loved in the monastery*
> *died suddenly. At the funeral the roshi was crying with the*
> *other mourners. One of the disciples saw the roshi's grief and*
> *asked,*
> *"But master, why are you crying? We thought you under-*
> *stood?"*
> *"Yes, yes," said the roshi impatiently, as if his meditation were*
> *being interrupted. "I do, I do. But when else do I get a chance*
> *to cry."*

This expression of Zen is considerably different from
the detached and disembodied presence that is so characteristic of the spiritual tradition in India:

> *The ideal man of Indian Buddhism is clearly a superman, a*
> *yogi with absolute mastery of his own nature. . . . But the*
> *Buddha or awakened man of Chinese Zen is "ordinary and*
> *nothing special". . . .*[6]

The irony in Zen is that the most important things in
life—birth, love, death—come of themselves. They require
no "mastery" of one's "own nature." Indeed, like happiness
and grief and the Tao itself, they are easy and unavoidable:

> *After all, the real secrets are what everybody knows. As*
> *Confucius said, "To know that you know, and to know that*
> *you don't know—that is the real wisdom."*[7]

The unspoken conspiracy of all religions—and the
Buddhism of Zen Buddhism is not an exception—is their
seemingly irresistible inclination to make metaphysical what
is not so, and then to organize into complexity what is inher-

ently simple. The wonder of Bankei was his ability to understand this and offer an alternative to the process:

> A *Shinshu priest once boasted that his master had such miraculous power that he could hold a brush in his hand on one bank of a river while his attendants on the other bank could hold a piece of paper, and the teacher could write the holy name of the Buddha through the air.*
> *"Can you do such a wonderful thing?" the priest asked Bankei.*
> *Bankei replied, "Perhaps your fox can perform that trick, but that is not the matter of Zen. My miracle is that when I feel hungry, I eat; and when I feel thirsty, I drink."*[8]

Alan Watts, who was free-spirited and iconoclastic enough to be entirely sympathetic with Bankei's everyday Zen, wrote in *The Way of Zen*:

> *But in Zen there is always the feeling that awakening is something quite natural, something startlingly obvious, which may occur at any moment. If it involves a difficulty, it is just that it is much too simple.*[9]

The words "natural," "obvious," and "simple" are expressions of Zen's Taoist character. Because the Tao is natural, it is obvious; because it is obvious, it is simple. How different this is from the scholarly division of Zen Buddhism into five ascending levels of sophistication: *bompu, gedo, shojo, daijo,* and *saijojo*.[10]

But sophistication followed far enough has a curious habit of returning to simplicity. The most sophisticated *saijojo* is described as being like *bompu*. Because *saijojo* reaches a condition in which there is no striving and no struggle, because there is faith that each person is a Buddha and trust that enlightenment will occur naturally, there is no need to "self-consciously strive for enlightenment."[11] *Saijojo's* sophisticated subtlety is *bompu* but without the trouble. In both *saijojo* and *bompu*, enlightenment arises spontaneously in a manner akin to the Taoist experience of *tzu-jan*. If being a Buddha is as unavoidable as following the Tao, the only requirement for enlightenment is to return to the simplicity of the beginning by learning how to let go of everything complicated. This letting go, with its gentle easiness of nonstriving and nonstruggle, is experienced in even the highest practice as something quite ordinary.

If everyday Zen is so ordinary, why does Zen seem so difficult? If the Tao cannot be avoided, why does it seem so elusive? Simply because the ordinary passes unnoticed in the guise of being ordinary. To be noticed the ordinary must somehow be made extraordinary. This is done by escaping the ordinary, by establishing a separation and a distance from it. When the ordinary is no longer available, it becomes special. Since the most important experience is ordinary, the extraordinary nature of the ordinary is only recognized from a condition of inner emptiness. Finding then, by both paradox and necessity, is the process of losing so the ordinary can be rediscovered. This is what T.S. Eliot describes in the *Little Gidding* section of his *Four Quartets*.[12] The search continues until the beginning is found, then this place is recognized and known for the first time. Such an experience happens in total simplicity, and costs the struggling psyche virtually everything as it collapses and reconstitutes itself in the clarity of its original beginning. In traditional Zen literature this return to the beginning is perhaps best illustrated in the *Ox Herding Pictures*.

The ten drawings and the accompanying commentaries are attributed in Zen Buddhist history to a Ch'an master of the twelfth century, Kuo-an (Japanese: Kakuan). But there were earlier Ch'an depictions of the bull in five to eight illustrations,[13] the last drawing simply being the empty circle of Buddhist nothingness. These pictures, in turn, were based on earlier Taoist bulls[14] in which the same circle was understood as the absolute receptivity of emptiness. Such a fully inclusive condition was recognized as the only access to the Way of Taoism. Thus emptiness was the means by which humans could connect to the great and pervasive harmony that moved through everything. Emptiness was access to a simple but fundamental wisdom. Through its receptivity came wholeness and harmony, and then an easy release to a natural course of action. The original *Ox Herding Pictures* were not about Buddhist detachment but Taoist connectedness.

To the eight bulls of Ch'an Buddhism, Kuo-an drew a ninth and a tenth, illustrating the difference between the Chinese and the Indian notion of realization. "Returning to the Source" and "In the World" were added to the empty circle of complete receptivity and harmony to make perfectly clear the Taoist theme of the *Ox Herding Pictures*.

"Returning to the Source," the ninth illustration, represents reentering the freshness of the beginning after having experienced wholeness and harmony through the conceptual emptiness of the Tao. Here the suchness of the world is apparent. The ordinary, once unnoticed, suddenly becomes extraordinarily vivid from the distance of separation—dramatically different yet paradoxically the same. Previous understandings, those based upon ideas and willful struggle, are transformed. The new reality, now free of conceptual habits, is natural, concrete, and specific. Here is a Ch'an description and comment:

> *Too many steps have been taken returning*
> *to the root and the source.*
> *Better to have been blind and deaf from the*
> *beginning!*
> *Dwelling in one's true abode, unconcerned*
> *with that without—*
> *The river flows tranquilly on and the flowers*
> *are red.*
>
> Comment: *From the beginning, truth is clear. Poised in*
> *silence, I observe the forms of integration and disintegration.*
> *One who is not attached to "form" need not be "reformed."*
> *The water is emerald, the mountain is indigo, and I see that*
> *which is creating and that which is destroying.*[15]

As expected from a Ch'an source, some of the terminology is Buddhist, but the flavor, the experience, the rhythmical movement and imagery are unmistakably Taoist.

The tenth drawing, "In the World," illustrates the practical, Taoist side of Ch'an. Enlightenment alone is not enough. The transforming insight of the circle and suchness is not actualized until the resulting wisdom is carried into the village for sharing and influence. The sage becomes an involved participant in the community, inconspicuously helping, guiding, harmonizing, and enlivening:

> *Barefoot and naked of breast, I mingle*
> *with the people of the world.*

> *My clothes are ragged and dust-laden, and I*
> *   am ever blissful.*
> *I use no magic to extend my life;*
> *Now, before me, the dead trees become*
> *   alive.*
> Comment: *Inside my gate, a thousand sages do not know me.*
> *The beauty of my garden is invisible. Why should one search*
> *for the footprints of the patriarchs? I go to the market place*
> *with my wine bottle and return home with my staff. I visit the*
> *wineshop and the market, and everyone I look upon becomes*
> *enlightened.*[16]

With the exception of "patriarchs," this quotation from the *Ox Herding Pictures* is pure Taoism. There is no monastic detachment, no *zazen*, no institution, barely a trace of Buddhism. Like the Taoist sage, the awakened seeker returns to the grace of the world to mingle again with the living community.

This grounded and connected involvement in the solidity of day-to-day life is what distinguishes the Zen from the Buddhism in Zen Buddhism and constitutes the social component of everyday Zen. A hint of this everyday quality is in Buddhism; it was one of the similarities that allowed the Chinese to facilitate the coexistence of Taoism and Buddhism as Ch'an. The Buddha, in addition to his meditative pose of inward detachment, is also depicted—even in India—as walking, standing, sitting, or lying. These four positions, all treated reverently, suggest that the path to enlightenment is embodied in all human activity, and that the whole experience of life is enlightenment itself. Indeed, the satori or kensho of Zen Buddhism is ostensibly this realization.

Ordinariness in both Ch'an and Zen Buddhism has

been nourished and encouraged by Taoism. The Chinese, who integrated this attribute into Ch'an through their sensitivity for subtlety and inconspicuousness, made it an essential part of their understanding of sageliness. The combined qualities of the sage and the ordinary were thus imparted to Zen such that its sense of enlightenment also fosters a disappearance into the common activity of daily life. Like the Taoist sage, each student of Zen moves toward a condition of being profoundly ordinary, and away from any position of special recognition, acclaim, or veneration. The best of the Zen tradition nourishes self-effacement and modesty, fosters a blending into common life to pass practically unnoticed. As if to guarantee this ordinariness, a classical Taoist paradox has been incorporated into the teaching of Zen. R.H. Blyth points out that the difference between those who are enlightened and those who are not:

> *is that you don't know the difference until you realize yourself*
> *to be no better than others, then you are better than others. But*
> *if you think this, you are not. Here is the paradox that rules*
> *the world. . . .*[17]

The source of this paradox is Taoism and its equivalence is expressed in the *Lao Tzu*:

> *A truly good man is not aware of his*
> *goodness,*
> *And is therefore good.*[18]

Such a paradox shifts Zen's focus of enlightenment away from the discipline of a specific practice toward a holistic way of being ordinary. This holistic perspective is one of the obvious similarities between Taoism and Zen. The sage of Taoism may sit and meditate, but the goal of the inner practice is to transform the process of living into an artful union with the outer world. Every meditator, whether the Buddha or Bodhidharma, must eventually get up and eat, work, walk, talk, and engage in the world. The world is unavoidable, and all wisdom is measured by the inevitable reconciliation that must take place with it. The nature of this reconciliation, a harmonious and balanced way of being in which the dichotomy of subject and object disappear, is really the common aim of the Taoist and Zen practice. In the words of Suzuki Roshi, a Soto master who came to teach in America in 1959:

> *There should not be any particular teaching. Teaching is in each moment.* . . .[19]

Zen, like Taoism, is organic and spontaneous. Institutions have compromised its essentially Taoist nature by narrowing and stiffening the practice, and by misplacing the discipline. But all institutions, whether the present ones or the T'ang monasteries of Ch'an China, have served their purpose for Zen and Taoism. To define and organize themselves they provide structure and order, and thereby they perpetuate an awareness that is very elusive indeed. Everyday Zen, like philosophical Taoism, runs the risk of being too subtle to be noticed at all, too ordinary even to be recognized. True wisdom needs some foolishness as a useful counterpart.

Formal Zen and everyday Zen serve each other. The order and discipline of one defines the spontaneity and free-

dom of the other. Without all the foolish talk of Zen, everyday Zen would be even more elusive.

Zen
in the West

en officially arrived in the West as Japanese Zen Buddhism, presented and interpreted by Buddhists during the 1950s and 1960s. Writers and roshis and Zen centers perpetuated the association of Zen with Buddhism.

But Zen was soon being discussed and represented by Westerners who were not Buddhists. Implicit in this expression was the notion that Zen and Buddhism were related but not synonymous.

Then came the popular literature that made Zen a household word. People who knew nothing about Buddhism could relate to the Zen experience through their ordinary lives. Zen Buddhism separated into its two components as it became part of the West's consciousness. Buddhism maintained its religious and philosophical qualities, while Zen returned to its secular origin. The separation was inevitable.

When institutionalized Zen Buddhism came to the West, it found itself disconnected from the stabilizing traditions of the Japanese culture. As it interacted with different attitudes and values in its new environment, it began to reconstitute itself. It relaxed its formality, and changed shape and expression. It also met other versions of itself: Son from Korea, Ch'an from Taiwan, and Vietnamese Zen. They softened the rigid boundaries of Rinzai and Soto, loosening the sense of how Zen might be practiced and approached.

Zen also came in contact with Taoism, which had arrived in the West somewhat earlier and was being taught and practiced with similar innovations. When the two traditions were explored in a forum of unprejudiced and honest curiosity, the distinctions that had defined them as exclusively Japanese or Chinese began to fall away. Their meeting in the West was a modern enactment of the first-century encounter in China of Taoism and Buddhism in which Taoism recognized a form of itself in the shape of Buddhism. In the fresh space of the West, without the old cultural habits that had narrowed perspectives, Taoism and Zen recognized their similarities. And Zen Buddhism continued to relax its structure.

This did not happen dramatically but it did happen quickly. It was evolution accelerated, the consequence of similar but different traditions from the East finding themselves in close proximity to each other in an atmosphere of open and trusting exploration. The similarities between Taoism and Zen became more apparent and their differences were defined more softly.

Eventually, everything changed. The West changed because of Zen. In his preface to *Zen Mind, Beginner's Mind*, Huston Smith notes that the arrival of Zen in the West:

> *has been likened in its historical importance to the Latin translations of Aristotle in the thirteenth century and of Plato in the fifteenth. . . .*[1]

But Zen also changed because of the West. Or, to put it more accurately, Zen itself remained unchanged but the structures of thought and belief that carried it, and therefore the processes for practicing Zen, these things changed because the Japanese system could not sustain itself in its new cultural context. The greatest changes took place in its formal expression: in its hierarchy, its institutional structure, and its Buddhism.

Traditional Zen Buddhism in Japan was structured vertically so that:

the person below was supposed to be loyal to the person above, and the person above was supposed to be responsible for the one below.[2]

This arrangement worked well in Japan where the society accepted hierarchical order. But in the West it was incompatible with egalitarianism, individuality, and the secularization of Zen Buddhism. Even the concept of the roshi was questioned.

In the traditional Japanese approach the presiding authority of the roshi is in contradiction with the feeling that enlightenment is inherently a personal experience. The roshi measures, assesses, and judges, while Zen itself advertises that one's insight is wholly intrinsic, wholly one's own, and that it cannot be found through study of *sutras*, through rational understanding, or even by being taught. In the West this contradiction is heightened by a strong sense of individuality and personal independence that has traditionally questioned the authority and authenticity of teachers. Katy Butler reports in *Whole Earth Review* the comments of a senior disciple at a Zen center:

In the Orient, every craft has transmission from master to disciple. Its purpose is to protect against unauthorized and self-appointed teachers. But this aggrandizement of transmission in the minds of young meditators has not served our interests. What is being authenticated? Every word and deed for the rest of someones's life? We have an idealized image of an enlight-

ened person. It's not, strictly speaking, accurate to speak of an
enlightened person, but rather of enlightened activity.[3]

Institutional Zen in the West has had difficulties with the authority and succession of roshis. The organizational demands and monetary costs of maintaining and operating a Zen center have also been problems.

Attitudes, less tangible influences, are forcing institutionalized Zen toward a less structured, lay form of practice in which individuals are in contact to varying degrees with teachers and literature, but are not immersed in a monastic life. They integrate into the wider community after discovering that enlightenment is actualized in being spouses, parents, workers, and citizens. This apparent informality returns Zen practice to the everyday world, and individual practitioners become more like Taoist sages than Zen Buddhist monks.

Zen and Buddhism, therefore, the two separate components of Zen Buddhism that coexisted so comfortably in Japan and China, were quickly separated in the West. Zen was one thing; Buddhism was another. The universality of Zen was intuitively recognized and accepted; the philosophical and religious character of Buddhism has remained somewhat foreign. So Buddhism, which became an asset to Zen in the East, became a liability in the West.

But a liability, seen differently, becomes an opportunity. As Zen became more independent of the religio-institutional structure that supported it in the East, it became more flexible and adaptable. Without the constraints of Buddhism's belief and philosophical system, Zen became looser and freer, more able to fit into the popular consciousness of the West. The more distinct Zen became from Buddhism, the more accessible it became.

Zen has now reached mainstream consciousness in the West. The word has entered the language and the term is commonly recognized. Of course, most people have no conceptual grasp of Zen, which is the best approach to it. But many people have a feeling for it. And this feeling is percolating through the culture, the subject of curiosity and consideration.

As evidence, consider the flood of books that recognizes Zen, not as an esoteric and mysterious practice of the East, but as an integral part of everyday living. Here is a sample of what is presently offered:

Zen and the Art of Changing Diapers,
   Sarah Arsone
Zen and the Art of the Macintosh,
   Michael Green
*Zen and the Art of Making a Living in the
Post-Modern World*,
   Laurence Bolt
Zen and the Art of Motorcycle Maintenance,
   Robert Pirsig
Zen Driving,
   K.T. Bergen
Zen in the Art of Child Maintenance,
   Michael Pastore and Larry Pastor
Zen in the Art of Climbing Mountains,
   Neville Shulman
Zen in the Art of Helping,
   David Brandon
Zen in the Art of Photography,
   Robert Leverant
Zen in the Art of Writing,

Ray Bradbury
Zen in the Markets: Confessions of a Zen Trader,
   Edward Toppel
The Zen of Hype: An Insider's Guide to the Publicity Game,
   Raleigh Pinskey
The Zen of Juggling,
   Dave Finnigan
The Zen of Running,
   Fred Rohß
The Zen of Seeing,
   Frederick Franck
The Zen Way to Be an Effective Manager,
   Radha
Zen Sensualism: The Union of Spirituality and Sexuality,
   Dale Watts

Of course, Zen has always been in the West, perhaps with a name, perhaps without one. It has always been the essential wisdom of nature, and the enlivening force in human insight and creativity. In his classic book on the subject, *Zen in English Literature and Oriental Classics*, R.H. Blyth illustrates that Zen has been present throughout Western literature in such authors as Shakespeare, Cervantes, Wordsworth, and Goethe. *The Gospel According to Zen* and *Zen and Christian* find Zen in Christianity. Douglas Hofstadter in *Gödel, Escher, Bach* identifies Zen in mathematics, art, and music.

The recent popularity and the identified ubiquitiousness of Zen can create the impression that the practice of it is—in the ordinary sense—easy. Zen's apparent easiness is disciplined and its apparent simplicity is deceptively elusive. It is too paradoxical, too deep and primal, to qualify as a fad.

Almost everyone knows about it, but almost no one knows what to do about it. So Zen has taken many shapes in the West. Alan Watts, in his usually inimitable way, sums up the situation in *Beat Zen, Square Zen, and Zen*:

> *But the Westerner who is attracted by Zen and who would understand it deeply must have one indispensable qualification: he must understand his own culture so thoroughly that he is no longer swayed by its premises unconsciously. . . . Lacking this his Zen will be either "beat" or "square," either a revolt from the culture and social order or a new form of stuffiness and respectability.*[4]

Any Zen but Zen itself is deliberate, affected, pretentious, and conspicuous. This is Zen as fad. When it is itself, it is so uncontrived and subtle that it goes nearly unnoticed, or it passes for luck or grace or some nameless equivalent. Like Taoism, it happens but few recognize it. And no one can deliberately do it.

In the West, Zen without Buddhism is beginning to function like Taoism. The more there is of it, the less apparent it is. The more it is practiced, the more ordinary it becomes.

PART II

Taoism and Zen:
The Philosophical
Similarities

*t*he Taoist source of Zen has been obscured by Buddhism's insistence that Zen be connected to India and the Buddha rather than to China and the *Lao Tzu*. But Japanese Zen Buddhism is not wholly responsible for this misassignment of source. The Chinese themselves are somewhat to blame: first, because Taoism has been popularly expressed with overlays of religious and esoteric practices that are far removed from the simple philosophical principles of its original teachings; and second, because Ch'an, the early Chinese form of Zen Buddhism, eventually became a Mahayana institution. When these historical convolutions and accretions are removed from Taoism and Zen, the two are revealed to be virtually identical.

The *Lao Tzu*, for example, cautions that the Tao is too ordinary to be understood, and Zen frequently advises that the most obvious is the most elusive. This element of shared simplicity, however, has not deterred the intellect from exercising itself by complicating and abstracting what is inherently plain and direct. Zen Buddhism and folk Taoism are just two of the most pertinent examples of this kind of intellectual obfuscation.

But, when history and intellect are cleared away, the elusiveness of Taoism and Zen is just the first of a large number of similarities that equate them. Both distrust words and systems. Both depreciate ego and a mindfulness that is deliberately self-conscious. Spontaneity is cultivated. The intuitive insight that arises from the integrity of a whole and balanced being is honored. Both trust that a harmonious relationship exists between the inner person and the outer world.

Strength and endurance are found in a kind of softness that is at once both yielding and unbending. Emptiness is espoused as a condition of total receptivity. An alert mindlessness is held to be the special condition of constant preparedness. The *Lao Tzu* and the teachings of Zen meet the paradox of duality by confronting it directly. Consequently, they are equally enigmatic because they resolve this essential dilemma by entering the contradiction; paradox, therefore, becomes the dynamic of their teaching. Both Taoism and Zen look inward for wisdom but apply it outwardly; their main purpose is full engagement in physical existence through the "cultivation of the inner life."[1]

Taoism and Zen work toward the same end with the same basic dynamics of teaching, but the language is sometimes different and the metaphors do not always coincide. This is due largely to the Buddhist company that Zen has kept in China and Japan. Taoism, for example, gives more overt attention to social matters than Zen; the *Lao Tzu* is laced with concern for the collective harmony and well-being of the community. Zen, in contrast, seems less concerned with such issues, even though its Mahayana context carries a strong social conscience. Closer reading of the whole Zen practice, however, reveals that its social concerns are merely being expressed in a Buddhist rather than a Taoist fashion. Here is Suzuki Roshi, a Soto master, describing the internal dynamics for Zen that effect the same social influence for Taoism:

> *So when you try hard to make your own way, you will help others. . . . Before you make your own way you cannot help anyone, and no one can help you.*[2]

In other words, both Taoism and Zen understand that the outer world can be properly influenced only through inner processes, and social concerns can be properly addressed only through the intuitive action that arises from a centered and balanced position. This inner process eludes description because it has to function intuitively and spontaneously; there can be no moral precepts to follow. How this inner condition affects the outer world is equally inexplicable, although a parallel exists in the way calm people have a calming influence on others.

Using words is risky for processes that distrust words. Therefore, any exploration of Taoism and Zen must offer the caveat that anything that can be said about them is incomplete, misleading, and largely wrong. Since there is no wordlessness without words, no selflessness without self, no softness without hardness, any word that is used also implies its opposite. Any resolution of opposites must still include those opposites. Any oneness requires the recognition of separateness, and any wholeness requires the recogition of parts. So Taoism and Zen are systemless systems that include both is and is-not; the Way is both known and not-known. One uttered word of explanation is wrong, but silence is not enough.

The essence of Taoism and Zen is in the art of the mystic who is not mystical, in the meticulous journey of those who have entered the mud of the ordinary. The answer is in the question; the resolution is in the paradox; the end is in the beginning. The challenge is to reach a peaceful reconciliation with the impossible.

Anyone who knows anything about Taoism and Zen will recognize that analyzing them so they can be considered and compared—indeed, writing anything about them—is fundamentally foolish. Yet, should anyone forget, foolishness is one of the paths to wisdom. Taoism offers constant reminders that parts and wholes are different views of the same ineffable Way; and Zen's full freedom is an experience that comes through protracted discipline. Paradox, paradoxically, leads to something not paradoxical. Words on the subject of Taoism and Zen are necessary folly; herein lies their justification. Out of indirection comes direction, out of confusion arises insight. Losing is a way of finding; out of the condition of is-not comes a sense of is.

The two traditions are approached with a discipline of mind and character that combines inner freedom with natural spontaneity. The Way is sensed directly, without verbalizing, theorizing, or philosophizing. Differences are experienced without differentiating. The world is entered by leaving it whole, undivided, and timeless. The instant is forever. This is not the temporal forever that was sought by the *hsien* of esoteric Taoism or is represented in the *nirvana* of Buddhism. It is the experiential forever that is found in the center of a single-pointed awareness as it moves in harmonious accord with the flowing present.

This condition is not described with absolutes because it falls outside the option of thought and words. The best sense of it is created when implied juxtapositions hang suspended in unresolved tension. The resolution of opposites seems to be directed toward some remote and advanced learning, but it is really grounded in the unfolding present, in the thoughtless condition before the construction of opposites began.

Consequently, Taoism and Zen do not evolve toward

some advanced knowing but, instead, revert to an earlier condition of simple clarity. The process of unlearning becomes
more important than learning; emptying is given precedence
over filling. Then, without apparent effort or struggle, without apparent thought or knowing, the unlearning somehow
engenders insight, and the emptiness is filled.

Wordlessness

*T*he essence of Taoism and Zen cannot be expressed in words, so both traditions express caution about using them. Paradoxically, of course, their cautionary advice is expressed in words, and both systems possess a core of oral and written literature. The dilemma is that words are to be avoided, yet they are unavoidable.

The problem with words is that they confuse the distinction between metaphorical experience and direct experience. The world of suchness does not correspond to any conceptual model expressed or invented by words. Care must be taken that the spell of words is not mistaken for direct awareness.

The *Lao Tzu* gently and repeatedly expresses this caution:

> *Because the mystery cannot be known or named,*
> *it is called the Tao.*[1]

> *The Tao that can be named . . .*
> *is not the nameless Tao.*
> *The Tao that can be known . . .*
> *is not the unknowable Tao.*[2]

This same idea is expressed throughout Zen literature. Sometimes it appears softly and poetically:

> *The wind is soft, the moon is serene.*
> *Calmly I read the True Word of no letters.*[3]

And sometimes it appears with the dramatic energy and shocking impact that is so typical of Zen:

Say this is a stick and I will beat you with it! Say this is not a
stick and I will beat you with it! Now, what will you say?

The challenge, of course, is to use words and not use words,
and never to mistake the word for the thing.

Philosophers in Chinese history became aware of the
distinction between the reality of direct experience and the
fiction created by the metaphorical spell of words. Their
insight had a parallel in the Greek logic of Zeno's paradox, in
which a runner who continues to cover half the remaining distance to a destination will never arrive. But the Chinese took
the lesson more seriously than thoughtful exercise:

> *During the fourth century B.C. it began to occur to the Chinese*
> *that words move in a world of their own, a region connected*
> *only in the most casual and precarious way with the world of*
> *reality. . . . Take a stick a foot long. Halve it. Tomorrow*
> *halve that half, and so on day after day. Ten thousand gener-*
> *ations hence there will still, theoretically speaking, be some-*
> *thing left to halve. But in reality we are obliged to stop short*
> *much sooner than this. . . . One can in fact . . . say things that*
> *sound all right, but mean nothing at all.*[4]

For the Chinese this was not an idle intellectual or
philosophical exercise. There were practical and crucial
implications—and an unavoidable conclusion. Words, they
decided, were the instruments of social intercourse and their
misuse could cause misunderstanding and discord. As Arthur
Waley writes:

> *For all Chinese philosophy is essentially the study of how men*
> *can best be helped to live together in harmony and good order.*
> *. . . [There is] nothing more dangerous than that theories and*

doctrines which belong only to the world of language should be
mistaken for truths concerning the world of fact.[5]

In this respect the Chinese concern for language differed from the mainly philosophical interests of the Greeks, and the spiritual disposition of the Indians who had brought Buddhism to China. For the practically minded Chinese, the metaphorical quality of language represented a threat and continued to be an issue in their thinking. Later, when Buddhism mixed with Taoism to become Ch'an, and when Ch'an migrated to Buddhist Japan to become Zen, this concern was carried with it. The Taoist concern for the misleading quality of words remained alive in Zen.

When Zen is considered without Buddhism, it shares with Taoism the same philosophical apprehension about words, an uneasiness that is based on the experiential distortion created by words as they attempt to explain what is essentially inexplicable. Consequently, words transfer the immediacy and power of direct experience into the fiction and vicariousness of metaphors. These metaphors are then mistaken for suchness or just-so-ness, as if naming a thing somehow bestows on it authenticity and irrefutability.

A commonly held misimpression of both Taoism and Zen is that they reject the use of words. They use words but they clearly understand the effects and the limits of them. This distinction is important. Both traditions are assiduously mindful of avoiding the pitfalls of a word system that builds its own structure of understanding and invents its own truths. So Taoism and Zen return to direct awareness. This is why the insight they engender is both ordinary and exceptional, both common and profound. Arriving seems to take place without leaving; the end somehow becomes the beginning.

Taoism and Zen seem enigmatic because words are turned against words to undo themselves so that the word system is prevented from spinning its own illusion of understanding. Words are not used to push insights beyond the meaning of words but to avoid the trap that is inherent in words themselves. Taoism and Zen are not metaphysical. But language is metaphorical and it very easily becomes metaphysical. So too much talk of Zen, in Zen's wonderfully succinct way of expressing a similar Taoist sentiment, is said to "stink of Zen." John Dykstra Eusden notes in *Zen and Christian*:

> Whoever writes anything about Zen is under the judgment of a
> seven-character expression which reads, "The instant you
> speak about a thing, you miss the mark." Warnings over defi-
> nitions, argument, and verbalization belong, in large part, to
> the influential Taoist inheritance of Zen Buddhism. The
> Taoist-Zen point of view reminds us that we cannot rest with
> neat phrases and logical delineations. "Words are the fog one
> has to see through," as one saying puts it.[6]

Buddhism has been a fog through which the clarity of Zen has had to shine. The following description from *Zen: Tradition and Transition* illustrates the point nicely:

> Though Zen focuses sharply on the delusive potential of lan-
> guage, it takes its own literature seriously. . . . Zen's warning
> against written works often had a political function—the
> emerging sect needed to distinguish itself from existing
> Buddhist schools that embraced major sutras. When Zen mas-
> ter Dogen addressed his own students, he taught that "an
> enlightened person always masters the sutras to full advan-
> tage."[7]

Zen Buddhism has been ambivalent about words because it has been ambivalent about itself. Is it Zen or is it Buddhism? Is there to be silence or sutras? Buddhism would ask, "What is the truth in the *sutras?*" Zen would ask, "What is the silence in the *sutras?*" When the truth and the silence are the same, why invoke the name of the holy Buddha and all his baggage of teachings?

Ambivalence can produce a foggy confusion or a creative clarity. Confusion is the result when the convolutions of Buddhist philosophy and theology attempt to coexist with the simple clarity of Zen.

This clarity has been amply illustrated in the many Zen stories which hang on the balancing edge of sense and nonsense. Here on this creative edge of ambivalence is the wonderful elusiveness of Zen's wisdom. But mix Buddhism with Zen and the result is unproductive confusion. The following story, abbreviated from *Zen Flesh, Zen Bones*, represents the clarity of the Zen view in the fog of institutionalized Buddhism:

> *The Zen master Mu-nan had only one successor. His name was Shoju. After Shoju had completed his study of Zen, Mu-nan called him into his room. "I am getting old," he said, "and as far as I know, Shoju, you are the only one who will carry on this teaching. Here is a book. It has been passed down from master to master for seven generations. I also have added many points according to my understanding. The book is very valuable, and I am giving it to you to represent your successorship."*
>
> *"If the book is such an important thing, you had better keep it," Shoju replied. "I received your Zen without writing and am satisfied with it as it is."*

"I know that," said Mu-nan. "Even so, this work has been
carried from master to master for seven generations, so you
may keep it as a symbol of having received the teaching. Here."
The two were talking beside a brazier of burning coals. The
instant Shoju felt the book in his hands he thrust it into the
flames.
Mu-nan, who never had been angry before, yelled, "What are
you doing!"
Shoju shouted back, "What are you saying!"[8]

The story is delightfully Zen but it is also disturbingly
Buddhist. How often have Buddhist habits resulted in an
uneven transmission of Zen teachings? For "seven generations," it seems, none of the masters had been in possession
of Shoju's wordless Zen.

The high praise for such wordless teaching raises an
issue that could be critical of Taoism. Like Zen's own inade-
quate words, the text of the *Lao Tzu* is serious about itself,
otherwise it would not have been written and preserved.
Accurate versions have been sought like the Holy Grail.
Translations abound. Some fifteen hundred commentaries
have been added to the core texts. For a system of understanding that cautions against the use of words, a great deal of
effort has been expended on them. But, just as Zen is not its
literature, Taoism is not the *Lao Tzu*. Both Taoism and Zen
literally or symbolically burn their own words:

Those who know . . . cannot explain.
*And those who can explain . . . do not know.*9

Language, like pure intellect, moves experience inexorably into the abstract, away from the finality of grounded
reality. This reality defies words. After all the fancy words

and profound thoughts, after all the sublime rhetoric and transcendent experience engendered by the spell of words, there remains the certain bounds set by the natural absolutes of physical existence. Life is punctuated by the blood of birth and the stillness of death. Words may fabricate abstractions and attempt to disconnect experience from this earthy condition. But all words, regardless of how high they soar, are ultimately rooted in the fact of substantiality, far closer to the soil of feeling and instinct than a deliberating consciousness often recognizes or readily admits. As Suzuki Roshi gently expressed it:

> *So how this physical body becomes a sage is our main interest. We are not so concerned about what . . . a sage is. A sage is a sage. Metaphysical explanations about human nature are not the point.*[10]

The *Lao Tzu*, in a similar manner, directs intellectual activity away from abstract considerations toward the direct experience of living. Half the text is given to the practical matter of social harmony and individual contentment.

Still, words exist. They cannot be dismissed. The *Lao Tzu* uses words and Suzuki Roshi uses them. And it is human nature to use words. Denying them is like denying walking or eating or loving. The trick is to use words without creating a metaphysical construct that takes on a life of its own. Both the Taoist and the Zen traditions have an oral and written literature. But the wisdom their sages offer rests on the understanding that the choice cannot be between words or silence; it can only be both words and silence. Indeed, a silent wordlessness would become an absolute, merely another metaphysic. The silence of Taoism and Zen is wholly inclusive,

197

embracing enough to allow a special kind of ambivalence that is neither certainty nor uncertainty.

This understanding of words and wordlessness is what distinguishes Taoism and Zen from Buddhism. The Indian tradition expresses distrust of words but it is inclined toward absolutism:

> Buddhist teachings often express a radical distrust of language in general. For example, in the Lankvatara, a sutra that was highly influential in the early development of Chinese Ch'an, the Buddha declares, "Words are not known in all the Buddha-lands," and "What one teaches, transgresses; for the truth is beyond words." And in the Vimalakirti Sutra, when the sage Vimalakirti is queried about the nature of non-duality, the concept that lies at the core of Mahayana Buddhism, his answer takes the form of a thunderous silence.[11]

Silence is wonderful but it is always defined by sound. Buddhism espouses only nonduality whereas Taoism and Zen embrace both duality and nonduality. In Taoism's terms there is both the polarity of yin-yang and the nonpolarity of the Tao; in Zen terms there is both the stick and not-the-stick.

Buddhism attempts to resolve duality with a metaphysical absolute, whereas Taoism and Zen suspend any resolution in the creative tension between the alternative extremes— both of which, incidentally, are absolutes. This is why the Way can never be conceptually located, why any effort to understand it is self-contradictory and self-defeating. The Way, once caught, would become an absolute that would stop the dynamic flow of insight, that would break the creative tension which exists as balanced stillness in Taoism and Zen.

Neither balance nor stillness is absolute; both are constantly shifting states of presence in the equilibrium of the moment. So Buddhism, by venerating the Buddha and making holy the sutras, becomes a religion; whereas Zen, in contrast, advises that the Buddha be killed.

Buddhism could not take itself seriously if it were truly Zen. This is why Taoism and Zen are playful but Buddhism is not. How can playfulness be avoided when a doctrine of wordlessness seriously expresses itself in words? Buddhism's joke on itself would be obvious if it were not so transfixed by the importance of its own words. It has forgotten that Mahakasyapa's wordless smile was an answer to the Buddha's worded question.

This playful perspective defines the Taoist and Zen understanding of wordlessness. The Way can be entered only without words. But it cannot be approached without words. Both words and silence are required. One leg will do for standing but two legs are required for walking. In a one-legged world there would only be silence and no one would eat when hungry.

The Way in Taoism and Zen is not a disembodied, absolute and static condition; it is a grounded and a dynamic one. The balance changes; the stillness moves. In the changing there is a moving balance. In the stillness there is a changing stillness. In the words there is a thundering wordlessness.

199

Selflessness

ny discussion of selflessness in Taoism and Zen is complicated by a word system that seems to offer as a choice only the two options of self and not-self. There is, however, a third option that includes both and neither. But this option is nearly impossible to articulate because of the inability of words to say two different, mutually exclusive things at the same time.

Although not-self is an important part of the Taoist and Zen experience, it is not the whole experience. Not-self melds into self, which is softened and kept but not rigidly defined or possessed. So selflessness is not a denial of self; instead, it is a kind of distancing that permits self to function in the context of not-self. The result is an undifferentiated continuum in which the two coexist in a dynamic and harmonious balance, each providing definition and perspective to the other. This is done through a process of losing and finding so there is both self and not-self similtaneously. The resulting condition is called selflessness but it embraces both self and not-self in a soft and inclusive wholeness.

Such a balanced coexistence is the only possible response to a philosophical dilemma that declares that any deliberate effort to deny or obliterate self merely serves to affirm it. In Zen's Buddhist language, this deliberate effort perpetuates duality; in Taoism's Chinese language, this same effort perpetuates mutual arising, *hsiang sheng*. The dilemma, however, is not real; it is the creation of language and philosophy. In actual experience, the dilemma simply dissolves into the balanced center between the invented poles of self and not-self as a genuine disinterest evolves. This disinterest is selflessness.

Although Taoism and Zen nominally see self as an impediment to following the Way, the matter is more complicated than eliminating self. Perhaps the complexity as well as the subtlety of the situation is best expressed in *haiku*, the poetic language of Zen. Three examples are offered here:

> *At our last parting*
> *Bending between boat and shore . . .*
> *That weeping willow.* —Shiki

> *A lost child crying*
> *Stumbling over the dark fields . . .*
> *Catching fireflies.* —Ryusui

> *Cruel autumn wind*
> *Cutting to the very bones . . .*
> *Of my poor scarecrow.* —Issa

A similar relationship to self is implict in Taoism. Although the sage is understood to be selfless, several chapters of the *Lao Tzu* are traditionally translated in the first person singular, rendering the image of an individual person who experiences confusion, sadness, and loneliness. The same sobering quality is implied in the Zen aphorism:

> *If you do not get it from yourself, where will you go for it?*

In Zen, as in Taoism, the search for the Way is an existential one that redefines the sense of self. It is worth noting here as a relevant aside, that the Chinese character for "meditation" is the source of the Japanese character for "Zen." On its left side is a radical associated with "religion" and "happiness;" the right side is chosen for the purpose of both pronunciation and meaning, but on its own is a character that means "alone."

Neither Taoism nor Zen denies the gamut of feelings that constitute human experience, but these feelings are received in a way that is tempered by a special perspective. Self is treated as a part of consciousness but not as the locus of consciousness. The larger center is the workings of the world itself, and in this context self finds rather than takes its place. However small or alone this self, a sense of belonging and appropriateness pervades whatever happens. All experience has a nurturing, deepening, and consoling quality. So, from Basho:

For a lovely bowl
Let us arrange these flowers . . .
Since there is no rice.

Circumstances are not always kind but they can be received with grace and patience.

Both Taoism and Zen can be understood in part as an adaptable response to the overbearing order and control of the societies that nurtured or adopted them. In China, Taoism seems to have occurred as a counterbalance to the rigidity of Confucianism. In Japan, Zen can be understood in the context of the tightly structured feudal order, both political and social, that has governed the Japanese for centuries. Taoism and Zen became processes for finding flexibility and freedom within this oppressive control.

Yet, paradoxically, neither one is ultimately a release, an escape from the societies that house them. Instead, they offer reconciliation. The sage, in archetypal Taoist terms, returns to the community to become one of its members, moving indistinctly and passing nearly unnoticed among all the others. And in Zen, as illustrated in the *Ox Herding Pictures*, the now enlightened seeker comes back to the village and reenters its life. The experience that has transformed the self is barely evident on the surface of appearances; the mountain is again the mountain, the sea is again the sea.

Zen acknowledges that the destruction and reconstitution of self begins and ends with each individual person. In Taoism this same understanding is expressed several times in the *Lao Tzu*:

> *Knowing others is understanding;*
> *   knowing self is wisdom.*
> *Force can master others;*
> *   but only strength can master self.*[1]

Rather than a static thing, self can be thought of as a shifting reference position for consciousness. Such a notion does not pose a philosophical problem for either Taoism or Zen. It is a problem, however, for an attitude that personalizes self, that defines it too narrowly and too rigidly. But this attitude can be transformed; it can be softened and expanded. Not even personality has to be taken personally.

Curiously, a less narrow attitude to self can best be cultivated by acknowledging it rather than denying it; paradoxically, the way to be free of a constraining self is to accept it. Both Taoism and Zen recognize this tactic as a method of properly placing self within the whole perspective of being. Two related ideas, already noted, are worth mentioning again because they are instructive here. The first is that all effort to negate self only succeeds in affirming it. The second is that self is not a thing but a reference position. A person who, by volition, undertakes the journey of inner discovery will gradually and inadvertently cultivate a softening, an opening, a releasing of any experience that is confining. At the end of this process, there is still a body that walks, eats, and talks; there is still a consciousness although it is no longer bound to a center that is rigidly defined as self. Everything in selflessness is the same as before, but with a difference. As T.S. Eliot pointed out in *Little Gidding*,[2] a profound simplicity is earned at the cost of a substantial self. The difference between the beginning and the end of the journey of discovery is nothing and everything.

Since there is a self, the beginning begins with self. In Suzuki Roshi's gentle way, he offers encouragement for this first step away from a narrow, confining center:

> *The best way is to understand yourself, and then you will understand everything.*[3]

This "yourself" eventually becomes a kind of universal self, the embodiment in one person of everything that is in all people. The same softening process that shifts understanding from a personal perspective to a human perspective also shifts to a boundless one. Confinement within a hard self is eventually replaced by the inclusive fluidity of selflessness. Selflessness cannot be reached deliberately; it cannot be cultivated or contrived. It just happens spontaneously as the conceptual habits of a confining consciousness give way to a consciousness that is nonconceptual. This is expressed in the *Lao Tzu*:

Through selfless action [fulfillment is attained.][4]

The sage has no mind of his own.[5]

As the selflessness of this new consciousness replaces the willfulness of the old one, a formless identity grows and enters the larger design of things. Flowers and frogs and fishes and stones are honored as equals. This is not imposed by any moral, ethical, or religious system. It happens spontaneously as self effortlessly dissolves into selflessness and an inevitable humility allows compassion. An empathetic awareness becomes deeper and wider as the narrow perspective of self falls away. In the words of Morinaga Soko Roshi:

> *Unless we . . . wean ourselves from this stubborn attachment to "I," our inherent wisdom is clouded and our inherent compassion is blocked.*[6]

As this weaning of "I" takes place, the full range of awareness is dramatically restructured toward a softer, more inclusive way of perceiving. It is the essence of a process that initiates all mystical experience.

This new consciousness creates a profound sense of insight and clarity, of peace and perspective. The world is experienced more directly and immediately as selfless insights see things the way they are rather than the way self wants them to be.

Like all mystical experiences, selflessness generates the paradoxical feeling of being both closer and farther away, as if distance somehow increases the closeness and closeness somehow increases the distance until oneness and separateness become indistinguishable from each other. A deep sense of belonging is balanced with a corresponding feeling of aloneness, a fullness is juxtaposed with an emptiness, as self recedes from its predominant position as the reference point of awareness.

The experience is irrefutable yet it cannot be explained. A profound compassion for everything is accompanied by a corresponding sense that each individual part of wholeness has its own course that belongs to the integrated pattern of everything. All details have context. And this deep awareness of context permits each person to move harmoniously within the moment-by-moment unfolding of a great wisdom.

This understanding is wonderfully expressed in the dramatic resolution of Shakespeare's *Hamlet*. This play, like all useful fiction, is an illustration of Picasso's definition of art as "a lie that makes us understand the truth." Hamlet smells treachery in the wagered swordfighting contest that he is to have with Laertes. But he also senses a resolution to the escalating rot that is consuming the state of Denmark.

> *But thou wouldst not think how ill all's here about my heart.*
> *But it is no matter.*[7]

His friend, Horatio, responds to Hamlet's premonition with the mind and self of ordinary awareness:

> *If your mind dislike anything, obey it.*[8]

But Hamlet is responding with a deeper awareness to a greater sense of order:

> *There is a special providence in the fall of a sparrow. If it be*
> *now, 'tis not to come; if it be not to come, it will be now; if it*
> *be not now, yet it will come. The readiness is all.*[9]

In each moment the wisdom of the future unfolds itself

in the power of the present. By awareness, compliance, and timing the world is entered through these moments. Moving with them rather than struggling against them requires a special sensitivity and perspective. Only selflessness is able to function within the context of this larger wisdom.

But this larger wisdom requires that self be acknowledged, for it, too, is part of a wholly inclusive unfolding. Since self cannot be eliminated by deliberate willfulness, it is diminished by a passive process, one that permits self to recede gently in its own way and in its own time. This happens by mindfulness alone. Nothing else needs to be done.

In the ritual of *zazen* such a passive process is symbolized and enacted by bowing. Suzuki Roshi writes:

> *After* zazen *we bow to the floor nine times. By bowing we are giving up ourselves. To give up ourselves means to give up our dualistic ideas.*[10]

The bowing is not a forceful act intended to induce not-self. If it were, self would simply continue to arise as the counterpart of not-self and the dance of opposites would persist. Bowing is a constant and patient reminder that the inner rebalancing must take place without deliberate effort.

This Zen realization and practice, when cast in Taoism's terminology, is spontaneity, *tzu-jan*. Deliberate effort in Zen is the treadmill of duality, and in Taoism it is the trap of mutual arising, *hsiang sheng*. Zen realizes, in the tradition of Taoism, that such a cycle can be broken only by not intending to break it. And this can happen only when selflessness is large enough to include self.

Softness

Softness in Taoism and Zen is a resilient strength that is not synonymous with acquiescence. It is a special kind of yielding that arises spontaneously from an inner integrity and discipline, somewhat like the strength of water comes from being unknowingly faithful to its own nature.

Such a softness is not easily cultivated. It requires sensitivity, discipline, and perseverance. Maintaining this integrity while knowing how and when to yield is an art that is difficult to master. And it is particularly difficult for the linear thinking that is so characteristic in the West.

This thinking is largely created by the notion of mind itself. It is one of the reasons, according to Frederick Franck, that Taoism and Zen did not flourish in the history of the West:

> *The Greeks could not for a moment give up their heads, their rational questions and rational answers. The Chinese, if it is not too rude to say so, had no heads from the beginning, and the same may be said of the Japanese, who have always hated logic and psychology, and perhaps always will. The Greeks were men, and the Chinese and Japanese were women, and women are always more right than men.*[1]

What does it mean to be "woman?" In terms of the female archetype it means being embracing and fluid, inclusive, and flexible. It means being nourishing and receptive, dark and mysterious. The female archetype is paradoxical, the way all final answers about thought and existence eventually undo themselves to become questions. "Woman" is the endless riddle that cycles forever between certainty and uncertainty, between knowing and not-knowing. It is living without final answers; it is being vitally alive without answerable questions and explainable reasons.

But this female archetype, for all its uncertainty and enigma, is true to an underlying principle that is definite and unavoidable—even though it remains indefinable. The seasons inexorably change and water always remains true to its own nature. Clouds appear and disappear in disordered order. There is structure in the tumult, patterns in the chaos. Such a principle is the underlying character of Taoism and Zen.

In Taoism this principle is symbolized by water, and is expressed as a simple teaching in the *Lao Tzu*:

> *By yielding . . .*
> *overcome.*
> *By bending . . .*
> *remain straight.*[2]

> *Softness overcomes hardness.*[3]

> *The formless is greater than form.*[4]

It is personified in Taoist thinking as the Great Mother, a world in which generosity, nurturing, and growth are counterbalanced by their opposites in an interplay of balanced completeness. All this is bound by the spontaneous nature of itself, an order that is called the Tao. Here all things move and dance in the changing of their inevitable rhythms. The changing and generosity are the softness; the order and inevitability are the hardness.

The hardness in Zen is obvious in the strictness of its monasteries and in the tactics of its teaching. Its softness is less conspicuous than Taoism's but it is nonetheless present, expressed obliquely but clearly in layered inferences. The skin of Zen seems tough, but its inner flesh is soft and yielding. The toughness is manifest in Zen's crusty discipline; the softness is apparent in its flexibility, adaptability, and compassion. But the skin and flesh hang on the hardness of invisible and indestructible bones. Their hardness is the resolute certainty of Zen itself. A traditional Ch'an story illustrates the layered softness and hardness, the compassion and strictness, that constitute Zen's seemingly paradoxical character:

For twenty years a wealthy woman had been sponsoring a monk by providing him with a hut and whatever material necessities he needed to sustain his simple life. But she began to wonder about his spiritual progress so she devised a plot to test it.

From a nearby village she acquired the assistance of a cooperative girl who agreed to ardently embrace the monk, profess her passion for him, and urge him to honor her desire.

The monk's response to the girl, which she related to the woman, was only a vague and diffident statement about, "An old tree grows on a cold rock in winter. Nowhere is there any warmth."

The woman, when she heard the girl's report, became angry. "For twenty years I have been feeding this fellow and he showed not one sign of warmth. He didn't need to satisfy your desire but he might have shown some understanding and compassion. He has learned nothing."

The story is about understanding and compassion but it is also about a way of relating to the world, a way of softening and opening that places moment by moment circumstances above the narrow rigidity of ideology so that principle is honored without being blinded by itself. Hardness coexists with softness.

Here is some wisdom from Ch'an that illustrates the same same idea in different words:

> *"What is the solution that accounts for every situation?" asked the Ch'an abbot.*
>
> *When no one could answer the question, he replied, "As the situation arises."*

This aphorism and the preceding story suggest a teaching that adheres meticulously to an indefinable principle. Because this principle is formless, it engenders a condition of continual readiness. Without any rules to follow, an appropriate response is possible to all situations. Spontaneity is permitted within the context of discipline.

This hard softness is a part of Taoism and Zen that is extremely difficult to grasp from outside the experience of the two traditions. It is not understood philosophically. Instead, it is sensed the way that an artist's aesthetic instinct unites inner with outer experience, so that each expression of inspiration is different, yet somehow the same. The softness has a hardness that yields to every situation but remains true to some inexplicable principle. Trying to define art, like trying to define Taoism and Zen, is a waste of time.

The fundamental attitude that is common to the Taoist and Zen experience is an inner softness that allows unconditional receptivity. It takes a special discipline to release the preconceptions and reflexes that prevent a fluid spontaneity of response. This is why the most powerful imagery in Taoism is water, and why the discipline of the Zen process is directed toward negation and doubt. Such emptying of certainty, even the deliberate cultivation of profound confusion, is really a means of softening, of opening, of becoming so inclusive that nothing is excluded. In such a process the unpredictable is never surprising.

Anyone who tries to understand Taoism or Zen is at first bewildered by them. This initial effect usually escalates to profound confusion, partly as the result of the elusive principle that underlies them. But the bewilderment and confusion are also a result of rigid systems of Western understanding that cannot bend to follow the crooked logic of these Oriental traditions. Taoism and Zen cannot properly be understood, but they can be experienced. Their inherently paradoxical character requires a soft approach. For anyone who persists in using a rigid one, the final effect is the collapse of any ability to understand systematically. This creates the ultimate softness: emptiness (Chinese: *k'ung*; Japanese: *ku*) and nothingness (Chinese: *wu*; Japanese: *mu*). It is worth noting here that *wu* is the Chinese word for the *satori* of Zen's inner awakening, and that emptiness and nothingness both belong to the female archetype.

Zen moves to the soft receptivity of emptiness and nothingness more methodically and deliberately than Taoism. Because the contemplative tradition of Taoism exists outside the institutional structure of Buddhism, it has proceeded organically by relating the wisdom in its literature to the dynamics of the world, and then noting what happens. Insight in Taoism gradually surfaces through a process of elimination, by discovering what is not the Way. This process continues until a "feeling" begins to coalesce. This feeling falls entirely outside the bounds of explanation or rules. It is

217

analogous to the artist's sense of beauty, the scientist's sense of natural symmetry, the athlete's sense of impeccable timing; these are comparable to both the Taoist and Zen experience. But the Zen approach, because of Buddhism, has been more structured than Taoism's organic process.

In Rinzai Zen, for example, the *koan* has been contrived to create an eventual intellectual crisis that leads to conceptual collapse, the so-called *kensho* or *satori* experience. The *koan* process is really an incisively calculated technique to induce a state of softness or receptivity through absolute uncertainty. The intellectual concentration and focus that are demanded by the *koan* exercise dissolve the constructs that obstruct the Zen experience. At a critical point in this process there is a falling away of intellectual order. The hardness of discipline is necessary to achieve this breaking point. What follows is a spontaneous arising of an elemental awareness that is, like the Way in Taoism, both indisputable and unexplainable. It is a grounded sense of being that is similtaneously indestructable and fragile, hard and soft. The whole inner process of working the *koan* is a calculated tactic to precipitate the questioning and the doubting, thereby inducing the softening and emptying. The hardness of a relentless and self-disciplined examination of the *koan* facilitates and defines the inner softening as an uncertain certainty. In this respect, Rinzai Zen is Taoism in a more focused, controlled, directed form.

The approach in Soto Zen is less dramatic than in Rinzai, but the disciplined erosion of hard and fixed concepts is the same. In this regard Soto is more like Taoism. But Taoist literature is also filled with philosophical conundrums and paradoxes that relate it to Rinzai Zen. In each of these traditions, however, the Way is finally accessible when softening has dissolved the structures of thought and feeling that obstruct spontaneous being.

The spontaneity that occurs is a condition of moment-by-moment insight unbounded by conceptual limits. This is not omniscience. It is rather a sense of contextual perspective that places each act and instant in the center of a balanced unfolding. It is also acceptance, a softening of position such that things are permitted to be received as they are without idealizing or romanticizing them, without denying or regretting them. This attitude is expressed nicely by R.H. Blyth in *Games Zen Masters Play*:

> *"Raising waves where there is no wind" is a famous expression in Zen, signifying that there is no problem in life. Things are as they are, and as they are becoming, and once you realize this in its active, not resigned, meaning, there is nothing really to worry about.*[5]

Blyth's words can be compared with those attributed to Chuang Tzu at the death of Lao Tzu. Here they have been adapted from Thomas Merton's *The Way of Chuang Tzu*:

> *The Master came into the world at the right time, and when his time was up, he left it again.*
> *He who awaits his time, who submits when his work is done, will find no room in this life for either sorrow or rejoicing.*[6]

Or these words from the *Lao Tzu*:

> *Each thing becomes and grows and fulfills itself,*
>   *and then returns to the nameless beginning.*
> *This is the way things are.*[7]

Or again from the Zen tradition:

[A]ll questioning is a way of avoiding the real answer which, as Zen tells us, is really known already.[8]

Fundamental to both Taoism and Zen is the tactic of avoiding the avoiding, a double negative that yields positive results. The eventual directness of this indirection is finally achieved by softening the defenses that obstruct what "is really known already." It takes inner strength to reach the "real answer" by no longer avoiding the unavoidable. This is not prescience. It is the recognition that the continuous unfolding of circumstances is expected, familiar, and appropriate. Finding this "known already" first requires emptying, the deep softening that feels initially like being totally lost and confused. Slowly, the implicit order is sensed then discerned as a peaceful balance moving softly and harmoniously in a vast mystery.

Oneness

ords are separateness; oneness is something more than words can say. Words cannot explain oneness, but they can point beyond themselves to something unsayable. If words are used in the spirit of suggesting and opening rather than defining and limiting, their use may not seem so futile.

Words that are used with a disciplined softness assume a generous shape. They become round and expansive instead of straight and confining. They intimate and inspire rather than demand and restrict. Their hardness mellows. And they begin to dissolve into a silence that opens into oneness.

When thoughts blow freely in the winds of words, each word means more than it means and each thought is unfettered by walls of notions. This is the spirit in which the words of Taoism and Zen are to be used. When words are allowed by the generosity of silence, the initial conditions are present for the oneness of Taoism and Zen. Oneness is large enough to include separateness.

Words used playfully and paradoxically come closer to oneness than those hard-crafted by intellect's exacting efforts. But intellect has its place. It can shape what is possible to say to make evident what cannot be said. Its sharp and cutting edge can slowly carve away everything that is separate, and thereby create a sense of the round and boundless form of oneness. The process is negative but necessary.

All the intellectual effort of words is a *kung-an*, a *koan*, that eventually undoes itself to leave a wordless oneness. Yet oneness cannot be sought without words. All words are a necessary futility. This is the spirit in which these words are offered.

From Taoist tradition comes these words from the *Lao Tzu*:

> *[The sage] is detached, thus at one with all.*[1]

Detachment invites opening and receptivity. It creates a distance that permits closeness, a separation that encourages intimacy. Indeed, the natural inclination of detachment is not to soar heavenward toward some abstract disembodiment but to reconnect to the grounded commonplace of the immediate and present. The experience is somewhat like the new seeing that comes from returning home after a long time away. Time and travel have created a separation from the familiar that is now revealed in fresh perspective. Everything is the same, all the old details are present but they are experienced intimately with an insightful and alive presence. The closeness happens because of the distance, and the oneness happens because of the separation. A delicate balancing of opposite perceptions sparks a bright and crisp awareness.

Closeness and distance are opposites. So are oneness and separateness. These opposites generate, define, and enhance each other. In Taoism and Zen this game of opposites is played within the reach of words to stretch insight beyond their reach. Here is Suzuki Roshi speaking like a Taoist sage:

> *When we talk about the negative side, the positive side is missing, and when we talk about the positive side, the negative side is missing. We cannot speak in a positive and a negative way at the same time. So we do not know what to say.*[2]

Yin and *yang* are the implicit archetypes in Taoism that correspond to Suzuki Roshi's opposites. The objective in both Taoism and Zen is to put the opposites together while leaving them apart. The opposites are resolved and not resolved. The result is that "we do not know what to say." Insight is pressed beyond words.

This paradox seems mind-boggling in the West because the conventions of language and the corresponding habits of thought limit the options that seem to be available: either it is plant or animal, true or false, mind or body, matter or energy. But the East, which once had a near monopoly on meaningful paradox, can no longer claim that distinction. Modern science has entered paradox in various places: in the particle-wave phenomenon of light; in the space-time fluidity of relativity; in the subject-object blending of quantum physics; in the evolution-emergence of systems theory; in the order-disorder relationship of the fresh study of chaos. These new explorations have been inadvertently connecting the West with the East's thinking.

The same violations of simple logic that are expressed in these recent scientific developments have been an essential ingredient in Taoist and Zen thinking for centuries. The purpose is to shift thought into a nonlinear mode and thereby arrive at an awareness that hangs alert in a suspended and unresolved balance. Some sense of this condition and its purpose is offered in the Zen observation:

The truth is that everything is One, and this of course is not a numerical one.[3]

This One is a sense of unity that includes all separateness.

The experience of oneness is holistic and cannot be

225

reached by the usual logical processes. At some point a crisis in linear thinking creates a leap of necessity, a discontinuity that is equivalent to the leap in quantum physics or the phenomenon of emergence in systems theory. A new state of awareness is reached without any apparent linear connection to the previous one. This style of thinking is an integral part of Taoism and Zen, making them seem so enigmatic:

> For in Taoism and Zen the world is seen as an inseparably interrelated field or continuum, no part of which can actually be separated from the rest or valued above or below the rest. It was in this sense that Hui-neng, the Sixth Patriarch, meant that "fundamentally not one thing exists," for he realized that all things are terms, not entities. They exist in the abstract world of thought, but not in the concrete world of nature.[4]

In other words, oneness is a seamless web of everything that transforms all separateness into distinctions that are recognized as arbitrary. Any word, any notion, any intellectual conceptualization, any serious invention by thought shatters the delicate spell of oneness. This is why talking about Zen is said to "stink of Zen," why "Those who know . . . cannot explain." In the mythological terms of the West, this spell of oneness was broken in the expulsion from the Garden. The goal of Taoism and Zen, in these same terms, is to return to this oneness while allowing the game of separateness.

When the context of anything is everything else, then all conceptual processes collapse in an empty receptivity, a kind of balanced stillness that is profoundly confusing and incomparably peaceful. The elusiveness of this sense is what the practice of Taoism and Zen attempts to reach and maintain; it is what the literature attempts to express. The *Lao Tzu* says it this way:

> *The greatest form has no shape.*
> *The Tao is hidden and without name.*[5]

Suzuki Roshi, with many other overtones, says the same thing on behalf of Zen:

> *Some people put stress on oneness, but this is not our understanding. We do not emphasize any point in particular, even oneness. Oneness is valuable, but variety is also wonderful.*[6]

Suzuki Roshi hints at the formless and the nameless rather than stating them. By placing together oneness with expressions of separateness, he makes explicit the paradox that is implied in the *Lao Tzu*. The "greatest form" has no conceptual structure and, therefore, has no equivalence in words. Efforts to explain oneness invariably chase themselves in circles.

The center of Taoism and Zen seems to be oneness. But when attention is focused on oneness, separateness becomes the center; when attention is focused on separateness, oneness becomes the center. Each negates itself as soon as attention is given to it. That is why all efforts to explain Taoism and Zen become statements followed by denials, positions echoed by contradictions. For example, both traditions have a profound empathy with everything, a sense of unity that overcomes the narrow perspective of selfishness; but they also have detachment, indifference, and separateness. Because of oneness, nothing matters; because of separateness, everything matters.

227

A system of thought that deliberately self-destructs by contradicting itself cannot be understood or explained by any consistent intellectual system. Consequently, Taoism and Zen defy definition. Both have refused to define themselves, and Zen in particular expresses itself and teaches in negative terms:

Not one, not two; not both, not neither.

For oneness, words must dance harmoniously with silence.

Contradiction eventually creates the experience of oneness. So, Taoism and Zen happily contradict themselves. They have a profound sense of empathy and caring for everything, and, at the same time, they have a detached indifference. In one instance the *Lao Tzu* declares:

The sage has no mind of his own.
He is aware of the needs of others.[7]

Yet, with equal conviction, it asserts elsewhere:

Heaven and earth are ruthless;
They see the ten thousand things as dummies.
The wise are ruthless;
They see the people as dummies.[8]

The world is a sacred place worthy of selfless dedication, yet it is a turmoil of fools and blind urges. All distinctions unify into oneness, out of which comes a diverse multiplicity of confused separateness. Both positions are held as equally valid.

These opposites represent the two fundamentally different ways of experiencing the world: one is a profound insight that integrates everything into a thoughtless oneness;

the other is the ordinary discriminations that attempt to navigate each person through the unpredictable particulars of day-to-day existence.

From invented separateness comes an unavoidable belonging. Of all the diversity that thoughts can imagine, each thing has its place in oneness.

Oneness is experienced as a great stillness, as an emptiness in which all separateness happens. The measure of this oneness is being still and receptive in the midst of all happening; the measure of separateness is being active and decisive in the center of stillness.

In this stillness, the greatest is fulfilled in the particular. And this is how oneness is found in separateness.

Emptiness

Emptiness (Chinese: *k'ung*, Japanese: *ku*) is a special kind of something. The walls of houses divide it into rooms. Bottles would be useless without it. The limits of all things are defined by it. Everything that exists is contained in emptiness. What is not, gives meaning to whatever is. Emptiness is what everything else cannot be.

Because emptiness is thought of as a condition of negation, conceptual thinking has difficulty with it. To consider emptiness, thinking must abandon the spaces that it fills with itself. In other words, emptiness is not an understanding; it is a condition of receptivity. So a phrase such as the "existence of emptiness" becomes an oxymoron because emptiness does not properly exist. No linguistic device can adequately deal with emptiness; words and their ordered structure constitute a conceptual frameword in which emptiness will not fit:

In the pursuit of learning,
everyday something is acquired.
In the pursuit of Tao,
everyday something is dropped.[1]

Emptiness is a key notion in Taoism and Zen, and negation is the only way of approaching it. Zen is often described as taking away everything that is not Zen. And the Tao is essentially discovered by learning what not to be and do. Mistakes, therefore, become a valuable source of information—perhaps the only source. The Way in both Taoism and Zen is approached by emptying, by abandoning what is not the Way, by eliminating questions rather than finding answers, by opening to what cannot be known. Because the

Way can be recognized but not explained, all concepts become obstructions that have to be cleared away. Emptiness, therefore, becomes the condition that provides maximum range and perspective, maximum flexibility and freedom to move and respond. Any conception or preconception limits by predisposing awareness and action.

Desire and attachment have similar effects. They are conditions of whole or partial fullness that obstruct the receptivity provided by emptiness. The following comments come from three separate chapters of the *Lao Tzu*:

> *Ever desireless, one can see the mystery.*
> *Ever desiring, one can see the manifestations*
> *These two spring from the same source*
> *but differ in name.[2]*

> *There is no greater sin than desire,*
> *No greater curse than discontent,*
> *No greater misfortune*
> *than wanting something for oneself.[3]*

> *He who is attached to things*
> *will suffer much.[4]*

In connecting desire and emptiness, R.H. Blyth offers the same advice on behalf of Zen:

> *Empty means with nothing clogging the mind, no trace of self-interest.[5]*

And this same principle is in Thomas Merton's version of *The Way of Chuang Tzu*:

> *If a man is crossing a river*

234

And an empty boat collides with his skiff,
Even though he be a bad-tempered man
He will not become very angry.
But if he sees a man in the boat,
He will shout at him to steer clear.
If the shout is not heard,
he will shout again,
And yet again, and begin cursing.
And all because there is somebody
in the boat.
Yet if the boat were empty,
He would not be shouting, and not angry.
If you can empty your own boat
Crossing the river of the world,
No one will oppose you,
No one will seek to harm you. . . .
Such is the perfect man:
His boat is empty.[6]

In traditional Zen literature the famous *mondo* or dialogue between a monk and Master Joshu expresses the same thought:

"I am empty of everything and there is nothing left in my
mind," said the monk to Joshu. "What do you say to that?"
Joshu said, "Cast that away."
But the monk persisted. "I have told you, there is nothing left
in me. I am completely empty. What can I cast away?"
"In that case," replied Joshu, "keep on carrying it."

So emptiness itself is a burden, and it, too, must finally be cast away.

This is also the case with such notions as ease, freedom,

spontaneity, timing, these practical manifestations of the Taoist and Zen practice. They can occur only without a conscious intention to make them happen. "I want you to forget what I just told you!" guarantees remembering. "Aren't we having a good time!" is the end of the fun. All sense of humility, too, must fall away from humility; it cannot be technically cast away because such a deliberate act is a contrived process that will just create a more subtle form of pride. Humility, like the emptiness being carried by Joshu's monk, must simply dissolve into emptiness. Any considered awareness of this process subverts the Way by converting it into something deliberate. Taoism and Zen both understand that the process of emptying can happen only without any kind of interference. Saying it, spoils it; thinking it, loses it; doing it, destroys it.

The famous Joshu *mondo* is an echo of an earlier teaching in Taoism:

> *Thirty spokes converge in a wheel's hub . . .*
> *It is the center whole*
> *   that allows them to turn.*[7]

The hole at the convergence of the thirty spokes is the emptiness that permits the wheel to turn. The same emptiness is the spaciousness that makes a room usable and a bottle useful. These images are really metaphors for philosophical principles to apply to ourselves. How can we move with the turning of the world if we have no emptiness within? How can we receive the world if we have no inner emptiness?

The sudden flash of enlightenment in Rinzai Zen, perhaps the result of work with a *koan*, is triggered by a profound inner confusion, an absolute collapse of understanding.

Thoughts stop thinking. The mind becomes still and empty. Without this emptiness no filling can take place. The Christian tradition has an equivalent of this inner crisis in the so-called dark night of the soul. In Zen the necessity of emptying is playfully illustrated in the story about the professor and the cup of tea:

> The Zen master Nan-in received a university professor who came to inquire about Zen. When they sat down for tea, Nan-in began to pour. The professor's cup filled and overflowed. The Zen master kept pouring.
> "Stop! Stop! said the professor. "It's full! No more will go in!"
> "Like this cup," said Nan-in, "you too are full. Until you are empty of all your opinions and speculations, how can you receive Zen?"

From the *Lao Tzu* come two examples that illustrate the same notion:

> *Empty and be full.*[8]

> *Empty yourself of everything.*
> *Let the mind rest at peace.*[9]

In Taoism and Zen the Way is followed by opening to emptiness. This following is unobstructed by concepts, preconceptions, and understanding or, finally, by volition itself. The appropriate receptivity only happens when emptiness arrives of itself. "Happens" is the appropriate verb since the process seems to be passive, culminating in an event that is not volitional. No one "does" it. The critical point is reached by letting go. And then "it" happens, as Eugen Herrigel recounts in *Zen in the Art of Archery*. How is it done? Herrigel offers the classic explanation:

> *By letting go of yourself, leaving yourself and everything yours behind you so decisively that nothing more is left of you but a purposeless tension.*[10]

This "purposeless tension" of Zen is the readiness of emptiness that awaits when opening is unconditional. It is exactly Taoism's understanding and use of emptiness.

Nothingness

he extension of emptiness is nothingness (Chinese: *wu*; Japanese: *mu*), the condition of total negation, the no-concept of no-concept. It is emptiness at its most allowing, if such a definition makes any semantic sense.

Whereas emptiness is relative, nothingness is absolute, a notion that cannot be conceived and does not have a conceivable counterpart. Emptiness almost seems conceptual because it can be juxtaposed with the fullness of what is, with what is tangible and finite. But nothingness is not remotely conceptual because it can be juxtaposed only with everything, with the infinite. Nothingness and everything become the same experience as they conceptually disappear in opposite directions into the one absolute. This absolute is like the unsayable, inexplicable, unknowable Way that manifests itself only in the particular. Nothingness is therefore closely related to the basic principles of Taoist and Zen teachings.

Zen, because of Buddhism's philosophical influence, has given much more attention to nothingness than Taoism. For Taoism, nothingness is too abstract to warrant much direct attention—emptiness is extreme enough. But for both traditions, nothingness is the defining background that gives meaning and perspective to the foreground of all experience.

Nothingness is not conceptually approachable. It is not intended to be. It is not a place; it is not even an idea. It is a device, a condition of mind that engenders insight. It is the distance that provides perspective to every thought. Like emptiness gives context to fullness, nothingness gives context to awareness. Awakening, therefore, is not a condition of absolute negation, it is a relationship between the opposite absolutes of what is and what is not, between everything and nothing.

The concern for nothingness in Zen is really a strategy to define awareness; emptiness also works, but historically the term has not been given the same superlative and philosophical qualities. Since nothingness is absolute emptiness, it causes absolute filling. In Rinzai Zen, the roshi uses the *koan* to measure the receptivity of the disciple by assessing the *mu*, the degree of nothingness. In Taoism, because of the principle of *hsiang sheng*, nothingness gives rise to everything, the same thoughtless inclusiveness and uninhibited receptivity that is measured in Zen's *mu*.

This tactic of arriving at everything by way of nothingness had been used in Taoist China long before it appeared in Japanese Zen. The following is condensed from an account by Chuang Tzu:

> *Four men . . . were having a discussion, saying, "Whoever*
> *believes Nothingness to be the head, Life to be the backbone,*
> *and Death to be the tail; whoever can know life, death, being,*
> *and non-being all as one, shall be our friend." The four*
> *looked at one another and smiled. And since they were in com-*
> *plete agreement, they became fast friends.*[1]

This use of nothingness and its implications for "knowing" is echoed later in Zen literature when Hui-neng (Japanese: Eno) says, "Arouse a mind resting on nothing."

Nothingness is the emptiness of being that is of key importance in both Taoism and Zen. One example from each tradition will suffice. The first, *The Lost Pearl*, comes from Thomas Merton's *The Way of Chuang Tzu*:

> *The Yellow Emperor went wandering*

To the north of the Red Water
To the Kwan Lun mountain. He looked around
Over the edge of the world. On the way home
He lost his night-colored pearl.
He sent out Science to seek his pearl,
* and got nothing.*
He sent Analysis to look for his pearl,
* and got nothing.*
He sent out Logic to seek his pearl,
* and got nothing.*
Then he asked Nothingness,
* and Nothingness had it.*

The Yellow Emperor said:
"Strange, indeed: Nothingness
Who was not sent
Who did no work to find it
Had the night-colored pearl."[2]

The second example is from a contemporary Zen story that tells of the visit of Queen Elizabeth II of England to a Zen monastery in Japan:

As the abbot was guiding the queen through the grounds she noticed, inscribed over the entrance gate, the character for nothingness. Since she could not read the kanji, she asked the abbot what the character meant. "God," he replied.

The "God" the abbot had in mind was not the anthropomorphized, patriarchal one of a conceivable deity; it was closer to the unsayable and unknowable YHWH, expressed as the tetragrammaton in the old Hebraic tradition. Just as this deeper, amorphous notion of God is found by the process of emptying to the total receptivity of "Thy will be done," so is the nothingness of Zen found. The abbot might have said "nothingness" to the Queen, or perhaps "everything," or "the Way," or even "Tao." At some profound level they all become the same means for entering the spontaneous ease of the world's unfolding. None of them can be explained, and the very act of trying destroys access to them.

The dilemma for Taoism and Zen in dealing with nothingness is often approached with remarkable similarity as both traditions try give verbal shape to a subject that falls outside the reach of words. Here is a contemporary rendering of the *Lao Tzu*:

> *The form that endures forever . . .*
> *is without form.*
> *Therefore those who follow the formless . . .*
> *find comfort and peace and fulfillment.*
>
> *Be nourished by what cannot be seen*
> *or heard or found.*
> *It is inexhaustible.*[3]

And here is Suzuki Roshi speaking for Zen. While trying to give some shape to Zen's sense of nothingness, he might as well be calling it the Tao and writing a chapter of the *Lao Tzu*:

> *So it is absolutely necessary for everyone to believe in nothing.*
> *But I do not mean voidness. There is something, but that*
> *something is something which is always prepared for taking*
> *some particular form, and it has some rules, or theory, or*
> *truth in its activity.*[4]

This nothingness in Zen, like the Taoist's Tao, is a pervasive, unknowable something that has all the attributes of nothing yet is somehow a something. It is experienced as a state of preparation that is the source of meaning and form, yet is not itself that meaning and form.

Now here is Chuang Tzu (this quotation has been used before but it has a new use in a new context), playfully expressing the same insight. He not only equates nothing and something but he also describes the delicate space between these polarities that is the razor's edge of the Taoist and Zen balance:

> *Now I am going to tell you something. . . .*
> *There is a beginning. There is no beginning of that beginning.*
> *There is no beginning of that no beginning of beginning. There*
> *is something before the beginning of something and nothing,*
> *and something before that. Suddenly there is something and*
> *nothing. But between something and nothing, I still don't really*
> *know which is something and which is nothing. . . .*[5]

This nothingness, which is also not-nothingness, is the common foundation of Taoism and Zen. Any effort to describe it is invariably wrong; any effort to remain silent is also wrong. The two options that are available—explanation and silence—are extremes that do not include the space between. "If you say this is a stick . . ." "Not this, not that; not both, not neither." "The Tao that can be named. . . ." Silence is balanced with the words of explanation; nothingness is balanced with the things and affairs of the world. Contradictions are not resolved; they are accepted and embraced. This is the only possible response to what is and what is-not.

245

Again the *Lao Tzu* offers some relevant words. They not only illustrate contradiction but they also give some sense to the same nothingness that Suzuki Roshi describes as the source of form and meaning:

Something mysteriously formed,
Born before heaven and earth.
In the silence and the void,
Standing alone and unchanging,
Ever present and in motion.[6]

A nothing and a something that is unchanging and in motion! A principle that is a process! A beginning that arose before the beginning! These are the same kinds of contradictions that produce the *koan*, that turn intellect against itself and leave all thinking collapsed in a wrecked heap, defined by nothingness.

These irresolvable juxtapositions in Taoism and Zen produce a creative tension that seems to move toward a resolution that never arrives. Every conceivable intellectual, gymnastic effort only succeeds in making the problem more subtle and the resolution more elusive. The intellectual dilemma then widens and deepens to become an emotional one until this one problem becomes all consuming. Possibilities offer promise, but impossibilities block options. The situation demands effort but thwarts trying. Frustration increases. Tension builds until a breaking point is reached. Then, spontaneously, a letting-go happens. Everything collapses, softens, becomes airy and light. And the problem falls away and disappears. The relief is palpable.

The first and most difficult step in reaching nothingness, the crucial phase, is reaching this point of crisis that demands a total surrender to the overwhelming complexity of understanding. Profound confusion is the beginning of this opening process that ends in filling. Such opening is conditional on uncertainty. Therefore, every certainty becomes a warning against pronouncements, against anticipation, against knowing. In the words of Zen:

> *The most dangerous thing in the world is to think you understand something.*[7]

From the traditional wisdom of Taoism the same idea is expressed less politely, "Knowing is the way of fools."

The wisdom, the peace, the grace of Taoism and Zen come from a special uncertainty. The result is a condition of perpetual preparedness, an easy readiness that takes an appropriate shape for every particular circumstance. Every answer occurs "as the situation arises." Each individual person becomes the balanced and shapeless center of the universe, dancing alone with the unpredictable order that swirls everywhere. Between the boundaries of birth and death, grace is both earned and given, happening regardless of struggle or surrender, or some seemingly magical combination of the two.

In a world full of people who are strewn between total confusion and absolute certainty, the Taoist and Zen challenge is the nearly impossible simplicity of reaching a deep insight that is wholly inclusive yet devoid of answers. The rewards are a wonderful relief and a quiet saddening. All awakening is shadowed by a loneliness, is sobered by a compassion of helpless caring. Taoism and Zen are not traditions that induce ecstasy; they do not arrive at the golden answer beyond questions. Their answer is in the profound doubt that lingers in a harmoniously charged nothingness. Their secret is to arrive by embracing and returning, and never again to feel the need to exclude and leave. So there is never a sense of separation from the ordinary and from the substance of ordinary experience. A feeling of deep empathy is pervasive. A simple awakening to a simple mystery is quite enough.

After awareness has been transformed by nothingness, everything is the same as before except that the old is now fresh, alive, and meaningfully ordered. When everything is the same but not the same, how can this new and ancient sense of beginning be conveyed to others? All effort to describe it seems like wasted platitudes:

> To know that there is nothing to know, and to grieve that it is
> so difficult to communicate this "nothing to know" to others—
> this is the life of Zen, this is the deepest thing in the world.[8]

The *Lao Tzu*, when expressed in contemporary language, clearly conveys the same feeling:

> Everyone else seems eager and dutiful . . .
>   but the deeper way seems lonely and confusing.
> Everyone else seems clear and definite . . .
>   but the deeper way seems dark and uncertain.
> What is a person to do when being adrift at sea,
>   when being blown aimlessly anywhere . . .
> Seems to be a more profound calling?
> When everyone else seems busy and purposeful,
> What is to be done with an urge that is confusing,
>   lonely . . . and different?
> When everyone else is guided by the affairs of
>   people . . .

248

What is this urge
that comes from the Great Mother?[9]

The "urge that comes from the Great Mother" is the Tao. It is the nothingness that is everything, the Way that Taoism shares with Zen. It can be neither lost nor found. It cannot be explained with words. It cannot be known with thoughts.

From the perspective of profound simplicity, all the struggle with words and thoughts and feelings, all the deep doubt and uncertainty and confusion, become necessary folly. This struggle is recognized as prerequisite to nothingness. It has generated the tension needed for arriving at a formless way of understanding.

Balance

alance is really balancing, not a static state but a dynamic process. It is a condition of perpetual arriving, of continual changing that is always adjusting to the shifting flow of circumstances. When balance becomes a reflexive reaction rather than a considered response, it is experienced as a stillness in the center of movement.

The Tao, in the language of Taoism, is said to be one *yin* and one *yang* in dynamic balance, opposites poised in that still moment when the imagined disparities of the world are experienced in sustained equilibrium. The different elements, whatever they may be, maintain their individual identities yet become something more than their separateness, as if the parts of wholeness are forever together in a moment-by-moment enchantment. This balance is like two dancers moving as one in a great rhythm of music, or two lovers moving as one in a great rhythm of passion. There is change yet nothing changes; there is changing yet perfect harmony.

This state of balance is a common experience. It is the stillness of the playing musician united with the unfolding eternity of the music; the motionless poise of the surfer in the shifting curl of a great wave; the plunging freefall of the skier at one with the silent waiting of the mountain. The Way does not exist outside the moment of balance. In the *I Ching* it is represented as #52, Kàn, when the *yang* of the mountain's upward thrust rests in momentary tranquility with the *yin* of the lake's downward waiting. It is that instant of seeming pause when all of the forces of the universe, as if waiting forever, are momentarily balanced in a massive stillness.

In the imagery of Chinese culture, this instant of perpetual poise is expressed through the duality of mountain and lake, *yang* and *yin*. Because of Buddhism's influence in China, Zen has expressed it as mind and body. The words are different but the process for attaining the balanced stillness is the same. As Suzuki Roshi explains:

> *This is the most important teaching: not two, and not one. Our body and mind are not two and not one. If you think your body and mind are two, that is wrong; if you think that they are one, that is also wrong. Our body and mind are both two and one.*[1]

Suzuki Roshi is alluding to the tension between these opposites, of finding and maintaining the inclusive point of balance that is both and neither. The paradox is kept alive. The challenge, therefore, is to live in the balanced dynamic between and within the invented opposites of body and mind. In the stillness is something other than stillness.

The balancing of apparent opposites, so much a part of Taoist philosophy, is readily apparent in Zen. Here again is Suzuki Roshi illustrating the same idea in different language:

> *Good is not different from bad. Bad is good; good is bad. They are two sides of one coin.*[2]

These words are a clear echo of the familiar ones from the *Lao Tzu*:

> *When beauty is recognized as beauty . . .*
> *ugliness is created.*
> *When good is recognized as good . . .*
> *bad is created.*[3]

254

The divided parts of good and bad are the two components of one wholeness. The nameless whole of two sides gives balance to the followers of the Tao. Suzuki Roshi's one coin of two sides is the same nameless center that gives composure to those who practice Zen. Oneness is the balance of having two legs. But the legs are not the balance. And the balance is not a oneness.

Both Taoism and Zen use the balance of this moving still point as the process for dealing with the inherent transience of everything. Change is ubiquitous and unavoidable, not such a terrible condition for anyone who does not take it personally, who is not attached to some abstract expectation of unchanging. This attitude to change is expressed in the Zen of Suzuki Roshi. He is quoted again because he so often sounds so much like a Taoist:

Actually, if you become honest enough, or straightforward enough, it is not so difficult to accept this truth.[4]

In terms of both Taoism and Zen, this acceptance provides access to a balance which lies within change. Balance also harmonizes the energy of opposites.

Of course, there are no opposites, just as there is no fixed state of balance. They are an intellectual convention, a convenience of mind, a habit of thinking that partitions wholeness into thought's duality. Perhaps opposites are simply projections of an internal bilateral symmetry, a brain fashioning everything into the left and right halves of its divided self. Fortunately, there is just one head; and two opposite hands can come together to symbolize a balanced wholeness.

Balance is not an unusual experience, not some esoteric device that is available only to the exceptionally self-disciplined or the diligent followers of the Way. It is common and unavoidable. Everyone has it and practices it. It is the inner condition that moves each person from one day to the next, that surmounts momentary frustration and deep trauma. It is the composure that instills patience, the calm that solves problems, the natural urge that inspires healing. The difference between this ubiquitous balance and its presence in Taoism and Zen is only a matter of attention. They cultivate balance until it becomes an inner process that is inseparable from being itself. Here is a Zen story that illustrates the point:

> Kasan was asked to officiate at the funeral of a provincial lord.
> He had never met lords and nobles before so he was nervous.
> When the ceremony started, Kasan [began to] sweat.
> Afterwards, when he had returned, he gathered his pupils together. Kasan confessed that he was not yet qualified to be a teacher for he lacked the sameness of bearing in the world of fame that he possessed in the secluded temple. Then Kasan resigned and became a pupil of another master. Eight years later he returned to his former pupils, enlightened.[5]

In its most demonstrable form, this balance is expressed in Zen as the *zazen* posture itself: the stability of the full lotus (if possible), the vertical steadiness of the straight back, the centered head, the hanging arms with hands cradled in the lap. *Zazen* is the physical enactment of Zen's internal balance, the cultivated stillness that meets every situation with peaceful equanimity. When this sitting practice is internalized, it becomes the model for all behavior, whether meditating formally or not. In the center of all changing there is a stillness that keeps balance regardless of circumstances. This explains in less esoteric terms the insistence by many roshis that Zen is nothing but *zazen*.

Perhaps the most dramatic illustration of this Zen balance is in a samurai story:

> *The code of* bushido *requires that a samurai avenge the killing of his lord. When he finally surprises the killer and raises his sword to strike, the intended victim spits in his face. The samurai sheathes his sword and walks away.*

Why did he not strike? Why did he leave without avenging his lord? Because *bushido* was also a Zen code, one that demanded action without anger, without passion, without personal attachment. In other words, with perfect balance. The samurai was angered by the insult of being spat upon, and could not act in that moment within the bounds of the code.

The practice of Taoism makes such dramatic examples unlikely. Nonetheless, its interest, as well as Zen's, is to cultivate this same inner balance. Before outer balance is possible, inner balance must be attained. Again, Suzuki Roshi:

> *But usually, without being aware of it, we try to change something other than ourselves, we try to order things outside us. But it is impossible to organize things if you yourself are not in order.*[6]

In a direct illustration of this advice, Carl Jung relates Richard Wilhelm's story of the rainmaker of Kiaochau. An old Chinese rainmaker was summoned from another province to end a devastating drought. He asked for nothing but a quiet little hut. There he locked himself in for three days. On the fourth day the drought ended. When Wilhelm asked him how he changed the weather, the old rainmaker denied direct responsibility:

> *I come from another country where things are in order. Here*
> *they are out of order . . . and I also am not in the natural*
> *order of things because I am in a disordered country. So I had*
> *to wait three days until I was back in Tao and then naturally*
> *the rain came.*[7]

The old rainmaker was echoing the words of the *Lao Tzu*:

> *Returning to the source is stillness,*
>   *which is the way of nature.*
> *The way of nature is unchanging.*[8]

This unchanging underlies the ordered flow of all changing. Taoist and Zen activity takes place within the context of its stillness, a condition that gives balance to all individual activity and to all natural processes. From the reference point of each individual person, outer balance can be effected only by inner balance; a person without this balance subverts the larger order and thereby invents circumstances to struggle against. The larger order, in turn, is a current of deeper balance that underlies what is called Nature—a view that is supported, incidentally, by the emerging science of chaos. This deeper balance is manifest in the designs and patterns of specific natural objects and in their spatial relationships to each other. Both Taoism and Zen have artistic traditions that are based on the aesthetics of such order. Like the shifting balance of Nature itself, this aesthetic has an instability and an imperfection as reminders that balance is neither absolute stillness nor absolute unchanging.

Here, again, is paradox, the logical dead end so often

encountered in Taoism and Zen—a stillness that is not still, an unchanging that changes, an emptiness that is full, a beginning before the beginning, a nothingness that is not voidness. Such difficulty is best treated with aesthetics rather than logic, for the essence of Taoism and Zen is the art of living rather than the philosophy of life. This essence is felt rather than understood. Consequently, Taoism and Zen have become inseparable from the artistic traditions in China and Japan; art has become for them a more appropriate language than reason and logic.

But even in the arts the expression of balance is created with diagonals and asymmetry. The balance is dynamic, made to seem unbalanced so that its changing character is suggested. Often the balance is implied rather than represented, placed outside the work, beyond the visual and intellectual eye of the viewer.

In the world of words, Suzuki Roshi is once more useful because he creates a feeling for the balance that underlies the practice of Taoism and Zen. Here he uses the modern metaphor of a train on railway tracks to describe the inner experience of Zen:

> *The sights we see from the train will change, but we are always running on the same track. And there is no beginning or end to the track. . . .*[9]

His comparison is like the timeless Tao with its level and balanced movement:

> *The path of the Tao is easy to follow.*
> *Only a little wisdom is needed*
> *   to walk its ancient and constant way.*[10]

All versions of this passage, whether from traditional translations of the *Lao Tzu* or the newly discovered *Ma-wang-tui texts*, use the image of a path or a road that is easy or level to travel. Another chapter echoes more of Suzuki Roshi's metaphor that "there is no beginning or end to the track. . . .":

> *Stand before it and there is no beginning.*
> *Follow it and there is no end.*
> *Stay with the ancient Tao,*
> *Move with the present.*[11]

To add yet another layer of correspondence between Taoism and Zen, consider the following lines from the *Lao Tzu* and compare them to the next quote from Suzuki Roshi:

> *Look, it cannot be seen—it is beyond form.*
> *Listen, it cannot be heard—it is beyond sound.*
> *Grasp, it cannot be held—it is intangible.*[12]

Now, here is Suzuki Roshi enlarging on his metaphor that the Way of Zen is like moving in a train on a railway track:

> *But when you become curious about your railway track, danger is there. You should not see the railway track. If you look at the track, you will become dizzy. Just appreciate the sights you see from the train. That is our way. There is no need for the passengers to be curious about the track. Someone will take care of it; Buddha will take care of it. But sometimes we try to explain the railway track because we become curious if something is always the same. We wonder, "How is it possible . . . ? What is [the] secret?" But there is no secret. Everyone has the same nature as the railway track.*[13]

Suzuki Roshi, of course, is a Zen Buddhist, so for his

"Buddha" substitute Tao, for his railway track substitute the Way, and for his "dizzy" and "curious" use lost and confused. But he might as well be describing Taoism. Just as "everyone has the same nature as the railway track," everything has the same nature as the Tao. This insight alone should offer some sense of balance since, in the largest possible sense, balance is unavoidable.

If balance is unavoidable, then why is it sought? Because, quite simply, people believe they don't have it. In both Taoism and Zen the objective—inasmuch as anything that cannot be done deliberately can be said to have an objective—seems to be to bring one's own balance into accord with the larger balance. This is neither difficult nor metaphysical. It is, in fact, ridiculously easy when, fundamentally, there is no imbalance. Because of the shapelessness of the Tao, all things are permitted to be themselves; because of the disciplined acceptance in Zen, nothing more is required than being one's self. Taoism and Zen share the insight that freedom is found and known within the confinement of what is. Nothing needs to be done or changed. This is why Taoists do not attempt to be supernatural; why Zen itself is so eminently ordinary. Both are grounded in the solidity and immediacy of the natural present. Both base their wisdom on the insight that each moment is required to be nothing more than itself. Balance is the full acceptance of each instant. As Frederick Franck writes in *Zen and Zen Classics*:

> *Zen means the freedom to be bound; we are bound by all within and without us.*[14]

Everything is bound by the nature of itself. Freedom is knowing how to live contentedly within these boundaries. Balance is remembering this freedom.

Balance comes easily when life is easy. The challenge for each person is to find the equanimity that maintains balance during unsettling circumstances. In Taoism and Zen this balance comes from a sense of unconditional openness, a spontaneous awareness that follows the contours of unfolding cirmumstances with a level and constant ease. To use Suzuki Roshi's words and metaphor once more:

> *The railway track is always the same. If it were to become wider or narrower, it would be disasterous.*[15]

The challenge, then, is to stay on the track, to cultivate the discipline and the sense of presence that keeps the wheels at the appropriate distance, that maintains the constant and balanced stance. But attention must not shift to the tracks because the ups and downs and curves of unfolding circumstances will then result in a loss of balance—like running blindfolded. The trick is to stay wholly present and to attend carefully to the world while feeling the balance within. This balance is kept in the empty center of each person but not at the center of attention. It becomes familiar rather than known, an inner and constant stance that provides readiness and stability. It accounts for every situation.

In the practice of Zen, because of Buddhism, the balancing process begins with the centering discipline of *zazen* and the disorienting-reorienting effects of the *koan*; they cultivate a state of total presence and empty receptivity. In Taoism the same condition is cultivated informally by the continual and unrelenting process of releasing from the hardness and certainty that obstructs softness and sensitivity. What occurs in both Taoism and Zen is a growing neutrality of attitude that permits the contours of circumstances to be followed without loss of balance, a particularly delicate task when this balance must be cultivated without attending to it.

The result is an instant and spontaneous adjustment to unfolding events. This is experienced as balance.

Taoism and Zen approach circumstances with a neutrality that is a balance of hardness and softness, of discipline and spontaneity. This is how the issue of duality applies to the principle of balance; both sides of everything exist similtaneously, with equal weight. By staying in balance, by moving in stillness, both self and not-self are accounted for. Both I and other, subject and object, coexist in balanced counterweight. The experience only becomes paradoxical when the balance is lost by consciously attending to it, by reflecting on it, or by trying to explain it. At this point the equilibrium is broken and, like the proverbial Zen centipede that gets entangled in its hundred legs when considering how to run, deliberation is undone by its own deliberations.

Balance is unconsidered and spontaneous. So such things as play, happiness, music making, love making—indeed, all being in the Taoist and Zen manner—are experienced as a balanced doing that happens without one thought of what to do.

Balance is also inseparable from emptiness, nothingness, softness, selflessness, and those other terms that constitute the language of Taoism and Zen. It is the operative principle, the implicit process that resolves the duality of opposites while leaving them intact. It is the shifting center, the changing middle, the dancing still point around which the parts of everything move.

Paradox

aradox defies explanation by confounding language. And it bewilders thinking that is bound by the conditions of language. Words have difficulty with a notion that *"seems contradictory, unbelievable, or absurd but that may actually be true in fact."*[1]

Taoism and Zen enter paradox; they do not explain it. They use paradox to create an insight that cannot be explained by any system of understanding. This is why Taoism and Zen initially seem so confusing. The deliberate cultivation of confusion is intended to generate an awareness that is neither logical nor linear. The result is awareness that is intuitive and spontaneous rather than rational and laborious. Paradox generates an inner tension that engenders moment-by-moment awareness without leaving any trail of connective explanation. Insight occurs by leaping rather than crawling. This process is fundamental to both the Taoist and Zen experience.

In Taoism: The Parting of the Way, Holmes Welch describes the essential paradox in the *Lao Tzu* to be that it:

> ... *lures us on with promises of power.... But in accepting these doctrines, we must reject the very rewards that have attracted us to them. We cannot practice ... unless we cease to care whether the world yields to us or not; and for that very reason it will yield.*[2]

This, too, is the classical Zen paradox: whatever is desired cannot be had; whatever is no longer desired comes of itself. Wanting gets in the way of having; seeking to know obstructs the knowing.

Richard Cavendish in *The Great Religions* expresses the Taoist paradox this way:

> *[T]he fundamental paradox is that union with Tao is not achieved by trying to achieve it. On the contrary, it is achieved by not trying to achieve anything, by ridding oneself of all desires.*[3]

Of course, the verbs that describe this process must be thought of in their passive rather than active sense because trying to rid "oneself of all desires" is a self-defeating process; any deliberate effort obstructs the union with Tao by infusing it with an element of personal willfulness. The paradox is pure Zen and is succinctly expressed in the Zen aphorism:

> *A sword cannot cut itself. Desire cannot overcome itself; self cannot understand itself; the Way cannot be followed by trying.*

The same paradox is the essential subject of Eugen Herrigel's *Zen in the Art of Archery*. It is wonderfully expressed in a dialogue when his teacher is trying to explain to him how to release the arrow without releasing it. Herrigel is told that the upper end of the bow pierces the sky and from the lower end hangs the Earth suspended by a delicate thread. The arrow must be released with such a smooth motion that the thread will not break. It is a matter of life and death:

> *"What must I do, then?" I asked thoughtfully.*
> *"You must learn to wait properly."*
> *"And how does one learn that?"*
> *"By letting go of yourself, leaving yourself and everything yours behind you so decisively that nothing more is left of you but a purposeless tension."*

*"So I must become purposeless—on purpose?" I heard myself
say.*

*"No pupil has ever asked me that, so I don't know the right
answer."*[4]

Paradox produces the condition of waiting, the "purposeless
tension" out of which comes the release, the resolution, the
leap of action or insight that is the core of the Zen and Taoist
experience.

Sometimes these paradoxes are obvious; other times
they are are implicit; sometimes they are layered in various
degrees of subtlety. Consider, for example, the Taoist principle of mutual arising, *hsiang sheng*, in which the opposites of
yin and *yang* are inextricably connected such that one generates the other. Choose one and the other is inevitably created.
The Tao is said to be one *yin* and one *yang* in dynamic balance, the still point between the opposites that is them but is
not them. Or, as the symbol for Taoism visually illustrates,
the Tao is approached by attending to the entire circle while
also attending to the rotating halves. In Zen's characteristically negative style, the process is, "Not this, not that; not both,
not neither."

The parallel in Zen that corresponds to Taoism's mutual arising is the philosophical notion of duality. Zen tends to
deal with issues of non-being and being, of mind and matter,
of detachment and connectedness, but does so exactly as
Taoism deals with *hsiang sheng*. Such a fundamental similarity
is not surprising. Despite a Buddhist influence on Zen, the
two traditions share the same root and style through their
common Chinese ancestry:

Without question, Ch'an and Zen contain many parallels to

Chinese yin-yang thought. The thrust of this traditional arche-
typal perspective was to stress balance and harmony between
female (yin) and male (yang), dark and light, soft and hard,
northside of a mountain and southside of a mountain, earth
and sky, negative and positive. In addition to harmonious
relationship, it was asserted that each quality or aspect con-
tained the seed or the germ of its opposite and would
inevitably mix with and even turn into that to which it was
originally opposed. Mutation and flow were thought to be
indispensable parts of yin-yang stability, balance, and unity.[5]

The language of Zen has become somewhat different from
Taoism's because of the Buddhist company it has kept, but
both seek insight and balance amid a "purposeless tension"
and both generate and sustain paradox for the same purpose.

To describe the same process with a slightly different
emphasis, here is Arthur Waley from *The Way and Its Power*:

But to the Taoists, Tao was at the same time within and with-
out; for in Tao all opposites are blended, all contrasts harmo-
nized.... In this identity of opposites all antinomies, not
merely high and low, long and short, but life and death them-
selves merge.[6]

Waley stresses the balance that results from the merging of
opposites. What is so logically taxing, however, is that this
harmonizing does not eliminate distinctions; indeed, it
requires them. The balance is found but the distinctions
remain. Harmonizing is not neutrality. As an equivalent in
Zen, here is R.H. Blyth from *Games Zen Masters Play*:

We have to live between the relative and the absolute, in both
at the same time.[7]

Paradox in Taoism and Zen is deliberately cultivated to create an ambivalence that feels impossible to resolve. The result is a deep confusion, a profound frustration that is intellectually debilitating and experientially freeing, both exasperating and envigorating. Think hard enough about paradoxes and sometimes it seems that they can almost be resolved. Then, just at the last moment, the solution slips into confusion, beyond intellect's reach. Then all the thought that has been invested feels like wasted effort, like absolute futility; the parts of thought that are needed for understanding will not fit together. Explanation fails. Language fails. That is exactly what is supposed to happen.

What is not widely recognized and accepted is that this failure is not peculiar to Taoism and Zen; it is pervasive and fundamental to all understanding. Any system of thought creates its own paradoxes, perpetuates them, and is incapable of resolving them. Initially, the problem seems to be a failure of language because understanding is processed with words. Words are clearly limited since every word is defined by every other word, and there are no words that are not in the dictionary. But paradox is deeper than language. It is a quality inherent in systems themselves.

The Austrian mathematician, Kurt Gödel, made this abundantly clear in his *Incompleteness Theorem* of 1931, but few philosophers have paid much attention because its consequences, like those for David Hume's *Treatise of Human Nature*, are too devastating for rational thought to contemplate seriously. Gödel's theorem seems innocent enough. It simply says:

This statement of number theory does not have any proof.[8]

As Douglas Hofstadter explains in *Gödel, Escher, Bach*, the important thing to remember is that in mathematical terms the theorem means that:

> *... proofs are demonstrations within fixed systems of propositions.*[9]

Or, to make the connection from mathematics to language and paradox, Hofstadter expresses the implications of Gödel's theorem this way:

> *The proof of Gödel's Incompleteness Theorem hinges upon the writing of a self-referential mathematical statement, in the same way as Epimenides paradox ["This statement is false."] is a self-referential statement of language.*[10]

In other words, each self-referential system cannot prove itself because it cannot get outside itself to do so. Every system builds in its own limitations by creating itself as a system. Expressed differently, no consistent system of thought can verify itself.

Words, of course, seem to make sense because they constitute a closed system that verifies itself. But the shortcoming of language is that it refers only to itself. If it attempts to get outside its own words, it violates its own conditions as a system and is no longer language.

Unfortunately for language, and for the logical thought that is so characteristic of philosophy in the West, the shortcoming in systems is even more serious than this. According to Gödel, every system eventually contradicts itself. Contradiction is inherent in all systems as a natural consequence of being closed. Paradox is the inevitable result as each system of understanding moves in a circle within the enclosure of itself. A paradox is a thought within any given system looping back to contradict itself. This defect is fundamental to every system but just happens to be most obvious in language.

In *Shifting Worlds, Changing Minds*, Jeremy W. Hayward is more specific in his application of Gödel's incompleteness theorem to language:

> *It says that any language system has to* either *contain statements that are contradictory, paradoxical, absurd;* or *be incomplete, open-ended, contain statements that are unprovable within that language system.*[11]

To put it bluntly, every statement of truth is either self-contradictory or incomplete. When this principle is translated into wider philosophical terms, it means that no system of thought can complete or justify itself. Straight thinking is a short illusion.

So the language system itself produces the indefinable, paradoxical character of Taoism and Zen. Both understand this clearly. That is why neither gives credibility to explanation, and why they devote their attention to processes that, using the system of words, seem to make no sense, or at least are paradoxical. The problem does not reside in Taoism or Zen but in the inherent limitations of a word system that attempts—with little modesty—to explain everything. When language explores far enough it invariably discovers its own contradictions and turns against itself. Its shortcomings appear in Taoism and Zen as paradoxes and *koans*, cracks that open to something other than systematic understanding.

So Taoism and Zen embrace paradox to escape paradox. They capitalize on their own systematic limitations to be free

273

from these same limitations. They play in paradox to avoid the confinement of the system that carries them, like an intellectual judo that turns the momentum of a deficiency into the force of advantage. Taoism and Zen purposefully contradict themselves. By colliding opposites together they deliberately create an unsettled condition, a conceptual confusion, so that something more than a systematic understanding is experienced. They are two expressions of the same system of thought that is actively engaged in subverting itself. Ultimately, they are not about the system that defines them.

Paradoxically, then, the Way of Taoism and Zen cannot be found in the system that bears their names. It resides outside the system. That is why the teachings of the two traditions never take themselves too seriously, and why the confusion that is generated by the collision of irreconcilable opposites is cultivated rather than avoided. Stillness and movement, detachment and involvement, abstraction and pragmatism, these attributes of a system of thought are deliberately juxtaposed to create disorientation. Profound confusion is the only way of escaping from the system that is called Taoism and Zen.

The collision of these contradictory opposites is quite apparent in institutionalized Zen, although it is somewhat confusing to those who do not expect paradox to be lived so unabashedly. On one side are the monastery, the meditation, the reverence, and the inner discipline; on the other is the earthy, practical, irreverent, spontaneous nature of Zen. For Taoism, because it did not officially institutionalize, these overt contradictions are not so apparent, but a monastery without walls can be thought of as the world at large, and the other contradictory ingredients are the same as Zen's. Or, to be more historically accurate, Zen's are the same as Taoism's.

274

For example, the *koan* of Rinzai Zen, the masterstroke of paradox and system destruction, traces its origin to Hui-neng, the Chinese patriarch from the Southern School of Ch'an. Hui-neng, who has all the qualities of a Taoist rather than a Buddhist, became recognized as the sixth Patriarch of Zen.

Paradox is much more Taoist than Buddhist. The Buddhist inclination is to move toward a resolution of duality—"not two, but one"—and thus become a religious system. The shortcoming of this Indian notion of oneness is that it denigrates separateness, distinction, and differences. Paradoxically, a larger oneness must exclude oneness to allow separateness. This paradox is what distinguishes the Taoist-like qualities of Chinese Ch'an from Mahayana Buddhism, and connects Zen to Taoism. The intellectual play that pervades Zen and elevates awareness while leaving it free from systems, is really a Taoist quality. Writes Frederick Franck:

But we must have unity as well as diversity, and so the word Zen usually refers to this depth of oneness in our depth of life. But just as deep is our experience of difference. For a thing to exist at all it must have this separateness; at the same time it has no existence if only separate.[12]

The effect of such a "unity as well as diversity" is a kind of perfection that is not perfect, an absolutism that is not absolute, an extraordinariness that is not extraordinary, a completion that becomes even more complete by renouncing itself. Zen, like Taoism, relies on the systemless. This is not like a religious system that relies on belief and consistency for its ultimate guidance. The viability of a systemless system is generated by the interaction of itself with itself to become wholly present in its own shapelessness. Its insights are opened by the dynamics of paradox. As Suzuki Roshi says when he is speaking like a Taoist with a Zen Buddhist accent:

> *But if you understand the secret of our practice, wherever you go, you yourself are "boss." No matter what the situation, you cannot neglect [the] Buddha, because you yourself are [the] Buddha.*[13]

This is Buddhism without Mahayana. It is the Zen in Buddhism and the Taoism in Zen. Make the necessary transposition of terms and Suzuki Roshi's awareness is precisely what Taoists understand by being with the Tao. The Tao is unavoidable because "you yourself" are it. But the paradox is that it cannot be deliberately practiced. Or, to cite Eugen Herrigel's memorable words again:

> *"So I must become purposeless—on purpose?" I heard myself say.*[14]

The "purposeless tension" generated by this paradox is the essential disposition of the Taoist and Zen practice. The paradox is not resolved; it dissolves into emptiness and remains suspended in a state of prepared waiting. When this waiting becomes effortless, the Way just happens of itself, and everything seems to move with a peaceful and spontaneous appropriateness.

Non-Doing

Non-doing (Chinese: *wu-wei*; Japanese: *mu-i*) is action or inaction that occurs spontaneously, selflessly, and unconditionally. Like many of the attributes shared by Taoism and Zen, the nature of non-doing itself defeats most efforts to explain it.

Consequently, non-doing is usually described in negative rather than positive terms: "By indirections find directions out."[1] It can be found only by discovering what it is not, by eliminating all the traces of deliberation, self, and restraint that obstruct it. Non-doing is found somewhat like a blind person cultivates a sense of unobstructed space by learning where to avoid obstacles, the way water finds its downward course. In Chuang Tzu's words:

> *The sound of water*
> *says what I think.*[2]

At a superficial level, non-doing seems to express itself in two forms: action and inaction. In each case a mixture of volition and passivity is accompanied by an attitude of apparent indifference. To a spectator, the action and inaction would appear to be different but from the inside they are experienced as the same. Thomas Merton's *The Way of Chuang Tzu* explains it this way:

> *The non-action of the wise man is not*
> *inaction.*
> *It is not studied. It is not shaken by*
> *anything.*
> *The sage is quiet because he is not moved,*

Not because he wills to be quiet. . . .
[His quietness] is the mirror of heaven and
earth
The glass of everything.
Emptiness, stillness, tranquillity,
tastelessness,
Silence, non-action: this is the level of
heaven and earth.
This is the perfect Tao.[3]

When non-doing appears as inaction it is peaceful, silent, and still; when it appears as action it is thoughtless, reflexive, and intuitive. As selfless action, it arises spontaneously out of the flowing continuity of events, like the movement of water is always appropriate to the circumstances of the moment. This apersonal momentum is what moves the fingers of the pianist; it seems as if no one is deliberately playing the piano, as if the player has become the instrument and the music is making itself. The same experience is cited as advice in R.H. Blyth's *Zen in English Literature and Oriental Classics*:

Draw bamboo for ten years, become bamboo, then forget all
about bamboo when you are drawing.[4]

This kind of selfless action somehow connects the artist of both East and West to a larger order, one that is akin to the Oriental understanding of the Way. Making beauty is like practicing Taoism and Zen. Beauty becomes the manifestation of some transcendent yet immanent order—it is relevant and noteworthy that in earlier times the artist's role was filled by the shaman. And sport, when it is engaged with the same inner discipline as the artist, has a quality that relates it to

280

non-doing. Even the simple art of living proceeds best without the fumbling deliberations of a self. Self narrows, confines, and obstructs the easy grace and natural joy of simply being; it spoils the freedom, prevents the spontaneity, fouls the timing that is inherent in an uncontrived life. Like non-doing, life is lived best when it is living itself. Suzuki Roshi was referring to non-doing when he said:

So if you are attached to the idea of what you have done, you are involved in selfish ideas.[5]

In this process there is an inner balance, an equilibrium that does not disturb the harmonious momentum of spontaneous happening. In Zen, as Suzuki Roshi notes:

Real calmness should be found in activity itself.[6]

From the Taoist tradition, Chuang Tzu observes the cause and consequences of lost calmness, of no longer practicing non-doing:

When an archer is shooting for nothing
He has all his skill.
If he shoots for a brass buckle
He is already nervous.
If he shoots for a prize of gold
He goes blind
Or sees two targets—
He is out of his mind!

His skill has not changed. But the prize
Divides him. He cares.
He thinks more of winning
Than of shooting—

*And the need to win
Drains his power.*[7]

Perhaps the most famous example in popular Zen literature of this active form of non-doing is in Eugen Herrigel's
account of his years of study with a Zen master of archery.
When Herrigel becomes aware that his time is Japan is limited and that his study cannot continue indefinitely, he asks his
teacher about the appropriate time for stopping. The master
says:

> *Once you have grown truly egoless you can break off at any
> time.*[8]

Later he asks how the shot can be loosed if "I" do not do it.
The master replies that:

> *"It" shoots. . . . "It" waits at the highest tension. . . . ["It"
> releases when you are] absolutely self-oblivious and without
> purpose. . . . You must act as if the goal were infinitely far
> off.*[9]

When Herrigel says he is having trouble understanding how
the target is hit, the master replies:

> *You are under an illusion . . . if you imagine that even a
> rough understanding of these dark connections would help you.
> These are processes which are beyond the reach of understand-
> ing. . . . The spider dances her web without knowing there are
> flies that will get caught in it. The fly, dancing nonchalantly on
> a sunbeam, gets caught in the net without knowing what lies in
> store. But through both of them "It" dances. So, too, the archer
> hits the target without having aimed—more I cannot say.*[10]

Pure Taoism! This "It" of the Zen master is the Tao of the Taoist tradition.

The other apparent expression of non-doing is inaction, a sensing of when to stand aside to let things do themselves, of allowing the momentum of circumstances to carry themselves. This, too, requires that self be put aside. From the *Lao Tzu* comes this Taoist advice:

> *Less and less is done*
> *Until non-action is achieved.*
> *When nothing is done, nothing is left undone.*
>
> *The world is ruled by letting things take*
> *their course.*
> *It cannot be ruled by interfering.*[11]

From a Zenrin poem comes the same understanding:

> *Just sitting quietly, doing nothing,*
> *Spring comes, and the grass grows by itself.*

In a haiku from Onitsura, this same notion is again expressed:

> *I know well*
> *That the June rains . . .*
> *Just fall.*

Such a close correspondence of non-doing in Taoism and Zen can be illustrated over and over. Consider the matter of influencing people. The *Lao Tzu* gives considerable attention to maintaining social harmony by leaving people undisturbed. Very clearly, this is not the same as neglect or indifference:

Governing a large country
is like cooking a small fish. . . .

When people are not provoked,
their lives are contented and full;
Because nothing disturbs the natural order,
everything stays in its proper place.[12]

Exactly how this is done is never explained. But people are undoubtedly guided by the same "It" that shoots the arrow and hits the target. The principle is clear. The process is in keeping with the Taoist notion of non-doing, *wu-wei*. Suzuki Roshi offers the same advice in the language of Zen:

> *To give your sheep or cow a large, spacious meadow is the way to control him. So it is with people: first let them do what they want, and watch them. This the best policy. To ignore them is not good; that is the worst policy. The second worst is trying to control them. The best one is to watch them, just to watch them, without trying to control them.*[13]

Such a passive technique for influencing others is precisely Taoism's method of "cooking a small fish"—attend to it but do not disturb it. This, in turn, is exactly the soft approach that *zazen* uses in controlling oneself. Just sit and watch the thoughts and feelings coming and going. Do not try to stop them. Do not interfere. Suzuki Roshi talks about the importance of an inner calmness and emptiness that remains undisturbed:

> *by the various images you find in your mind. Let them come, and let them go. Then they will be under control.*[14]

This process of effecting inner control is pure Taoism. Or,

when practiced for outward effect, it is the rainmaker explaining how to end a drought.

In the inner world of controlling oneself and in the outer world of influencing others, the principle of non-doing is the same. Everything is allowed to change in concurrence with an inherent and unknowable order that is synonomous with the Taoist and Zen notion of the Way—the "It" of Herrigel's archery master. In both Taoism and Zen an inner stillness is prerequisite to outer influence.

The control in the *zazen* practice of Zen is really a complete release of control, an inner stillness that ends mind's struggle with itself and permits responses to occur reflexively to the unfolding of outer events. The equivalent in Taoism is an unconditional softness that allows all experience—whether inner or outer—to flow harmoniously with the movement of all circumstances. The inner discipline of becoming undisciplined is the paradoxical art that lies at the center of the Taoist and Zen practice. Neither the results nor the influence can be predicted because there is no planning, no objective. Indeed, the rule is clear: any intentional mindfulness subverts the effect, any premeditated or deliberate cultivation of influence subverts the process by destroying the accuracy of its intuitive and reflexive spontaneity. Here again is Suzuki Roshi sounding more like a Taoist than a Zen Buddhist:

> *We say . . . to concentrate your mind on something is not the true purpose of Zen. The true purpose is to see things as they are, to observe things as they are, and to let everything go as it goes.*[15]

This ability "to see things as they are" is essential to non-doing because it is the insight that recognizes and accepts the wisdom in each thing's changing. Without recognition and acceptance, the softening that is able "to let everything go as it goes" could not happen.

The insight that sees the wisdom in each thing's changing is experienced as a stillness. It allows non-doing. The world moves yet the world is unchanged. The changing is still as it moves. That is why the Way of Taoism and Zen is understood to be a moving stillness, a still changing. Within the changing of everything, there is a pervasive stillness; within the stillness, everything changes. The stillness and the changing are experienced as the same, as if each has become the other in an unmoving balance of dancing wholeness.

From this balance of stillness and changing comes an intuitive, purposeless, selfless doing. It is experienced as a charged emptiness in which both action and inaction are spontaneous and unconsidered. Everything and nothing become the same. Everything is crucially important yet not one thing matters. Changing becomes still and stillness moves. And from this condition, non-doing happens of itself. As the *Lao Tzu* explains:

> *Proper lightness . . .*
> *springs from the root of heaviness.*
> *Proper action . . .*
> *springs from the root of stillness.*[16]

Spontaneity

*t*he allowing, the releasing, the inner freedom that gives rise to spontaneity cannot occur if any reservation exists about the source from which it arises. Spontaneity is subverted by a culture that has a defensive mythology.

The spontaneity that is such an important part of Taoism and Zen is based on a deep trust in the inherent wisdom of people and in the natural world that produced them. In *Tao: The Watercourse Way*, Alan Watts describes the situation like this:

> *If there is anything basic to Chinese culture, it is an attitude of respectful trust towards nature and human nature . . . a basic premise that if you cannot trust nature and other people, you cannot trust yourself. If you cannot trust yourself, you cannot even trust your mistrust of yourself. . . .*[1]

The intellectual judo of Watts's last sentence clears away volumes of philosophical argument. It also dispenses with the distrust that obstructs spontaneity. Children naturally have this trust. All learning is based on it. Love is based on it. And adults, without this inherent and pervasive sense of trust, could not take the personal or social risk of being wholly honest with themselves. Such a trust, which lies at the heart of Taoism and Zen, authorizes spontaneity.

Spontaneity, however, does not arise from an attitude of reckless disregard for either oneself or the world. It is neither casual nor negligent. It comes instead from a disciplined yet easy following of one's own intrinsic nature. Spontaneity is easy because it follows what is intrinsic; it is disciplined because it cannot waver from what is natural. From the deepest trust in oneself emanates the broadest trust in the world.

The idea of spontaneity arises from the ease and trust that pervade the Taoist and Zen sense of nature. In Zen these elements come together this way:

> *The seed has no idea of being some particular plant, but it has its own form and is in perfect harmony with the ground, with its surroundings. . . . And there is no trouble. This is what we mean by naturalness.*[2]

"No trouble" is what Taoists mean by spontaneous arising, *tzu-jan*. It is that condition of being in which the uncontrived self functions in accord with the larger nature of things. A baby has this connective accord because its learning has not yet interfered with its naturalness. But as soon as self-conscious deliberation appears, natural spontaneity begins to disappear. As Wordsworth said in *Intimations of Immortality*:

> *Shades of the prison house begin to close*
> *Upon the growing boy.*

The undermining of the natural condition of spontaneous being begins with the emergence of self and the consequent subject-object dichotomy that results. Later, this dichotomy is expressed as the mind-body and thought-action split. The inevitable consequence of these discriminations, of becoming enculturated, of learning and growing up, is the distraction of having to struggle with these invented divisions of wholeness. In a larger sense, however, the process is both natural and necessary because it provides the inner and outer structures of personal and social organization that are inherently human.

This same split in human awareness that initially interferes with childhood's spontaniety, eventually results in introspection and self-reflection; pure being is lost to consideration of being. This propensity of being to consider itself is both the blessing and the curse of the human condition. It is everyone's dilemma. It is also Hamlet's:

> *Thus conscience [read: self-consciousness]*
> *does make cowards of us all,*
> *And thus the native hue of resolution*
> *Is sicklied o'er with the pale cast of thought.*
> *And enterprises of great pitch and moment,*
> *. . . lose the name of action.*[3]

How is action to proceed appropriately and spontaneously without "the native hue of resolution" tripping over thoughtful deliberations? The answer is suggested in early Taoist literature. The impossible logistics of a centipede self-consciously coordinating its hundred legs first appears in the *Chuang Tzu*. This version by Thomas Merton is condensed for brevity:

> *Kui, the one-legged dragon . . .*
> *said to the centipede:*
> *"I manage my one leg with difficulty:*
> *How can you manage a hundred?"*
> *The centipede replied:*
> *"I do not manage them.*
> *They land all over the place*
> *Like drops of spit."*
> *. . . "The true conqueror is he*
> *Who is not conquered*
> *By the multitude of the small.*

> *The mind is this conqueror—*
> *But only the mind*
> *of the wise man."*[4]

Later, in a slightly different form, the centipede appears again in a playful Zen aphorism:

> *The centipede was happy, quite,*
> *Until a toad in fun*
> *Said, "Pray, which leg comes after which?"*
> *This worked his mind to such a pitch,*
> *He lay distracted in a ditch,*
> *Considering how to run.*

Learning how to run again, how to return to a mature version of childhood's thoughtless spontaneity, is both easy and difficult. In Zen's terms this is done by intellect undoing intellect, by mind beating out mind:

> *Only when you have no thing in your mind and no mind in*
> *things are you vacant and spiritual, empty and marvelous.*[5]

In Taoism's terms, such a marvelous quality as spontaneity results from unlearning learning, from discarding the constraints imposed by all cultural habits and returning to what is thoughtlessly human. The Lao Tzu expresses it like this:

> *Give up learning and put an end*
> *to your troubles.*[6]

> *Give up sainthood, renounce wisdom*
> *And it will be a hundred times better*
> *for everyone.*[7]

The access to spontaneity in Taoism and Zen is achieved by exactly the same process. The marvelous results are identical. In both traditions the very thought of what to do interferes with the doing—doing is one thing, thinking about doing is quite another. So, in the unfolding spontaneity of moment-to-moment being, doing is allowed to do itself. It just happens without interference from deliberation. Philip Kapleau notes this in *The Three Pillars of Zen*:

> *One who thinks of himself as kindhearted and sympathetic is truly neither.*[8]

Interestingly enough, in support of Zen's connection to Taoism, he validates this pronouncement with a footnote from the *Lao Tzu*:

> *The truly virtuous is not conscious of his virtue. The man of inferior virtue, however, is ever consciously concerned with his virtue and therefore he is without true virtue. True virtue is spontaneous and lays no claim to virtue.*[9]

The Taoist sage and the Zen master are not virtuous because they have no concept of virtue that they are deliberately trying to effect. Indeed, there is no *they* who are self-consciously doing. Doing is doing itself.

This is what Suzuki Roshi means when he is explaining that giving should be an act of the "big I" rather than the "small I."[10] He illustrates a more subtle understanding of the process when he recounts:

> *Dogen-zenji said, "To give is non-attachment." That is, just not to attach to anything is to give.*[11]

In other words, Zen's understanding of giving takes place

without attachment, without connection to any intention or recipient. Such giving is equivalent to the *Lao Tzu's* spontaneous "true virtue" that "lays no claim to virtue."

This Taoist sense of virtue shares with Zen a standing aside from self so that things are left to do themselves. Detachment from doing permits doing to arise thoughtlessly and spontaneously, without the labored self-involvement that imparts ulterior motives. Such doing, consequently, becomes something more than ordinary doing because it is allowed to happen within the flow of a larger, selfless wisdom. The highest form of doing in Taoism and Zen occurs without any interference from a deliberate or contriving self. The doing is happening but *no one* is doing it.

Many events in the literature of Taoism and Zen describe this experience. It is the substance of Herrigel's adventure with the art of archery. Here is another example condensed from *Zen Flesh, Zen Bones*:

> The Obaku temple in Kyoto has above its entrance gate the
> character for "The First Principle." It was drawn by Kosen
> two hundred years ago.
> As Kosen drew the character, a bold pupil was with him.
> "That is not good," he told Kosen after the first effort.
> "How is that one?"
> "Poor. Worse than before," pronounced the pupil.
> Eighty-four First Principles later Kosen was still without the
> approval of the pupil.
>
> When the young man stepped outside for a few moments,
> Kosen thought: "Now is my chance to escape his keen eye," and
> he wrote hurriedly, with a mind free from distraction.
> "A masterpiece," pronounced the pupil.[12]

This freedom from distraction allows the spontaneity that is key to the practice of Taoism and Zen. And here is an equivalent story from the Taoist tradition. It has to do with a cook and his skill at butchering oxen:

> *Prince Wen Hui remarked, "How wonderfully you have mastered your art."*
> *The cook laid down his knife and said, "What your servant really cares for is Tao, which goes beyond mere art. When I first began to cut up oxen, I saw nothing but oxen. After three years of practicing, I no longer saw the ox as a whole. I now work with my spirit, not with my eyes. My senses stop functioning and my spirit takes over."*[13]

Everyone has experienced the opposite effect. It happens when self-consciousness gets in the way of doing and the most familiar acts can no longer be performed. The shift of attention causes doing to stumble over itself in what might be called the "the centipede syndrome." It results when doing becomes too intentional. Deliberate trying gets in the way of doing when doing is no longer trusted to do itself.

This trust is founded on the insight that the unfolding of circumstances proceeds with an inherent wisdom that is greater than one's own deliberateness, and that individual volition is a part of that wisdom but not all of it. All individual activity can be attuned to this unfolding by being receptive to its movement and by softening to its course. Learning continues and skills are honed but they are understood and expressed as an integral part of a larger wisdom than one's own interests. Spontaneity happens when there is no interference with this larger wisdom.

Spontaneity begins with a subtle and delicate detachment, a gentle and patient distancing from what is learned, from what is considered, and from what is owned as personal. The purpose of detachment in Taoism and Zen is to provide the necessary space in which direct and spontaneous action can occur. Such distancing prevents the doing from being crowded by deliberation. At the same time, it permits a special closeness.

Slowly, by standing aside from oneself, the doing begins to happen easily because it is unimpeded by ownership. Deliberation recedes. Distancing reveals an inner center of balanced emptiness that is full yet devoid of explanation, always ready because it is always receptive. This empty center is a formless wisdom that is entered by gently opening to its emptiness. The distancing, the separation, the detachment creates an opening that fills with spontaneity.

This empty source of spontaneity is the "mind within the mind," an expression used in early Taoism and modern Zen, what Hui-neng alluded to when he purportedly said that, "The essence of mind is intrinsically pure.

It is helpful to think of this inner space as a process rather than a thing, as a condition of consciousness that experiences but does not conceptualize. This "essence of mind" is really a thoughtless emptiness, a no-mind (Chinese: *wu-hsin*; Japanese: *mushin*), a receptivity that responds but is unself-consciousness and undeliberating.

The still and empty center out of which doing arises of itself is unimpeded by thoughtfulness. This doing is insightfully intuitive. It occurs like a reflex, coming from inner sensitivity rather than considered responses to outer appearances. The Ch'an question asks and then answers:

"What is the solution that accounts for every situation?"
"As the situation arises."

The solution occurs directly, without an intermediary condition of concepts. Such doing arises from the fullness of the empty center, like the aesthetic hunches that lead an artist toward the creation of beauty. There is preparation but no formula. The *Lao Tzu* says:

> *Therefore the sage is guided by what he feels*
> *and not by what he sees.*[14]

The Way in Taoism and Zen is more accurately an aesthetic process of being than a philosophy of life. Living means cultivating an intuitive spontaneity that becomes one with the unfolding of circumstances. This spontaneity, arising from trust, reconnects the divided inner and outer.

The spontaneous arising, *tzu-jan*, is really authorized by trust. This is mentioned once again because, without trusting that the intrinsic self can exist in accord with the nature of the Way, no basis exists for allowing spontaneity. As Alan Watts said:

> *[W]ithout this underlying trust in the whole system of nature*
> *you are simply paralyzed.*[15]

So spontaneity must derive from both the inner world that is called self and the outer self that is called the world. Ultimately, the process for attaining spontaneity requires total acceptance and complete trust because the inner and the outer cannot be separated into I and it—each is the other. So Taoism and Zen do not attempt to transcend anything; neither self nor the world. They remain grounded within the circle of direct experience, connected to it but not oppressed by it. They work within all systems of thought to negate the confining effects of these systems. This is succinctly illustrated by Suzuki Roshi when he quotes Dogen-zenji as saying:

> To study Buddhism is to study ourselves. To study ourselves is to forget ourselves.[16]

Make the necessary transposition, of course, and read "Zen" for "Buddhism." But the idea is clearly the desystemization of systems. Now compare the words from Dogen with the words from the *Lao Tzu*: "The sage has no mind of his own."[17]

This is what Paul Reps means in *Zen Telegrams* when he writes:

> *cucumber*
> *unaccountably*
> *cucumbering*[18]

The cucumber is wholly engaged in being a cucumber—no ambivalence, no doubt, no reservations, no questions. Yet, it is wholly selfless. It has disappeared into its selfless self. It is so occupied with being a cucumber that it cannot not be a cucumber. The challenge in Taoism and Zen is to discover an equivalent way of being.

The total lack of contrivance in Taoism and Zen is the source of spontaneity. The cucumber has the secret. And this offers another explanation of how inner becomes one with the outer. Here again is Suzuki Roshi speaking with his Buddhist accent:

> To have some deep feeling about Buddhism is not the point; we just do what we should do, like eating supper and going to bed. This is Buddhism.[19]

When all doing is happening with the spontaneity of just being ordinary, this is living the practice of Taoism and Zen. The simplicity of this process becomes difficult only when considered. Attach a self, and spontaneity becomes impossible because all doing is now confined by a conceptual point of reference and owned by a source that purports to manage the doing.

To have a Zen mind is to return to the freshness of a beginner's mind, to return to the uncarved block, the *p'u* of Taoism. The separateness of inner and outer is forgotten so they reunite. The result is a whole awareness that is fully present. Yet, because of its lightness and its transparence, it is not aware of itself. In a self that is not aware of self, spontaneity just happens. Again from Suzuki Roshi:

> *When we forget ourselves, we actually are the true activity of the big existence, or reality itself. When we realize this fact, there is no problem whatsoever in the world, and we can enjoy our life without feeling difficulties.*[20]

At the center of this experience of "no problem" is a stillness that changes, a changing stillness that is like the flowing of water—the water moves but the river remains unchanged. The river is the stillness; the flowing of the water is the moving circumstances. The trust that the river will remain is not diminished by the water's changing:

> *Zen is not something that changes and grows; it is the changing and the growing itself.*[21]

So Zen is process, the dynamic of balancing that occurs within omnipresent change. In a curious reversal of semantics, the changing becomes the unchanging. Or, to express the same idea with a hint of the balance that is the hallmark of Taoism, trust the changing more than the change.

At the center of Taoism and Zen is an amorphous balance, a certain softness that remains the same in spite of changing circumstances. This balance changes spontaneously while maintaining its shapeless center, like water thoughtlessly takes the shape that every situation demands while retaining its integrity as river. This analogy is useful, but it is misleading because neither Taoism nor Zen conceptualizes either the water or the river.

Nonetheless, the metaphorical quality of water appears frequently in the literature of both traditions. Although the metaphor is less overt in Zen, water's attributes are still implicit in a great deal of its description. Again, here is Suzuki Roshi speaking like a Taoist:

> *The important thing in our understanding is to have a smooth, free-thinking way of observation. We have to think and to observe things without stagnation. We should accept things as they are without difficulty. Our mind should be soft and open enough to understand things as they are. When our thinking is soft, it is called imperturbable thinking. This kind of thinking is always stable. It is called mindfulness.*[22]

This soft mindfulness that Suzuki Roshi describes is virtually identical to Taoism's understanding of water.

But the comparisons go further. The softness of water, which is so representative of movement in Taoist thought, is also the perfect image for the spontaneity that Taoism shares with Zen. Regardless of obstacles, water finds its downward course: through, around, under, or over. When an opportunity occurs, water moves spontaneously. When not moving, it rests in a condition of easy and constant readiness. Here again is

Suzuki Roshi, this time describing the state of readiness in Zen:

> *If we are prepared for thinking, there is no need to make an effort to think. This is called mindfulness. Mindfulness is, at the same time, wisdom. By wisdom we do not mean some particular faculty or philosophy. It is the readiness of the mind that is wisdom.*[23]

Readiness, then, is more than a synonymn for a spontaneous doing. It is also an empty and thoughtless condition of responsiveness that is the source of insight. In this effortless readiness of Zen is an intuitive wisdom that is identical to the *te*, the virtue-power of Taoism. From the integrity that is possessed by each thing being unpretentiously itself, comes the larger wisdom of the Way.

When people are naturally themselves, when they are unfashioned by any preconception about what they ought or ought not be, and who they might or might not be, they inadvertently become one with the wholeness of things. This does not make them "perfect" according to some narrow system of idealistic judgment. But it does give them an integrity of being that intuitively and spontaneously follows a wisdom that is greater than themselves.

301

Ordinariness

So close, so immediate, so ordinary. And yet, for all the heroic effort to follow the Way of Taoism and Zen, it remains frustratingly elusive. As Alan Watts noted:

> . . . in Zen there is always the feeling that awakening is something quite natural, something startlingly obvious. . . .[1]

How can the obvious be so elusive? Why is the easy so difficult? The *Lao Tzu* expresses the same dilemma for Taoism:

> These words are easy to understand,
>   and these teachings are easy to follow.
> But no one understands the words,
>   and no one follows the teachings.[2]

The elusiveness of the ordinary should not surprise anyone who remembers that the little words are the most difficult to define, that the commonest of human experiences are the most difficult to understand. Why? Because such things are themselves the fundamentals of thought and experience. The ordinary is immune to understanding because it cannot be placed outside human experience for examination. The ordinary is the frame of reference that defines all answers. And all questions, too. What is red, love, dead, or salty? Such questions can only be answered in terms of blue, hate, alive, or sweet.

Asking such questions converts direct experience into linguistic and conceptual metaphor. Their answers, too, are also metaphor, representations that are no longer direct expe-

305

rience. So the real answer to any fundamental question is experience itself.

The first mistake is asking the first question. It obscures the clarity of pure being by superimposing a convention of metaphor upon it and then expecting that this system of words will be able to say something meaningful about an experience that is only itself. The dog cannot catch its own tail; the circle of thinking cannot find its first thought. The ordinary is absolute.

Ordinary experience, just being natural, is the answer to all fundamental questions. People who do not understand this are like the man in the Zen adage who rides a donkey in search of the donkey he is riding. Such answers are so elusive because they are the questions.

From the early tradition of Ch'an comes a dialogue reported in Chapter 19 of the *The Gateless Gate* (Chinesse:*Wumen kuan*; Japanese: *Mumonkan*):

> *"What is the Tao?" asked Chao-chou.*
> *"Your ordinary mind is the Tao," said Nan-ch'uan.*
> *"How can it be found?"*
> *"By searching for it, it is lost."*
> *"But," persisted Chao-chou, "without searching, how can it be found?"*
> *Nan-ch'uan replied, "The Tao is neither found nor lost, neither known nor not-known. It belongs to no category. Knowing it is impossible; not-knowing it is folly. Understanding the Tao is like understanding empty sky. This has nothing to do with opposites?"*

The trick is to be wholly empty while remaining receptive to concrete and specific experience. The boundless mystery of life is vividly explained merely by being alive. Ask someone who is about to die. Just being alive is what makes the ordinary so extraordinary. Being fully present explains the meaning of life; being wholly empty provides the receptivity that understands this explanation. There is nothing else to know. After the diver has taken the greatest breath and plunged into the darkest depth in search of the deepest truth, the answer can only live in the bright air of the surface. This is why all mythological heroes who survive the journey of their quest finally return to the place where they began. The end is the beginning. The ordinary is the answer.

But the dive, like the quest, is necessary. The shedding of the ordinary permits the diver to resurface and breathe again. The old is made new. The heavy becomes light. The ordinary is transformed into the extraordinary. The sun is brighter and warmer. And the trees are freshly ablaze with green. The dive is so difficult because the knowing that is known but not recognized must be wholly lost to be rediscovered. Each person must trust that the dark sinking will be followed by a sure rising, and that the struggling consciousness will flood again with empty sky.

Moment by moment the same old ordinary reappears, rejuvenates, and teaches. Here is Mahakasyapa's smile offered to the Buddha's flower. Here is the child's birth-cry, the smell of fresh grass, the dew on the morning spiderweb. The eye sees. The ear hears. And the heart softly understands. The cycle of time, seasons, and generations continues on its profoundly ordinary course. Basho writes:

See: surviving sons
Visit the ancestral grave . . .
Bearded, with bent canes.

307

A traditional Zen story, related in a number of versions, describes the same insight:

> *An old master was commissioned to write a verse celebrating the birth of the first son of the emperor.*
> *On his finest piece of paper he wrote, "Grandfather dies, father dies, son dies."*
> *The emperor was furious and summoned the master to explain himself.*
> *The old man replied, "This is the proper order of things. If the father should die before the grandfather, this would be a tragedy. If the son should die before the father, this, too, would be a tragedy. How else," asked the master, "would you prefer it?"*

Trusting and accepting the ordinary is a theme that runs through the heart of Taoism and Zen. From the *Lao Tzu*:

> *In dwelling, be close to the land.*
> *In meditation, go deep in the heart.*[3]

And from the *The Gospel According to Zen*:

> *The song of the birds, the voices of insects, all are means of conveying truth to the mind; in flowers and grasses we see messages of the Way. The scholar, pure and clear of mind, serene and open of heart, should find in everything what nourishes him.*[4]

Being ordinary, being naturally simple, is the balanced center between words and the invented poles of opposites. Ordinariness is the neutral position that does not generate the dance of metaphor or abstraction. It is just being, totally free from unjustified pretention or unnecessary humility.

Perhaps this condition of balanced wholeness is best expressed in literature as *haiku*, a succinct verse form that conveys ordinary experience without intellectually coloring it. In the world of words, *haiku* comes closest to capturing the poignant extraordinariness of the ordinary, to saying something that is similtaneously lofty and grounded. Again, Basho:

> *Come! Let's go see*
> *The real flowers . . .*
> *Of this painful world.*

Beauty and pain are both embraced in the wisdom of the ordinary. Both are accepted and trusted so that the balanced wholeness of personal experience becomes one with natural wisdom. The *Chuang Tzu* offers this affirmation of the ordinary:

> *The great earth burdens me with a body, causes me to toil in*
> *life, eases me in old age, and rests me in death. That which*
> *makes my life good, makes my death good also.*[5]

It is important to live the moment with both the head and the heart while knowing in the bones that the flow of life's course has a simple and inexorable appropriateness. So the *Lao Tzu* declares:

> *It is . . . important*
> *To see the simplicity,*
> *To realize one's true nature. . . .*[6]

This "true nature" is ordinariness. When it is wholly trusted, living is imbued with an easy grace, a plain humility, and a simple elegance. Those who unconditionally accept the absolute of the ordinary have a grounded presence, a fullness that allows the complete range of human experience within the equilibrium of a natural balance. The Taoist sage or the Zen master is not some disembodied spirit that is detached from the affairs of the heart and flesh. Here is a description from Fung Yu-lan's translation of the *Chuang Tzu*:

> *His mind is free from all thoughts. His demeanor is still and*
> *silent. His forehead beams with simplicity. He is cold as*
> *autumn, and warm as spring, for his joy and anger occur as*
> *naturally as the four seasons.*[7]

The "joy and anger" occur naturally and spontaneously but they have been balanced by a subtle detachment that places them in the perspective of "the four seasons," the round wholeness of the birth-death cycle. With this perspective the "mind is free from all thought" and the "demeanor is still and silent." A special closeness owns the full range of human experience, yet a delicate distance keeps them from becoming disquietingly personal. The owning expresses itself as a groundedness; the distancing expresses itself as an easiness and a grace. In such a balanced condition, simplicity is not tempted by indulgence; the ordinary necessities are enough. So excesses are not moral issues in Taoism and Zen; they are merely distractions. This attitude in Taoism appears as:

> *The five colors blind the eye.*
> *The five tones deafen the ear.*
> *The five flavors dull the taste.*
> *Racing and hunting madden the mind.*
> *Precious things lead one astray.*[8]

The following example from the Zen tradition is nearly the

identical observation, couched with the same intention to maintain inner balance:

> Strong wine, fat meat, peppery things, very sweet things, these
> have not real taste; real taste is plain and simple.
> Supernatural, extraordinary feats do not characterize a real
> man; a real man is quite ordinary in behaviour.[9]

To stress the importance of ordinariness in Taoism and Zen, their teachings sometimes use earthy examples. Here is a Taoist dialogue between Chuang Tzu and Tung Kwo reported in Thomas Merton's *The Way of Chuang Tzu*:

> Master Tung Kwo asked Chuang:
> "Show me where the Tao is found."
> Chuang Tzu replied:
> "There is nowhere it is not to be found."
> The former insisted:
> "Show me at least some definite place where
>   the Tao is found."
> "It is in the ant," said Chuang.
> "Is it in some lesser being?"
> "It is in the weeds."
> "Can you go further down the scale of
>   things?"
> "It is in this piece of tile."
> "Further?"
> "It is in this turd."[10]

The essential teaching of this Taoist dialogue appears later in *The Gateless Gate*:

> A monk asked Ummon, "What is Buddha?"
> "It is shit-wiping stick," replied Ummon.[11]

The profane is sacred. The ordinary is wisest. The higher people rise from their connection to the ground the farther they move from essential wisdom. Great people without a countervailing humility are more than foolish; they are also dangerous.

The final word on this subject is adapted from the traditional literature of *Chuang Tzu*. It does not stress the danger of foolishness, but it does illustrate the importance of ordinariness:

> *With his bamboo pole Chuang Tzu was fishing peacefully from the bank of the Pu River. Two officials from the Imperial Court approached him.*
> *"Master Chuang," they announced, "as duly authorized by the Prince of Chu, we hereby appoint you Prime Minster."*
> *Chuang Tzu kept fishing, never glancing up from the river.*
> *"I am told," he said, "that on an altar in the temple of the Court there is a sacred tortoise. It is three thousand years old. It is wrapped in rare silk, venerated and honoured. Now, do you see that tortoise over there on the riverbank? Which would you rather be, the dried old tortoise shell in the temple or that live tortoise dragging its tail in the mud?"*
> *"For the tortoise it would be better to be alive, dragging its tail in the mud," said one of the officials.*
> *"Then," said Chuang Tzu, "leave me here to drag my tail in the mud."*

Playfulness

*t*he playfulness that is so conspicuous in Taoism and Zen is not an indication of superficiality. Rather, it is an expression of the profound insight that lies below the surface of appearances. Sobriety struggles with the world; playfulness dances with it.

The instinct that holds life as valuable must also hold it as worthless. Without this balance of opposite measures, life would be a commodity too valuable to spend on living. Without the reckless and defiant laugh, life could not properly risk, change, flourish, and spend itself. As Robert Louis Stevenson wrote in his essay, *Aes Triplex*:

> *We may trick [ourselves] with the word life in its dozen senses until we are weary of tricking; we may argue in terms of all the philosophies on earth; but one fact remains true throughout—that we do not love life, in the sense that we are greatly preoccupied about its conservation; that we do not, properly speaking, love life at all, but living. . . .*

This insight recognizes that life lives itself by tricking everyone to follow what it demands. Anyone with a sense of humor will realize how this joke places all sobriety in the context of playfulness.

So playfulness always has a double edge; it is the levity offering balance to a game that is deadly serious. Its apparent irreverence is really an affirmation and a celebration of life's own freedom to be itself. Playfulness balances what would otherwise be discouragingly heavy and weary. Without both halves, the whole of life would be crippled.

Since the rules of life are absolute and irrevokable, what

choice is there but to accept them gracefully and play within their confinement? When placed beside the serious finality of life, the rules of people seem relative, arbitrary, and often foolish. But people take them seriously. So these rules are seen for their serious whimsy and they too become the ground of play.

What is the difference between the absolute and the arbitrary? Nothing. For opposite reasons play treats them as the same. The inevitability of destiny deserves a smile; and the nonsense of others also deserves a smile. There is no better option.

Therefore, in the middle of a cold winter night at a Zen monastery, Tanka burns the wooden Buddha for warmth. And Shoju, to keep ablaze the living vitality of Zen, throws into a fire the written teachings of seven generations of masters. Chuang Tzu's crooked tree stands as a monument to the usefulness of being useless. Even the *Lao Tzu*, with its notably sober tone, gives considerable attention to playing with the serious efforts of moralists and officials who try to control and organize what insists on happening of itself. The game of life makes its own rules, and the wise have little option but to adopt them as their own. After thoughtfully reading this old Chinese masterpiece it is difficult to conform to propriety and convention without a smile.

But playfulness is serious. Behind its lightness is the deep smile of insight, the belly laugh of a cosmic joke:

In Zen, laughter is not merely permitted, it is insisted upon.[1]

The insight feeding this laughter comes from a gentle distancing that sees the human condition in the context of the greater Way. The view comes from a balance of detachment and involvement, from someplace where a compassionate perspective sees the magnificent silliness of human endeavor. All its busyness, its invented pomp and rituals, its individual and collective folly, is serious nonsense. And the grandness of self-importance is the empty bubble so easily popped by the common act of dying. Without this perspective, even the sorry drama of personal tragedy would somehow misrepresent itself. Distancing creates a clarity so that when it meets the seriousness of life, they remember their togetherness and greet each other with smiles and laughter.

Perspective is prerequisite for playfulness. The human condition is best experienced from an intimate and accepting distance. Consider the old hunchback called Shu:

His chin rested on his navel, his shoulders rose up over his head, and his neck bone pointed to the sky. His five vital organs were upside down, and his hips were level with his ribs. By sewing and taking in laundry, he made enough to feed himself. By winnowing and sifting grain, he earned enough to support ten people. When the authorities were raising an army, he came and went without having to hide. When a big public project was planned, he was assigned no work. When the government was giving free grain to the sick, he received three measures and ten bundles of firewood. If a man whose body is strange can live to the end of his natural life, how much easier it is for a man with strange behaviour.[2]

This is playfulness with a serious edge, nonsense with an uncommon sense. From Zen comes a story that is very different but the method in the madness is the same:

Two Zen teachers, Daigu and Gudo, were invited to visit a lord. Upon arriving, Gudo said to the lord: "You are wise by

nature and have an inborn ability to learn Zen."
"Nonsense," said Daigu. "Why do you flatter this blockhead?
He may be a lord, but he doesn't know anything of Zen."
So, instead of building a temple for Gudo, the lord built it for
Daigu and studied Zen with him.[3]

Bunsei's delightful fifteenth-century drawing, *The Three Laughters of Tiger Ravine,* shows a Taoist, a Confucian, and a Buddhist circled together in uproarious laughter. Apparently the Buddhist had taken a vow never to leave the monastery but, in the enthusiasm of visiting with his two friends, he inadvertently wanders over the bridge of the ravine that defines the monastery's grounds. The distant roar of a tiger breaks the spell of their visit and they realize the vow of confinement has been broken. They clasp each other's hands and laugh.[4] This is the playful spirit that supercedes vows and teachings and ideologies.

Even death, hardly a subject for playful treatment, receives a dusting of lightness in Taoism and Zen. Chuang Tzu beats on a bowl and sings at the death of his wife to show that:

> *. . . if I were to start bawling and bewailing her, I would merely show that I did not understand destiny.*[5]

Acceptance of death as a statement of fulfillment and an act of completion is illustrated in a traditional Zen story:

> *An old abbot had decided to stop eating and die. The monastery was poor, the winter was cold and the food was scarce. Unable to contribute any longer, the old man realized he was a drain on the scant resources. His students gathered around him, beseeching him to eat and remain with them. But*

the old man was resolved. His life was fulfilled and his teaching was completed.

But, his students pointed out, dying in mid-winter would be a miserable time for a funeral, for the grave-digging and all the other necessities that would have to follow his death. Could he not choose a more comfortable time of year to die?

So the old abbot ate again until spring. Then he fasted, and died.

For every Zen story that playfully deals with death there seems to be another that comes from the Taoist tradition. Here again is a sample from the *Chuang Tzu*. When one of a group of three friends died, Confucius sent a disciple to help the other two chant the required obsequies. The disciple arrived to discover that one of the surviving friends was singing his own song and the other was playing the lute. The rest of the story is recounted in Thomas Merton's *The Way of Chuang Tzu*. They sang:

"Hey, Sung Hu!
Where'd you go?
Hey, Sung Hu!
Where'd you go?
You have gone
Where you really were.
And we are here -
Damn it! We are here!"
Then the disciple of Confucius burst in on them and exclaimed:
"May I inquire where you found this in the rubrics for obsequies, this frivolous carolling in the presence of the departed?"
The two friends looked at each other and laughed: "Poor fellow," they said, "he doesn't know the new liturgy!"[6]

This story, of course, is a Taoist joke at the expense of the Confucians. But it is also a joke about death and life. The "new liturgy" is a defiant response to the confining effect of all conventions and traditions, and therefore to all understanding. Neither Taoism nor Zen is comfortable with those conditions that intrude on spontaneity, that obscure insight, that limit the full range of personal responsiveness.

Playfulness is a kind of reverent disregard for imposed limits, a kind of happy defiance. It is warm spirited and positive for those with the perspective to see beyond stodgy propriety. In archetypal terms, the clown has always been the sage, wisdom dressed in a laugh. In practical terms, playfulness is the disruption that unbalances to create a wider and more durable balance.

Playfulness disrupts because it arises from a knowing that is other than meaning. It is the act that emanates from the unknowable midpoint between the poles of tragedy and absurdity. It disrespects convention because it answers to insights that cannot be explained. It is a constant and unpredictable reminder that all things are greater than the systems that contain them. Playfulness is trust dancing with an indefinable order.

Suchness

f all the attributes shared by Taoism and Zen, perhaps suchness is the most difficult to describe. It is simply what is—experience without any complications from questions, considerations, concepts, or thoughts. Suchness is a just-so-ness that allows things to be themselves. It is reached by emptying, by unlearning, by forgetting all the constructs of thinking that have been imposed by enculturation. The *Lao Tzu* offers frequent instructions to this effect. One example will suffice:

> *In the pursuit of learning,*
> *everyday something is acquired.*
> *In the pursuit of Tao,*
> *everyday something is dropped.*[1]

In *Zen and Zen Classics*, the same notion is expressed by Frederick Franck:

> *What is Zen? Zen is the unsymbolization of the world and all*
> *the things in it.*[2]

This "unsymbolization" is an essential step in the realization of suchness. Awareness is freed of symbolic thinking so it can return to direct experience. Suchness happens when perception is released from conceptual constructs so "the world and all the things in it" can be perceived without interpretation through ideological, philosophical, or intellectual tampering. Suchness is everything intrinsically itself. It is the result of direct experience without any interference by symbolism, metaphor, judgment, prejudice, or systems.

That is why suchness cannot be explained by the

metaphorical character of language. Language invariably fails to capture suchness because words immediately transform direct experience into the shape and form of the system that is trying to express it. Suchness has no analogy, no symbolic, representational, or abstract equivalent of itself. The dilemma that language has with suchness is analogous to the in-here/out-there enigma that quantum mechanics faces when examining the subatomic world. This is the same subject-object split that is illustrated so nicely by Alan Watts in *The Way of Zen*:

> *When we look for things there is nothing but mind, and when we look for mind there is nothing but things.*[3]

Look in mind to find mind; look in things to find things; look in words to find words. But words chase themselves in circles trying to explain things that are not words. There are words but they are themselves; and they are not to be confused with anything else.

The best that language can do is point to suchness, for it is no more in words than a destination is in a finger's pointing. Look where the words point. Suchness is there in the emptiness that fills with awareness—not magical, not metaphysical, not even transcendent. Suchness is profoundly ordinary. This is why it is so elusive. As R.H. Blyth writes on behalf of Zen:

> *. . . with satori or without it, the world is unchanged.*[4]

Or, as Suzuki Roshi says when he is speaking as a Zen master but sounding like a Taoist sage:

> *. . . it is a heretical view to expect something outside this world.*[5]

So suchness has something to do with acceptance, with an unconditional receptivity to the world just as it is. It is uncolored by words, concepts, or self-interest. It is reality experienced directly with an unconcerned mind, with a totally neutral attitude, with an absolute indifference that is fully present in the fullness of each moment.

Furthermore, suchness is only suchness when it is so engaged in experience that it is wholly unaware of itself; it has no subject-object split. It has no self at its center so it cannot occur when a separate "I" is experiencing. It happens spontaneously, and can be neither forced nor uncontrived. It is not volitional because it is not connected to self or doing or knowing or desiring. Suchness happens of itself when awareness hangs suspended in the receptivity of emptiness.

In Taoism and Zen, suchness is accommodated by emptying. This is the process of clearing away the attitudes, the judgments, the roles, and all the conditioned patterns of thinking and feeling that shape ordinary experience. This means no questions, no answers, no explanations, no justifications, no rationalizations, no utilitarianism. It also means no moralizing, no personifying, no empathizing. In brief, none of the ways in which experience is directed by purposefulness, self-centeredness, and the dispositions of learning.

A clarity of insight occurs when perception is unconstrained and unregulated by the controlling character of culture. Suchness is awareness without sanctions, without restraint, without interpretation, or organization. It is pure awareness, pure experience dancing lightly in the whole freedom of absolute emptiness.

Much of the long spiritual tradition of the East has been directed toward attaining this freedom of awareness. In the

West, with the exception of a few religious mystics such as Meister Eckhart, the practice and experience have not been common. In both East and West, however, religion usually clouds suchness with some notion of divinity. Suchness disappears promply when it becomes associated with religion.

Perhaps the first and best secular example of suchness in the West is described by the eighteenth-century French philosopher, Jean Jacques Rousseau. On his island refuge in Switzerland's Lake of Bienne he had an experience that did much to revolutionize European thought and prepare the modern West for Eastern thinking. Sir Kenneth Clark in *Civilisation* describes Rousseau's experience:

> *In listening to the flux and reflux of the waves, he tells us, he became completely at one with nature, lost all consciousness of an independent self, all painful memories of the past or anxieties about the future, everything except the sense of being. "I realized," he said, "that our existence is nothing but a succession of moments preceived through the senses."*[6]

This was Rousseau's glimpse of suchness. His experience was the result of clearing away "everything except the sense of being." He came to the same awareness that is nurtured in the practice of Taoism and Zen.

Suchness is being wholly present in the selfless moment. And time without self is timeless. This was the experience of time probably mistaken by the *hsien* Taoists to mean physical time and then interpreted as eternal life.

Selflessness experiences without time. Such timelessness is also the stillness and the full emptiness of Taoism and Zen. Chapter 47 of *The Gateless Gate* describes this moment:

> *An instant realization sees endless time.*

Endless time is as one moment.

When one comprehends the endless moment

He realizes the person who is seeing it.[7]

This "person" is no one and everyone, pure awareness unbounded by the limits of a defined center called self. Suchness is experienced without person, without time, in a condition of receptive emptiness. Here again is *The Gateless Gate* expressing this same understanding in different words:

. . . *if you free yourself from birth and death, you should know where you are.*[8]

This "where" is the suchness of everything; this "you" is the suchness of self. Everything is as it is; self is an emptiness brimming with inexplicable awareness.

As a consequence of emptying, there is fullness, and a perpetual freshness of perception that is akin to living a timeless, precultural existence. So the analogy of childhood is often used to describe suchness. The *Lao Tzu* makes several references to this state. Two are cited here:

Become as a little child once more.[9]

Those who follow the Tao

seem like newborn infants.[10]

Zen stories are saturated with conduct that seems superficially childish.

But the process employed in Taoism and Zen is not a reversion to childhood; it is the emptying of adulthood. The reference to childhood is metaphorical. Suchness, then, has a freshness, an innocence, an immediate presence about itself that is devoid of the values of all learning. The apparent air of

327

childhood is really the simple clarity of experience released from values, utilitarianism, shoulds, musts, and what ifs. This quality is illustrated in a Zen story, adapted here from *Zen Flesh, Zen Bones*:

> *Hakuin was praised by his neighbors for living a pure life. When a beautiful young woman in the village confessed to her parents that she was pregnant with Hakuin's child, they angrily confronted him.*
> *His only reply was, "Is that so?"*
> *After the child was born it was brought to Hakuin, who by now had lost his reputation and credibility as a teacher. Without a question he took the child and cared for it.*
> *A year later the young woman could no longer endure her dishonesty. She confessed that the real father was a young man who worked in the fishmarket.*
> *The parents went immediately to Hakuin to beg for his forgiveness and to retrieve the child. Without a pause he gave it to them. "Is that so?" was his only reply.*[11]

The essential nature of suchness is profound neutrality, inner stillness, and clarity that sees through the contesting poles of right and wrong, guilt and innocence, justice and injustice:

> *Lucid means seeing unreason as clearly as reason, reflecting ugliness as serenely as beauty.*[12]

Suchness has no room for the conflict of good and bad. It has no invented demon-ghosts whose constant cunning must be warded off with an inner posture of persistant vigilance. An understanding like this offers only perpetual struggle; even the walls of Heaven could be breached by the forces of Hell, and the nothingness of Nirvana could be assailed by the evil of Desire. The neutrality of suchness is as open and trusting as the child.

The essential prerequisite for this neutrality is trust, an innocence that allows emptying to take place and be filled with whatever should come. Trust also allows the uninterrupted unfolding of moment-by-moment experience. So Alan Watts's insightful observation is once more appropriate:

> *If we cannot trust ourselves, then we cannot trust our distrust of ourselves.*[13]

This "ourselves" is not self-centeredness. It is experience without self as the center of experience, what Mencius (371-289 B.C.) meant when he said, "Everything is complete within us."
Or, to quote once more the Zen aphorism, which says the same thing somewhat differently:

> *If you do not get it from yourself, where will you go for it?*

The irony in Taoism and Zen is that self, like language and culture, is eventually discovered to be a construction that cannot be kept if suchness is to be experienced. The advice to "get it from yourself" is an invitation to step into thin air. The plunge through emptiness to suchness begins by discovering the changing insubstantiality of self.

The idea of self is a reference that confines awareness. It is what Joseph Campbell meant when he said in *The Power of Myth*:

> *Fear is the first experience of the fetus in the womb. . . . Fear is the first thing, the thing that says "I."*[14]

A preoccupation with I, like an obsession with fear, is debilitating. So self, in Taoism and Zen, is not *the* center but *a* center, a soft and flexible persona this is worn for the practical purpose of identification. This was Alan Watts's point when he said that he was not really Alan Watts, he was only called Alan Watts. An absolute self eventually cracks under the accumulated weight of itself; a hard and rigidly defined self eventually breaks because it cannot adjust to the changing nature of its own experience. Ralph Waldo Emerson wrote in his essay *Self-Reliance*, "A foolish consistency is the hobgoblin of little minds."

Insight reveals self to be a "foolish consistency." As "little minds" become larger the need for consistency and definition declines, and the bending self becomes progressively more amorphous until it finally disappears in all but name. Indeed, self cannot reach suchness carrying the weight of its own awareness.

Awareness that is not personalized is not burdened or confined, is not encumbered or distracted. Then suchness just happens. The experience is clear, unequivocal, and unquestionable. It has to be trusted simply because there is nothing else to trust. This is what Joseph Campbell meant when he was asked about faith, "I don't have to have faith. I have experience."[15]

This experience is the indefinable ground of all being, Rousseau's "succession of moments perceived through the senses." It is the irrefutable and formless foundation of existence itself, the source of the inner balance, peace, and stillness that is the wisdom of Taoism and Zen. Suchness is reached by letting go of everything, by completely trusting the inner process of emptying. That is the only way emptiness can fill with suchness.

Trust permits the emptying that allows the filling. Emptying, therefore, is not an end in itself, although it must be treated as such. Otherwise it could not properly become the unconditional receptivity of emptiness.

This emptiness fills with suchness, a kind of ordinariness that is more than ordinary. Its quality is perhaps best illustrated by the comments of a blind man who said of listening attentively to Bankei's voice:

> *Whenever he expressed happiness, I heard nothing but happiness, and whenever he expressed sorrow, sorrow was all I heard.*[16]

The blind man recognized Bankei's suchness as an unambigious clarity of presence. Bankei would have known it as an unambiguous clarity of experience. This clarity is ordinariness unmitigated by questions, doubts, or confusion.

But confusion is the inevitable result of trying to explain suchness. Suchness itself cannot be explained because it is so ordinary; and the ordinary cannot be explained because it is so much like suchness. They are the same yet not the same because a subtle change of attitude has come and gone but left an indelible effect. Suchness is the ordinary with a difference of perspective that has been remembered in emptiness and then appropriately forgotten. The remembering restores equanimity and balance to all experience, and the forgetting allows that experience to proceed naturally. The difference is everything yet nothing.

Perhaps this descriptive dilemma is best dealt with by the words of Alan Watts in *The Way of Zen*. His efforts to explain the philosophy of Hui-neng, that pivotal character in the history of Ch'an and Zen, say much that bears directly on suchness. But his words also weave together a number of other pertinent themes and solidify a case for Zen's origin in Taoism:

> *Hui-neng's position was that a man with an empty conscious-*
> *ness was no better than "a block of wood or a lump of stone."*
> *He insisted that the whole idea of purifying the mind was*
> *irrelevant and confusing, because "our own nature is funda-*
> *mentally clear and pure." . . . The true mind is "no-mind"*
> *(wu-hsin), which is to say that it is not to be regarded as an*
> *object of thought or action, as if it were a thing to be grasped*
> *and controlled. The attempt to work on one's own mind is a*
> *vicious circle. To try to purify it is to be contaminated with*
> *purity. Obviously this is the Taoist philosophy of naturalism,*
> *according to which a person is not genuinely free, detached, or*
> *pure when his state is the result of an artificial discipline. He*
> *is just imitating purity, just "faking" clear awareness. Hence*
> *the unpleasant self-righteousness of those who are deliberately*
> *and methodically religious.*[17]

Here the ingredients of emptying, trusting, filling, naturalness, spontaneity, clarity, and suchness are all woven together. Furthermore, Watts argues that the essential core of Taoist philosophy, naturalism, can be identified as the essential concern of Zen. He also suggests that the spirit of inner freedom they share is incompatible with the institutionalized religion of Buddhism.

The suchness of being oneself without bearing the mark of trying to be "deliberately or methodically" so, connects spontaneity, ordinariness, and non-doing with trusting, emptying, and filling. Integrating all these elements into an unpretentious daily practice is an incredibly difficult task; it requires a naturalness that is so unassuming it could only arise out of the unequivocal neutrality of emptiness.

Emptiness is the cleansing condition that allows suchness to arise as fullness. This experience cannot be manufactured by effort or will; it cannot be devised or contrived by thought. Like the Way of Taoism and Zen, suchness just comes of itself. "It" happens when "It" is ready. Then a new awareness is born from the old. And the end is recognized as the beginning.

ΠΟΤΕS-PART OΠΕ

Preface
1. The *Lao Tzu* is the current nomenclature for the *Tao Te Ching*; the *Chuang Tzu* is sometimes referred to as *Inner Chapters*.
2. Frederick Franck, *Zen and Zen Classics* (New York: Vintage Books, 1978), p. 4.

Introduction
1. Arthur Waley, *The Way and Its Power* (New York: Grove Press, 1958), p. 20.
2. Ibid., p. 44.
3. Victor H. Mair, trans., *Tao Te Ching* (New York: Bantam Books, 1990), p. 146.
4. Ibid., p. 145.
5. Ibid., p. 146.
6. William Barrett, ed., *Zen Buddhism: Selected Writings of D.T. Suzuki* (New York: Doubleday Anchor Books, 1956), p. 60.
7. Seung Sahn, "*A Time of Complete Transformation*," Primary Point, 3:2, June 1986, p. 2.
8. Frederick Franck, *Zen and Zen Classics* (New York: Vintage Books, 1987), p. 211.

Lao Tzu
1. Holmes Welch, Taoism: *The Parting of the Way* (Boston: Beacon Press, 1966), p. 1.
2. Victor H. Mair, trans., *Tao Te Ching* (New York: Bantam Books, 1990), p. 152.
3. Ibid., p. 131.

4. Robert G. Henricks, trans., *Lao-Tzu: Te-Tao Ching* (New York: Ballantine Books, 1989), p. xiv.

Chuang Tzu

1. Burton Watson, trans., *Chuang Tzu: Basic Writings* (New York, Columbia University Press, 1964), p. 1.
2. Ibid., p. 13.
3. Gia-fu Feng and Jane English, trans., *Chuang Tzu: Inner Chapters* (New York: Vintage Books, 1974), p. 35.
4. Burton Watson, op.cit., p. 5.
5. Ibid., p. 5.
6. Gia-fu Feng and Jane English, trans., op.cit., p. vii.

Taoism: A Brief History

1. Holmes Welch, *Taoism: The Parting of the Way* (Boston: Beacon Press, 1966), p. 163.
2. Ibid., p. 123.
3. Ibid., p. 124.
4. Robert G. Henricks, trans., *Lao-Tzu: Te-Tao Ching* (New York: Ballantine Books, 1989), p. xi.
5. Holmes Welch, op.cit., p. 143.
6. Ibid., pp. 144-5.
7. Ibid., p. 145.
8. Ibid., p. 146.
9. Ibid., p. 146.
10. Ibid., p. 147.
11. Ibid., p. 147.
12. Ibid., p. 148.
13. Ibid., p. 146.
14. Ibid., p. 158.
15. Ibid., p. 124.
16. Ibid., p. 159.

Buddhism in China

1. Richard Cavendish, *The Great Religions* (London: Contact, 1980), p. 93.
2. Arthur F. Wright, *Buddhism in Chinese History* (Stanford: Stanford University Press, 1971), p. 33.
3. Holmes Welch, *The Practice of Chinese Buddhism* (Cambridge: Harvard University Press, 1967), p. 372.
4. Martin Collcutt, *Five Mountains: The Rinzai Zen Monastic Institution of Medieval Japan* (Cambridge: Harvard University Press, 1981), p. 7.
5. Arthur F. Wright, ed., *Studies in Chinese Buddhism* (New Haven: Yale University Press, 1990), p. 38.
6. Burton Watson, trans., *Chuang Tzu: Basic Writings* (New York: Columbia University Press, 1964), p. 12.
7. Bradley Smith and Wan-go Weng, *China: A History in Art* (New York: Doubleday, 1972), p. 123.
8. Alan Watts, *The Way of Zen* (New York: Vintage Books, 1957), pp. 78-81.
9. Ibid., p. 80.
10. Ibid., p. 81.
11. Ibid., p. 83.
12. Arthur F. Wright, op.cit., p. 79.
13. Bradley Smith and Wan-go Weng, op.cit., p. 129.
14. Ibid., p. 129.
15. Frederick Franck, *Zen and Zen Classics* (New York: Vintage Books, 1978), p. 18.
16. Charles A. Moore, ed., *The Indian Mind: Essentials of Indian Philosophy and Culture* (Honolulu: University Press of Hawaii, 1978), p. 86.
17. Gia-fu Feng and Jane English, trans., *Lao Tzu: Tao Te Ching* (New York: Vintage Books, 1972), ch. 13.

18. Burton Watson, op.cit., p. 3.
19. Richard Cavendish, op.cit., p. 94.
20. Ibid., p. 93.
21. Ibid., p. 58.
22. Victor H. Mair, trans., *Tao Te Ching* (New York: Bantam Books, 1990), p. 145.

Bodhidharma
1. Ernest Wood, *Zen Dictionary* (New York: Penguin, 1957), p. 19.
2. William Barrett, ed., *Zen Buddhism: Selected Writings of D.T. Suzuki* (New York: Doubleday Anchor Books, 1956), p. 64.
3. Earnest Wood, op.cit., p. 18.
4. Alan Watts, *The Way of Zen* (New York: Vintage Books, 1957), p. 84.
5. William Barrett, ed., op.cit., p. 65.
6. Ibid., p. 65.
7. Victor H. Mair, trans., *Tao Te Ching* (New York: Bantam Books, 1990), p. 152.
8. John R. McRae, *The Northern School and the Formation of Early Ch'an Buddhism* (Honolulu: University of Hawaii Press, 1986), p. 15.
9. William Barrett, ed., op.cit., pp. 61-2.
10. Ibid., p. 62.
11. Ibid., p. 62.
12. Alan Watts, op.cit., p. 84.
13. Ibid., p. 80.
14. Ibid., p. 83.
15. Ibid., p. 83.
16. Ibid., p. 85.
17. Ibid., p. 83.

18. Ibid., p. 84.
19. John R. McRae, op.cit., p. 101.
20. Arthur Waley, *The Way and Its Power* (New York: Grove Press, 1958), p. 120.
21. Alan Watts, op.cit., p. 85.

Ch'an

1. Norman Waddell, trans., *The Unborn: The Life and Teaching of Zen Master Bankei* (San Francisco: North Point Press, 1984), p. 54.
2. Ibid., p. 55.
3. Kenneth Kraft, ed., *Zen: Tradition and Transition* (New York: Grove Press, 1988), p. 34.
4. Ernest Wood, *Zen Dictionary* (New York: Penguin, 1957), p. 25.
5. Kenneth Kraft, ed., op.cit., pp. 138-9.
6. Ibid., p. 131.
7. Ibid., p. 130.
8. Ibid., p. 130.
9. Ibid., p. 131.
10. Ibid., p. 131.
11. John Dykstra Eusden, *Zen and Christian: The Journey Between* (New York: Crossroads, 1981), pp. 37-8.
12. Christmas Humphreys, *A Western Approach to Zen* (Wheaton: Quest, 1987), p. 15.
13. Alan Watts, *Beat Zen, Square Zen and Zen* (San Francisco: City Lights Books, 1959).
14. Alan Watts, *The Way of Zen* (New York: Vintage Books, 1957), pp. 88-9.
15. William Barrett, ed., *Zen Buddhism: Selected Writings of D.T. Suzuki* (New York: Doubleday Anchor Books, 1956), p. 53.

16. Ibid., p. 54.
17. Ibid., p. 54.
18. Ibid., p. 67.
19. Kenneth Kraft, ed., op.cit., p. 144.
20. Ernest Wood, op.cit., p. 49.
21. Arthur Waley, *The Way and Its Power* (New York: Grove Press, 1958), p. 120.
22. Alan Watts, *The Way of Zen*, p. 98.
23. John Dykstra Eusden, op.cit., p. 38.
24. Ernest Wood, op.cit., p. 124.
25. Ibid., p. 124.
26. Bradley Smith and Wan-go Weng, *China: A History in Art* (New York: Doubleday, 1972), p. 123.
27. Ibid., p. 123.
28. Arthur F. Wright, *Buddhism in Chinese History* (Stanford, Stanford University Press, 1971), p. 78.
29. Philip Kapleau, *The Three Pillars of Zen* (New York: Anchor/Doubleday, 1980), pp. 23-5.
30. Alan Watts, *The Way of Zen*, p. 109.
31. Ibid., p. 111.
32. Frederick Franck, *Zen and Zen Classics* (New York: Vintage Books, 1978), p. 220.
33. William Barrett, ed., op.cit., p. 53.

Hui-Neng
1. Frederick Franck, *Zen and Zen Classics* (New York: Vintage Books, 1978), p. 211.
2. Kenneth Kraft, ed., *Zen: Tradition and Transition* (New York: Grove Press, 1988), p. 134.
3. Ibid., p. 139.
4. Alan Watts, *The Way of Zen* (New York: VintageBooks, 1957), p. 91.

5. William Barrett, ed., *Zen Buddhism: Selected Writings of D.T. Suzuki* (New York: Doubleday Anchor Books, 1956), p. 67.
6. Ibid., p. 67.
7. Ibid., p. 69.
8. Kenneth Kraft, ed., op.cit., p. 136.
9. William Barrett, ed., op.cit., p. 54.
10. Ibid., p. 53.
11. Ibid., p. 55.
12. Ibid., pp. 69-70.
13. Robert Sohl and Audrey Carr, eds., *Games Zen Masters Play: Writings of R.H. Blyth* (New York: Mentor Books, 1976), p. 167.
14. Kenneth Kraft, ed., op.cit., pp. 35-6.
15. Alan Watts, *Tao: The Watercourse Way* (New York: Pantheon Books, 1975), p. 90.
16. Kenneth Kraft, ed., op.cit., p. 37.
17. William Barrett, ed., op.cit., pp. 79-80.
18. Ibid., pp. 74-9.
19. Ibid., p. 72.
20. Kenneth Kraft, ed., op.cit., p. 138.
21. Ibid., p. 134.
22. Ibid., p. 134.
23. Ibid., pp. 136-7.
24. Ibid., p. 137.
25. Ibid., p 129.
26. Ibid., pp. 129-30.
27. Ibid., p. 138.
28. Alan Watts, *The Way of Zen*, p. 99.
29. Ibid., p. 100.
30. Ibid., p. 101.
31. Ibid., p. 101.

32. Ernest Wood, *Zen Dictionary* (New York: Penguin, 1957), p. 6.

Zen in Japan
1. Kenneth Kraft, ed., *Zen: Tradition and Transition* (New York: Grove Press, 1988), p. 140.
2. Alan Watts, *The Way of Zen* (New York: Vintage Books, 1957), p. 107.
3. Philip Kapleau, *The Three Pillars of Zen* (New York: Anchor/Doubleday, 1980), p. 373.
4. Ibid., p. 369.
5. Ibid., p. 52.
6. Kenneth Kraft, ed., op.cit., p. 157.
7. William Barrett, ed., *Zen Buddhism: Selected Writings of D.T. Suzuki* (New York: Doubleday Anchor Books, 1956), p. 55.
8. Martin Collcutt, *Five Mountains: The Rinzai Zen Monastic Institution of Medieval Japan* (Cambridge: Harvard University Press, 1981), p. 79.
9. Frederick Franck, *Zen and Zen Classics* (New York: Vintage Books, 1978), p. 181.
10. Ibid., p. 181.
11. John Dykstra Eusden, *Zen and Christian: The Journey Between* (New York: Crossroads, 1981), p. 40.
12. Richard Cavendish, *The Great Religions* (London: Contact, 1980), pp. 113-14.
13. Ibid., p. 115.
14. John Dykstra Eusden, op.cit., p. 43.
15. Ibid., p. 43.
16. Ibid., p. 43.
17. Nahum Stiskin, *The Looking-Glass God* (Tokyo: Autumn Press, 1972), p. 150.

18. Frederick Franck, *Zen and Zen Classics* (New York: Vintage Books, 1978), p. 181.

19. Ibid., p. 211.

Zen Without Buddhism

1. Ernest Wood, *Zen Dictionary* (New York: Penguin, 1957), pp. 65-6.

2. Paul Reps, *Zen Flesh, Zen Bones* (Tokyo: Charles E. Tuttle, 1957), p. 153.

3. Robert Sohl and Audrey Carr, eds., *Games Zen Masters Play: Writings of R.H. Blyth* (New York: Mentor Books, 1976), p. 168.

4. Ibid., p. 168.

5. M. Conrad Heyers, *Zen and the Comic Spirit* (London: Rider, 1974), pp. 105-6.

6. Frederick Franck, *Zen and Zen Classics* (New York: Vintage Books, 1978), p. 181.

7. Robert Sohl and Audrey Carr, eds., op.cit., p. 133.

8. Ibid., p. 133.

9. Ibid., p. 151.

10. Ernest Wood, op.cit., pp. 64-5.

11. John Dykstra Eusden, *Zen and Christian: The Journey Between* (New York: Crossroads, 1981), p. 35.

12. Alan Watts, *Tao: The Watercourse Way* (New York: Pantheon Books, 1975), p. 89.

13. Robert Sohl and Audrey Carr, eds., op.cit., p. 152.

14. Christmas Humphreys, *A Western Approach to Zen* (Wheaton: Quest, 1987), p. 136.

15. Shunryu Suzuki, *Zen Mind, Beginner's Mind* (Tokyo: Weatherhill, 1973), pp. 53-4.

16. Paul Reps, op.cit., p. 112.

17. Alan Watts, *The Way of Zen* (New York: Vintage, 1957), p. 45.
18. Frederick Franck, op.cit., p. 10.
19. Ibid., p. 6.
20. Paul Reps, op.cit., p. 142.
21. Kenneth Kraft, ed., *Zen: Tradition and Transition* (New York: Grove Press, 1988), p. 178.
22. Zenkei Shibayama, *A Flower Does Not Talk: Zen Essays* (Tokyo: Charles E. Tuttle, 1972), p. 81.

Nonin and Bankei
1. Kenneth Kraft, ed., *Zen: Tradition and Transition* (New York: Grove Press, 1988), p. 151.
2. Ibid., p. 143.
3. Ibid., p. 143.
4. Ibid., p. 143.
5. Ibid., p. 143.
6. Norman Waddell, trans., *The Unborn: The Life and Teaching of Zen Master Bankei* (San Francisco: North Point Press, 1984), p. 37.
7. Ibid., pp. 4-5.
8. Ibid., p. 5.
9. Ibid., p. 10.
10. Ibid., p. 48.
11. Ibid., p. 51.
12. Ibid., pp. 48-9.
13. Paul Reps, *Zen Flesh, Zen Bones* (Tokyo: Charles E. Tuttle, 1957), p. 23.
14. Alan Watts, *The Way of Zen* (New York: Vintage, 1957), p. 108.
15. Norman Waddell, op.cit., pp. 56-7.

16. Ibid., p. 57.
17. Ibid., p. 57.
18. Ibid., p. 70.

Everyday Zen

1. Shunryu Suzuki, *Zen Mind, Beginner's Mind* (Tokyo:Weatherhill, 1973), p. 42.
2. Alan Watts, *The Way of Zen* (New York: Vintage Books, 1957), p. 169.
3. Ibid., p. 152.
4. Ibid., p. 151.
5. Robert Sohl and Audrey Carr, eds., *Games Zen Masters Play: Writings of R.H. Blyth* (New York: Mentor Books, 1976), p. 123.
6. Alan Watts, *Beat Zen, Square Zen and Zen* (San Francisco: City Lights Books, 1959).
7. Robert Sohl and Audrey Carr, eds., op.cit., p. 137.
8. Nancy Ross, ed., *The World of Zen* (New York: Vintage Books, 1960), p. 84.
9. Alan Watts, *The Way of Zen*, p. 77.
10. Philip Kapleau, *The Three Pillars of Zen* (New York: Anchor/Doubleday, 1980), pp. 44-9.
11. Ibid., p. 49.
12. M.H. Abrams, ed., *The Norton Anthology of English Literature* (New York: Norton, 1962), p. 1970.
13. Philip Kapleau, op.cit., p. 313.
14. Paul Reps, *Zen Flesh, Zen Bones* (Tokyo: Charles E. Tuttle, 1957), p. 165.
15. Ibid., p. 152.
16. Ibid., p. 154.
17. Robert Sohl and Audrey Carr, eds., op.cit., p. 153.

18. Gia-fu Fend and Jane English, trans., *Lao Tzu: Tao Te Ching* (New York: Vintage Books, 1972), ch. 38.
19. Shunryu Suzuki, op.cit., p. 127.

Zen in the West
 1. Shunryu Suzuki, *Zen Mind, Beginner's Mind* (Tokyo: Weatherhill, 1973), p. 9.
 2. Kenneth Kraft, ed., *Zen: Tradition and Transition* (New York: Grove Press, 1988), p. 187.
 3. Kathy Butler, "Events are the Teacher," CoEvolution Quarterly, Winter 1983, p. 115.
 4. Alan Watts, *Beat Zen, Square Zen and Zen* (San Francisco: City Lights Books, 1959).

NOTES–PART TWO

Introduction
1. Holmes Welch, *Taoism: The Parting of the Way*
   (Boston: Beacon Press, 1966), p. 169.
2. Shunryu Suzuki, *Zen Mind, Beginner's Mind*
   (Tokyo: Weatherhill, 1973), p. 111.

Wordlessness
1. Ray Grigg, *The Contemporary Lao Tzu* (unpublished),
   ch. 69/25.
2. Ibid., ch. 45/1.
3. Zenkei Shibayama, *A Flower Does Not Talk: Zen
   Essays* (Tokyo: Charles E. Tuttle, 1972), p. 264.
4. Arthur Waley, *The Way and Its Power*
   (New York:Grove Press, 1958), pp. 59-60.
5. Ibid., p. 64.
6. John Dykstra Eusden, *Zen and Christian: The Journey
   Between* (New York: Crossroads, 1981), p. 31.
7. Kenneth Kraft, ed., *Zen: Tradition and Transition*
   (New York: Grove Press, 1988), p.4.
8. Paul Reps, *Zen Flesh, Zen Bones*
   (Tokyo: Charles E. Tuttle, 1957), pp. 80-1.
9. Ray Grigg, op.cit., ch. 19/56.
10. Shunryu Suzuki, *Zen Mind, Beginner's Mind*
    (Tokyo: Weatherhill, 1973), p. 56.
11. Kenneth Kraft, ed., op.cit., p. 113.

Selflessness
1. Ray Grigg, *The Contemporary Lao Tzu* (unpublished),
   ch. 77/33.

2. M.H. Abrams, *The Norton Anthology of English Literature* (New York: Norton, 1962), p. 1970.
3. Shunryu Suzuki, *Zen Mind, Beginner's Mind* (Tokyo: Weatherhill, 1973), p. 111.
4. Gia-fu Feng and Jane English, trans., *Lao Tzu: Tao Te Ching* (New York: Vintage Books, 1972), ch. 7.
5. Ibid., ch. 49.
6. Kenneth Kraft, ed., *Zen: Tradition and Transition* (New York: Grove Press, 1988), p. 24.
7. William Shakespeare, *The Tragedy of Hamlet, Prince of Denmark*, V, ii, 213-14.
8. Ibid., V, ii, 218.
9. Ibid., V, ii, 220-4.
10. Shunryu Suzuki, *Zen Mind, Beginner's Mind* (Tokyo: Weatherhill, 1973), p. 43.

Softness

1. Frederick Franck, *Zen and Zen Classics* (New York: Vintage Books, 1978), pp. 13-4.
2. Ray Grigg, *The Contemporary Lao Tzu* (unpublished), ch. 67/22.
3. Ibid., ch. 6/43.
4. Ibid., ch. 6/43.
5. Robert Sohl and Audrey Carr, eds., *Games Zen Masters Play: Writings of R.H. Blyth* (New York: Mentor Books, 1976), p. 168.
6. Thomas Merton, *The Way of Chuang Tzu* (New York: New Directions, 1965), p. 57.
7. Ray Grigg, op.cit., ch. 60/16.
8. Robert Sohl and Audrey Carr, eds., op.cit., p. 101.

Oneness
1. Gia-fu Feng and Jane English, trans., *Lao Tzu: Tao Te Ching* (New York: Vintage Books, 1972), ch. 7.
2. Shunryu Suzuki, *Zen Mind, Beginner's Mind* (Tokyo: Weatherhill, 1973), p. 90.
3. Philip Kapleau, *The Three Pillars of Zen* (New York: Anchor/Doubleday, 1980), p. 103.
4. Alan Watts, *Beat Zen, Square Zen and Zen* (San Francisco: City Lights Books, 1959).
5. Gia-fu Feng and Jane English, trans., op.cit., ch. 41.
6. Shunryu Suzuki, *Zen Mind, Beginner's Mind* (Tokyo: Weatherhill, 1973), p. 119.
7. Gia-fu Feng and Jane English, trans., op.cit., ch. 49.
8. Ibid., ch. 5.

Emptiness
1. Gia-fu Feng and Jane English, trans., *Lao Tzu: Tao Te Ching* (New York: Vintage Books, 1972), ch. 48.
2. Ibid., ch. 1.
3. Ibid., ch. 46.
4. Ibid., ch. 44.
5. Robert Sohl and Audrey Carr, eds., *Games Zen Masters Play: Writings of R.H. Blyth* (New York: Mentor Books, 1976), p. 64.
6. Thomas Merton, The Way of Chuang Tzu (New York: New Directions, 1965), pp. 114-15.
7. Ray Grigg, *The Contemporary Lao Tzu* (unpublished), ch. 55/11.
8. Gia-fu Feng and Jane English, trans., op.cit., ch. 22.
9. Ibid., ch. 16.

10. Eugen Herrigel, *Zen in the Art of Archery* (New York: Vintage Books, 1971), p. 35.

Nothingness
 1. Gia-fu Feng and Jane English, trans., *Chuang Tzu: Inner Chapters* (New York: Vintage Books, 1974), p. 128.
 2. Thomas Merton, *The Way of Chuang Tzu* (New York: New Directions, 1965), p. 74.
 3. Ray Grigg, *The Contemporary Lao Tzu* (unpublished), ch. 79/35.
 4. Shunryu Suzuki, *Zen Mind, Beginner's Mind* (Tokyo: Weatherhill, 1973), p. 117.
 5. Gia-fu Feng and Jane English, trans., op.cit., p. 35.
 6. Gia-fu Feng and Jane English, trans., *Lao Tzu: Tao Te Ching* (New York: Vintage Books, 1972), ch. 25.
 7. Robert Sohl and Audrey Carr, eds., *Games Zen Masters Play: Writings of R.H. Blyth* (New York: Mentor Books, 1976), p. 128.
 8. Ibid., p. 95.
 9. Ray Grigg, op.cit., ch. 64/20.

Balance
 1. Shunryu Suzuki, *Zen Mind, Beginner's Mind* (Tokyo: Weatherhill, 1973), p. 25.
 2. Ibid., p. 103.
 3. Ray Grigg, *The Contemporary Lao Tzu* (unpublished), ch. 46/2.
 4. Shunryu Suzuki, op.cit., p. 104.
 5. Paul Reps, *Zen Flesh, Zen Bones* (Tokyo: Charles E.

Tuttle, 1957), p. 77.

6. Shunryu Suzuki, op.cit., p. 27.

7. Carl G. Jung, "Mysterium Coniunctionis," *Collected Works, Vol. 14* (Princeton: Princeton University Press, 1963), pp. 419-20.

8. Gia-fu Feng and Jane English, trans., *Lao Tzu: Tao Te Ching* (New York: Vintage Books, 1972), ch. 16.

9. Shunryu Suzuki, op.cit., p. 54.

10. Ray Grigg, op.cit., ch. 16/53.

11. Gia-fu Feng and Jane English, trans., op.cit., ch. 14.

12. Ibid., ch. 14.

13. Shunryu Suzuki, op.cit., p. 54.

14. Frederick Franck, *Zen and Zen Classics* (New York: Vintage Books, 1978), p. 10.

15. Shunryu Suzuki, op.cit., p. 54.

Paradox

1. David B. Guralnik and Joseph H. Friend, eds., *Webster's New World Dictionary* (Toronto: Nelson, Foster & Scott, 1962), p. 1060.

2. Holmes Welch, Taoism: *The Parting of the Way* (Boston: Beacon Press, 1966), p. 40.

3. Richard Cavendish, *The Great Religions* (London: Contact, 1980), p. 92.

4. Eugen Herrigel, *Zen in the Art of Archery* (New York: Vintage Books, 1971), p. 35.

5. John Dykstra Eusden, *Zen and Christian: The Journey Between* (New York: Crossroads, 1981), p. 42.

6. Arthur Waley, *The Way and Its Power* (New York: Grove Press, 1958), pp. 52-3.

7. Robert Sohl and Audrey Carr, eds., *Games Zen*

   Masters Play: Writings of R.H. Blyth (New York: Mentor Books, 1976), p. 162.

8. Douglas R. Hofstadter, *Gödel, Escher, Bach: An Eternal Golden Braid* (New York: Vintage Books, 1980), p. 18.

9. Ibid., p. 18.

10. Ibid., p. 17.

11. Jeremy W. Hayward, *Shifting Worlds, Changing Minds: Where the Sciences and Buddhism Meet* (Boston: Shambhala, 1987), p. 250.

12. Frederick Franck, *Zen and Zen Classics* (New York: Vintage Books, 1978), pp. 5-6.

13. Shunryu Suzuki, *Zen Mind, Beginner's Mind* (Tokyo: Weatherhill, 1973), p. 76.

14. Eugen Herrigel, op.cit., p. 35.

Non-Doing

1. William Shakespeare, *The Tragedy of Hamlet, Prince of Denmark*, II,i,66.

2. Alan Watts, *Tao: The Watercourse Way* (New York: Pantheon Books, 1975), p. 90.

3. Thomas Merton, *The Way of Chuang Tzu* (New York: New Directions, 1965), p. 80.

4. R.H. Blyth, *Zen in English Literature and Oriental Classics* (New York: Dutton, 1960), p. 58.

5. Shunryu Suzuki, *Zen Mind, Beginner's Mind* (Tokyo: Weatherhill, 1973), p. 63.

6. Ibid., p. 46.

7. Thomas Merton, op.cit., p. 107.

8. Eugen Herrigel, *Zen in the Art of Archery* (New York: Vintage Books, 1971), p. 58.

9. Ibid., pp. 58-62.

10. Ibid., pp. 64-5.
11. Gia-fu Feng and Jane English, trans., *Lao Tzu: Tao Te Ching* (New York: Vintage Books, 1972), ch. 48.
12. Ray Grigg, *The Contemporary Lao Tzu* (unpublished), ch. 23/60.
13. Shunryu Suzuki, op.cit., p. 32.
14. Ibid., p. 32.
15. Ibid., p. 33.
16. Ray Grigg, op.cit., ch. 70/26.

Spontaneity
 1. Alan Watts, *Tao: The Watercourse Way* (New York: Pantheon Books, 1975), p. 32.
 2. Shunryu Suzuki, *Zen Mind, Beginner's Mind* (Tokyo: Weatherhill, 1973), p. 108.
 3. William Shakespeare, *The Tragedy of Hamlet, Prince of Denmark*, III, i, 83-8.
 4. Thomas Merton, *The Way of Chuang Tzu* (New York: New Directions, 1965), pp. 89-90.
 5. H. Dumoulin and R.F. Sasaki, *The Development of Chinese Zen After the Sixth Patriarch* (New York: First Zen Institute, 1953), p. 48.
 6. Gia-fu Feng and Jane English, trans., *Lao Tzu: Tao Te Ching* (New York: Vintage Books, 1972), ch. 20.
 7. Ibid., ch. 19.
 8. Philip Kapleau, *The Three Pillars of Zen* (New York: Anchor/Doubleday, 1980), p. 146.
 9. Ibid., p. 146.
10. Shunryu Suzuki, op.cit., p. 65.
11. Ibid., p. 66.
12. Paul Reps, *Zen Flesh, Zen Bones* (Tokyo: Charles E.

Tuttle, 1957), pp. 39-40.

13. Gia-fu Feng and Jane English, trans., *Chuang Tzu: Inner Chapters* (New York: Vintage Books, 1974), p. 55.

14. Gia-fu Feng and Jane English, trans., *Lao Tzu: Tao Te Ching*, ch. 12.

15. Alan Watts, *Tao: The Watercourse Way* (New York: Pantheon Books, 1975), p. 32.

16. Shunryu Suzuki, op.cit., p. 79.

17. Gia-fu Feng and Jane English, trans., *Lao Tzu: Tao Te Ching*, ch. 49.

18. Paul Reps, *Zen Telegrams* (Tokyo: Charles E. Tuttle, 1959), p. 27.

19. Shunryu Suzuki, op.cit., p. 75.

20. Ibid., p. 73.

21. Frederick Franck, *Zen and Zen Classics* (New York: Vintage Books, 1978), p. 15.

22. Shunryu Suzuki, op.cit., p. 115.

23. Ibid., p. 115.

Ordinariness

1. Alan Watts, *The Way of Zen* (New York: Vintage Books, 1957), p. 77.

2. Ray Grigg, *The Contemporary Lao Tzu* (unpublished), ch. 35/70.

3. Gia-fu Feng and Jane English, trans., *Lao Tzu: Tao Te Ching* (New York: Vintage Books, 1972), ch. 8.

4. Robert Sohl and Audrey Carr, eds., *The Gospel According to Zen* (New York: Mentor, 1970), pp. 105-6.

5. Gia-fu Feng and Jane English, trans., *Chuang Tzu: Inner Chapters* (New York: Vintage Books, 1974), p. 123.

6. Gia-fu Feng and Jane English, trans., *Lao Tzu: Tao Te Ching*, ch. 19.
7. Fung Yu-lan, *Chuang Tzu: A New Selected Translation* (New York: Paragon, 1963), p. 113.
8. Gia-fu Feng and Jane English, trans., *Lao Tzu: Tao Te Ching*, ch. 12.
9. Robert Sohl and Audrey Carr, eds., op.cit., p. 105.
10. Thomas Merton, *The Way of Chuang Tzu* (New York: New Directions, 1965), p. 123.
11. Robert Sohl and Audrey Carr, eds., *Games Zen Masters Play: Writings of R.H. Blyth* (New York: Mentor Books, 1976), p. 139.

Playfulness
1. Nancy Ross, ed., *The World of Zen* (New York: Vintage Books, 1960), p. 183.
2. Gia-fu Feng and Jane English, trans., *Chuang Tzu: Inner Chapters* (New York: Vintage Books, 1974), p. 87.
3. Paul Reps, *Zen Flesh, Zen Bones* (Tokyo: Charles E. Tuttle, 1957), p. 84.
4. John Dykstra Eusden, *Zen and Christian: The Journey Between* (New York: Crossroads, 1981), p. 72.
5. Gia-fu Feng and Jane English, trans., op.cit., p. 44.
6. Thomas Merton, *The Way of Chuang Tzu* (New York: New Directions, 1965), p. 55.

Suchness
1. Gia-fu Feng and Jane English, trans., *Lao Tzu: Tao Te Ching* (New York: Vintage Books, 1972), ch. 48.
2. Frederick Franck, *Zen and Zen Classics* (New York: Vintage Books, 1978), p. 10.

3. Alan Watts, *The Way of Zen* (New York: Vintage Books, 1957), p. 131.
4. Robert Sohl and Audrey Carr, eds., *Games Zen Masters Play: Writings of R.H. Blyth* (New York: Mentor Books, 1976), p. 105.
5. Shunryu Suzuki, *Zen Mind, Beginner's Mind* (Tokyo: Weatherhill, 1973), p. 103.
6. Kenneth Clark, *Civilisation* (London: BBC, 1971), pp. 272-74.
7. Paul Reps, *Zen Flesh, Zen Bones* (Tokyo: Charles E. Tuttle, 1957), p. 158.
8. Ibid., p. 126.
9. Gia-fu Feng and Jane English, trans., op.cit., ch. 28.
10. Ray Grigg, *The Contemporary Lao Tzu* (unpublished), ch. 18/55.
11.Paul Reps, op.cit., p. 22.
12. Robert Sohl and Audrey Carr, eds., op.cit., p. 64.
13. Alan Watts, *Tao: The Watercourse Way* (New York: Pantheon Books, 1975), p. 32.
14. Joseph Campbell, *The Power of Myth* (New York: Doubleday, 1988) p. 5.
15. Ibid., p. 208.
16. Paul Reps, op.cit., p. 48.
17. Alan Watts, *The Way of Zen* (New York: Vintage Books, 1957), p. 93.

About the Illustrator–William Gaetz

Art, philosophy, and religious studies have been the consuming interests of William Gaetz. He is both an accomplished vocalist and classical pianist. His studies in Zen and Metaphysics have earned him teaching certification in California. After years of expressing his creativity through photography, he embarked on the path of Chinese brush painting under the tutelage of Master Professor Peng Kung Yi. This is the medium that Mr. Gaetz feels best fulfills his spiritual needs and comes closest to expressing that which truly cannot be expressed.

The Tao of Zen is the third book by Ray Grigg that Mr. Gaetz has been generous enough to illustrate. He has used traditionally styled landscapes to represent the perspective of the author's scholarly consideration of Taoism and Zen, and then details from these landscapes for the supporting chapters.

Mr. Gaetz presently lives in Victoria, British Columbia, where he was born on September 23, 1934. Here he continues to paint under the Chinese name of Koy Sai. His work is shown in Victoria galleries, hangs in homes and businesses throughout Canada and the United States, and can be seen in other books by Ray Grigg, *The Tao of Being* and *The Tao of Sailing*.

357